Differentiation
in the
Elementary Grades

Issaquah School District
Teaching & Learning Services
565 NW Holly St.
Issaquah, WA 98027

Kristina J. Doubet
Jessica A. Hockett

Differentiation
in the
Elementary Grades

Strategies to Engage and Equip All Learners

Foreword by **Carol Ann Tomlinson**

ASCD
Alexandria, VA USA

1703 N. Beauregard St. • Alexandria, VA 22311-1714 USA
Phone: 800-933-2723 or 703-578-9600 • Fax: 703-575-5400
Website: www.ascd.org • E-mail: member@ascd.org
Author guidelines: www.ascd.org/write

Deborah S. Delisle, *Executive Director;* Robert D. Clouse, *Managing Director, Digital Content & Publications;* Stefani Roth, *Publisher;* Genny Ostertag, *Director, Content Acquisitions;* Julie Houtz, *Director, Book Editing & Production;* Miriam Calderone, *Editor;* Masie Chong, *Graphic Designer;* Mike Kalyan, *Director, Production Services;* Keith Demmons, *Production Designer;* Andrea Hoffman, *Senior Production Specialist*

Copyright © 2018 ASCD. All rights reserved. It is illegal to reproduce copies of this work in print or electronic format (including reproductions displayed on a secure intranet or stored in a retrieval system or other electronic storage device from which copies can be made or displayed) without the prior written permission of the publisher. By purchasing only authorized electronic or print editions and not participating in or encouraging piracy of copyrighted materials, you support the rights of authors and publishers. Readers who wish to reproduce or republish excerpts of this work in print or electronic format may do so for a small fee by contacting the Copyright Clearance Center (CCC), 222 Rosewood Dr., Danvers, MA 01923, USA (phone: 978-750-8400; fax: 978-646-8600; web: www.copyright.com). To inquire about site licensing options or any other reuse, contact ASCD Permissions at www.ascd.org/permissions, or permissions@ascd.org, or 703-575-5749. For a list of vendors authorized to license ASCD e-books to institutions, see www.ascd.org/epubs. Send translation inquiries to translations@ascd.org.

ASCD® and ASCD LEARN. TEACH. LEAD.® are registered trademarks of ASCD. All other trademarks contained in this book are the property of, and reserved by, their respective owners, and are used for editorial and informational purposes only. No such use should be construed to imply sponsorship or endorsement of the book by the respective owners.

Excerpts from Common Core State Standards © Copyright 2010. National Governors Association Center for Best Practices and Council of Chief State School Officers. All rights reserved.

All web links in this book are correct as of the publication date below but may have become inactive or otherwise modified since that time. If you notice a deactivated or changed link, please e-mail books@ascd.org with the words "Link Update" in the subject line. In your message, please specify the web link, the book title, and the page number on which the link appears.

PAPERBACK ISBN: 978-1-4166-2454-7   ASCD product #117014   n10/17
PDF E-BOOK ISBN: 978-1-4166-2455-4; see Books in Print for other formats.
Quantity discounts are available: e-mail programteam@ascd.org or call 800-933-2723, ext. 5773, or 703-575-5773. For desk copies, go to www.ascd.org/deskcopy.

Library of Congress Cataloging-in-Publication Data
Names: Doubet, Kristina, 1969- author. | Hockett, Jessica A., author.
Title: Differentiation in the elementary grades : strategies to engage and
    equip all learners / Kristina J. Doubet and Jessica A. Hockett ; foreword
    by Carol Ann Tomlinson.
Description: Alexandria, Virginia : ASCD, [2017] | Includes bibliographical
    references and index.
Identifiers: LCCN 2017023400 (print) | LCCN 2017036586 (ebook) | ISBN
    9781416624554 (PDF) | ISBN 9781416624547 (pbk.)
Subjects: LCSH: Individualized instruction. | Mixed ability grouping in
    education. | Education, Elementary.
Classification: LCC LB1031 (ebook) | LCC LB1031 .D64 2017 (print) | DDC
    371.39/4--dc23
LC record available at https://lccn.loc.gov/2017023400

27 26 25 24 23 22 21 20 19 18   1 2 3 4 5 6 7 8 9 10 11 12

Soli Deo gloria

Differentiation
in the
Elementary Grades

Foreword:
Learning from Literature— and Children

By Carol Ann Tomlinson

A century ago, Dorothy Canfield Fisher wrote a children's book called *Understood Betsy* (1917) that has continued to appeal to young readers across the decades. It's a story about 9-year-old Elizabeth Ann, later known as Betsy, whose world is upended when she has to leave the neat and highly structured world she has known in a city to move to rural Vermont and live with her mother's relatives. Everything in her new surroundings seems so alien to Elizabeth Ann. For starters, her "new" aunt calls her Betsy—and she treats Betsy as though she were capable of doing useful things rather than merely being taken care of. When it's time to go to school, she tells Betsy how to walk across fields and over fences to get to the one-room schoolhouse that will welcome her. In the city, people walked her to and from school, holding her hand all the way.

The new school is disorienting as well. There are little kids and big kids all in the same room. The teacher appears delighted to include Betsy in the class and has her read aloud so that she can get a sense of Betsy's starting point as a reader. Because Betsy reads fluidly and with feeling, the teacher lets her read a very long passage. Although that is something Betsy has always wanted to do, it makes her feel as if the teacher doesn't know how to "do school"; in her old school, where students were carefully sorted by age into separate rooms, each student read one sentence during reading time, with the next student picking up the sentence that followed.

During math time in Betsy's new school, she comes close to tears. She doesn't know how to work the problems she is given, and she feels like a failure.

Later in the day, the teacher tells Betsy that tomorrow she will work with the level seven readers and with the level three math group. Confused, Betsy says to the teacher, "How can I be level seven in reading and level three in math when I'm in Grade 2?" The teacher responds, "What's the point of reading things that are way too easy for you or working on math problems you don't understand? And what difference does it make what groups you're in? You're just you, aren't you?"

It seems so reasonable. When a teacher works from that perspective, it's not a problem if the students aren't a matched set chronologically. She figures out where a student is in a sequence of learning and helps the student move ahead. The day is ordered so that sometimes everyone works together. Sometimes students work alone. Sometimes they help one another. Sometimes they work in small groups. The goal, informed by common sense and reality rather than by research in psychology and neuroscience, is to create a growth-centered learning environment that contemporary researcher John Hattie would call a "plus-one classroom": a place where each student can expect to move ahead at least one step a day from his or her entry point.

Other research supports teaching learners in their zones of proximal development or at a level of moderate challenge. Betsy's teacher in the one-room schoolhouse predated that research in both psychology and neuroscience. What she had to work from, however, was not trivial. She constructed her practice on the basis of common sense and observation. "Why," she might have asked, "would you assume all students in your classroom need to be taught the same things on the same day at the same rate and with the same support system?" Had she ever visited Betsy's school in the city, she might have added, "Do you really think all 7-year-olds are alike as learners?"

Almost 100 years after Betsy joined that one-room schoolhouse, Mr. Clifton, an elementary math teacher in Lisa Graff's book *Absolutely Almost* (2014), helps 5th grader Albie consider some ideas much like those of Betsy's teacher. Albie is struggling with math—and almost everything else in school, for that matter. He just wants to be "good" in his subjects, as he believes everyone else is. Albie knows Mr. Clifton is on his side and wants to help him enjoy math, but Albie wants a quick solution, an act of magic. Mr. Clifton is more pragmatic when he says to Albie, "You can't get where you're going without being where you are."

As teachers, we know Mr. Clifton is right. You can't learn fractions if you haven't learned to multiply. You can't write a persuasive paragraph if you can't yet write a sentence.

Today's classrooms don't group adolescents with 1st graders, but students who read at a 1st grade level do share classrooms with students who read like adolescents. Students who have only ever known English as their language of communication share classrooms with students who are encountering English for the first time. Students whose independence outstrips their years learn alongside students who have the barest sense of self-efficacy.

Some would argue that the wise course is to further sort students, so that they learn only with others who are "like" them—so that teachers don't have to teach students whose entry points into grade-level curriculum vary significantly. I'd argue the opposite—that there is great opportunity and richness in helping students learn to see the strengths that each human being brings to a community and that we are extended as human beings when we come to understand the array of perspectives and experiences that constitute our world.

That richness and opportunity, however, can be realized only when teachers grasp and respond to the twin realities that learners differ and that we only help them flourish by enabling them to move forward from their current points of development—academically, socially, and emotionally. Pressures to bypass those realities come at teachers from every side every day.

Certainly a powerful antidote to the pressures that favor one-size-fits-all teaching comes in the form of informed and practical toolkits that help us craft mental images of what a student-focused classroom could look like, inspire us to turn those images into actions, and support us in succeeding as we do so. This book is such a toolkit.

Kristina Doubet and Jessica Hockett understand differentiated classrooms at a deep, rather than a surface, level. Because the philosophy of differentiation is a belief system for them, it is worth the investment of a significant portion of their personal and professional lives. They understand the complexity of teaching in general and of teaching that responds to students more than to mandates. They also understand that all of us can achieve complex goals with sound guidance and a stepwise approach.

In this book, these two authors provide sound, research-based explanations of differentiation, informed guidance on how to grow in confidence and competence with student-focused instruction, and a robust array of examples of differentiation in many subjects and all elementary grade levels. Their work encompasses all key facets of effective differentiation: learning environment, curriculum, formative assessment, responsive instruction, and classroom leadership and management. Its already impressive trove of examples of classroom applications of differentiation is further enhanced with online forms and tools.

This is a book that, like differentiation itself, can meet teachers who are at varying points of development as educational practitioners, serving as a catalyst for growth wherever they are in their trajectories. This book merits reading and rereading —studying and restudying—over the course of a career. I have learned from these two over many years and will continue to learn from them as a student of this book.

A number of years ago, I met an elementary teacher in Canada whose devotion to her students both as individuals and as a group was evident from our earliest conversations. One winter Friday afternoon, she had taken her students ice-skating. As they came back to their room at school and were putting away their coats, gloves, and hats, a student asked, "Did anybody notice how many different sizes of ice skates we wore today?" Another student pointed to the coat rack and said, "I guess we shouldn't be surprised. It's just like our clothes sizes." A third chimed in, "It's how we learn."

The teacher, Mrs. Gilewicz, generally concluded the week by asking her students to write a reflection on something that had taken place during the week. Overhearing the students' conversation, she asked them to write their reflection this week on "different-size learning." She shared their writing with me, and I've always appreciated at least three things about their thoughts each time I return to them. First, it was evident (as it nearly always is in school) that the students' writing was developing at quite different rates. Some of them wrote almost eloquently, some minimized words and sentence length, and others included drawings as a more successful way of making their points than words yet afforded them. Second, it was evident to me through their work that their teacher had helped them develop a common understanding of what differentiation is and how it can make a classroom better for its inhabitants. Third, in that understanding, I saw a child's sense of what Betsy's teacher and Albie's teacher were trying to convey to those fictional children: "It's good to be who you are, and to grow in your own way." Here are just a few excerpts from Mrs. Gilewicz's 5th graders.

David: "If everybody had to learn the *same* thing in the *same* way at the *same* time, it would be too easy for some people and too hard for others. We'd be frustrated or bored a lot of the time because everybody is different, not the *same*."

Jeremy: "What would happen if we had to learn everything just alike? Well, we'd probably ask not to go to school. Thank goodness our class isn't like that."

Shelby: "Different-size learning is the way we are in all subjects because no one is the same in a subject. People are just different in learning."

Rebecca: "Without different-size learning, we wouldn't learn so much. When we work so it's right for us, we grow. We work our way up."

Danyk: "If we all had to learn everything alike, it would be just plain disastrous. A better thing is to be myself and work so it works for me."

Shaun: "If it weren't for different-size learning, we would have no challenge at all. Lots of people have lots of different learning abilities. Without different-size learning, we would be frustrated, or else start anticipating everything. If you destroy the balance between student and challenge, you plunge the school into chaos, a sort of educational Dark Age."

Kudos to each of you who works daily to meet young learners where they are and mentor them forward!

Carol Ann Tomlinson
Former high school and middle school teacher
William Clay Parrish, Jr. Professor & Chair of Educational Leadership, Foundations, and Policy, Curry School of Education, University of Virginia
Charlottesville, VA

Acknowledgments

We could not have written this book without the generosity and support of many people.

We are first grateful to the incredible teachers and leaders we have had the privilege to work with over the years. You have shared your deep well of experience, giving us glimpses into your triumphs and struggles. Your compassion and commitment to your students both humble us and push us forward. In particular, our work with educators in Evanston/Skokie School District 65 (IL) has shaped and sharpened our understanding of what it means to teach well in diverse settings.

In addition, teachers and leaders in the following schools and districts have grown our expertise by opening the doors of their classrooms and inviting us into what they think and do: Amistad Dual Language School (NYC), Antioch School District 34 (IL), Arlington Heights School District 25 (IL), Bialik Hebrew Day School (Toronto, Canada), Charles E. Smith Jewish Day School (MD), Emma Lazarus High School for English Language Scholars (NYC), Garnet Valley Schools (PA), Harrisonburg City Schools (VA), Hempfield Area School District (PA), Jefferson County Schools (KY), Mannheim School District 83 (IL), North Shore School District 112 (IL), Rockingham County Schools (VA), and Winnetka School District 36 (IL). A special thanks to Charlottesville City and Albemarle County (VA) Schools, in which we both worked as research assistants on an immersive study of K–2 classrooms for the National Center for Research on Gifted Education at the University of Virginia.

We are indebted to friends and colleagues who generously lent their expertise and encouragement during the composing and editing process. Lara Galicia, Frances Collins, and Hedy Helfand shared pragmatic wisdom about teaching in diverse contemporary classrooms that helped us set our course. Amanda Sawyer kept us sharp mathematically, Eric Imbrescia offered important reflections on the first portion of the manuscript, and Lin-Manuel Miranda encouraged us to write "nonstop." We are especially thankful to Christine Trendel and Kelly Ellington, who read the manuscript in its entirety, offering us detailed suggestions and thoughtful feedback.

Your insights were invaluable. Michelle Cude, Suzanne Farrand, Joel Heckethorn, Kori Hockett, Brian Knox, Lenore Layman, Jamilla Pitts, Amy Platt, Kyle Schultz, and Gena Southall: thank you for being eager cheerleaders of our work.

To our editing team at ASCD, Genny Ostertag and Miriam Calderone: our thanks for helping us hone our message and bring our ideas to life.

Our talented colleagues in the differentiation effort continue to be a true blessing. Jennifer Beasley, Catherine Brighton, Marla Read Capper, Eric Carbaugh, Cheryl Dobbertin, Kelly Hedrick, Holly Hertberg-Davis, Marcia Imbeau, Jane Jarvis, Tonya Moon, Wil Parker, Chad Prather, Judy Rex, Nanci Smith, Cindy Strickland, and Christine Trinter: your expertise, examples, and support inspire us.

We are grateful as well for leaders in the field of education whose work has influenced or nurtured us both individually and together. These include Grant Wiggins, Jay McTighe, Lynn Erickson, Carolyn Callahan, Joe Renzulli, Sally Reis, Jann Leppien, Del Siegle, LouAnn Lovin, and Susan Mintz.

Carol Ann Tomlinson, our advisor and mentor, launched us on this journey and has remained beside us, providing sage wisdom and insight, in the decades since. You will always be our teacher.

Our love and gratitude to the kids who are dearest to our hearts: Mason, Harley, Jake, Marissa, and Josh. You remained at the forefront of our thinking as we wrote each word.

To our families: Jessica's husband, Tim, and our parents, Don and Patti Faber and Eldon and Susan Doubet—you have loved and supported us throughout our lives as well as the process of writing this book. Thank you.

Finally, and most importantly, praise and thanksgiving to our gracious Heavenly Father, who teaches us "to act justly, to love mercy, and to walk humbly" (Micah 6:8). May this book reflect Your heart.

Introduction:
Differentiation Gets an Upgrade

The Challenge

Elementary school classrooms in the United States today are blessed with students from a rich range of racial, ethnic, cultural, linguistic, and socioeconomic backgrounds. This vibrant diversity expands students' understanding of what makes us *us*, and helps equip them to become productive, empathetic, and ethical citizens who can thrive in an ever-changing global society.

At the same time, the country's commitment to educating all children well has driven the push for more rigorous standards. These standards are meant to ensure that today's children are ready for tomorrow's world. A high-quality education is no longer the province of the few or the affluent, but the right of every child in every community.

These two factors—greater student diversity and increased academic rigor—mean that today's teachers have greater accountability for a more heterogeneous population of students than ever before. In many schools, appraisal of teachers' performance is based at least in part on their ability to ensure the progress of every student, regardless of background, native language, motivation, or school experience.

These realities present every teacher with a fundamental, persistent question: "How do I divide time, resources, and myself so that I am an effective catalyst for maximizing talent in all my students?" (Tomlinson, 2014a, p. 2). Herein lies the challenge.

Differentiation: Meeting the Challenge

Good teachers have always recognized and responded to the inherent diversity in their classrooms. At minimum, they understand that they have content and skills to teach, students who need to learn those things, and differences among the students that make one-size-fits-all approaches ineffective. This, in essence, is *differentiation*. A teacher who differentiates instruction (Tomlinson, 2014)

- Creates an atmosphere in which students' unique qualities and needs are as important as the traits they share.
- Uncovers students' learning needs through pre-assessment and formative assessment and tailors tasks accordingly.
- Plans experiences and tasks that are bound together by common and important learning goals.
- Presents varied approaches and avenues for students to take in, process, and produce knowledge.
- Varies grouping configurations frequently and strategically as a way of granting access to learning goals, providing support and challenge, and building community.
- Orchestrates fluid routines and management systems.

For many elementary teachers, cultivating a differentiated classroom is a natural and intuitive response. Most kindergarten teachers, for example, understand and *delight in* the fact that the 30 faces they see belong to individuals as unique as their fingerprints. Embracing and planning for the variance is what skilled teachers just *do*.

Yet not everyone "does" differentiation the same way. In reality, there are significant misconceptions about what actually constitutes defensible differentiated instruction. Figure I.1 addresses some of those misconceptions and their respective "truths" (Tomlinson, 2003, 2014a).

Figure I.1 | What Differentiation Is and Is Not

Differentiation *Is*	Differentiation *Is Not*
. . . A philosophy rooted in effective teaching and learning.	. . . A bag of tricks or set of strategies that can be plunked into low-quality curriculum.
. . . Regularly examining evidence of student learning and making thoughtful instructional decisions accordingly.	. . . Either an every-moment necessity or a once-in-a-blue-moon "event."
. . . Tailoring instruction in response to patterns in student needs.	. . . Writing individualized lesson plans for every student.
. . . Designing respectful tasks and using flexible grouping.	. . . Sorting or pigeonholing students into static groups or levels.
. . .A way *up* to standards and learning goals.	. . . . A way *out* of standards and learning goals.
. . .Critical to improving instruction for *all* students.	. . . More important for certain groups of students (e.g., students with IEPs or English language learners).

Source: From *Differentiation in Middle and High School: Strategies to Engage All Learners* (p. 3), by K. J. Doubet and J. A. Hockett, 2015, Alexandria, VA: ASCD. Copyright 2015 by ASCD.

Upgrading Differentiation: Ensuring Continued Growth and Progress

Don't good elementary teachers *already* differentiate? Because differentiation is a journey rather than a destination, it's something a teacher can never truly be finished with. A teacher's efforts to plan for students' needs improve with time, practice, and feedback in the same way that new technologies are constantly "upgrading" to improve the user experience.

For many elementary-grades teachers, upgrading involves shifts in beliefs about what differentiation is, as well as changes to methods and approaches that, in some cases, have become automatic or widely accepted or otherwise gone unquestioned. In the following sections, we discuss five commonly adopted practices that impede true differentiation and explain how to upgrade them to more sophisticated applications of differentiation.

1. Designing differentiated tasks vs. tasks that are just "different"

Variety is a hallmark of a differentiated classroom, but that variety should come in *how* students learn, not in *what* they learn. Differentiated tasks, therefore, are not just "different"; they are designed to address a given set of learning goals with different levels of scaffolding, within different areas of interest, or via different methods for taking in, processing, or demonstrating understanding, knowledge, and skills. An "upgraded" approach would ensure that students arrive at the same learning destination even if they get there through a variety of learning paths.

2. Designing engaging *and* substantive tasks vs. tasks that are just "fun"

Elementary teachers recognize how important it is for children to find joy in learning. They want their students to be excited about what they're doing in school and take pride in what they produce. Sometimes, in an effort to make sure that students are actively engaged, teachers lose sight of the goals and purpose of a task and, in the name of differentiation, substitute "fun" for substance. Teachers with an upgraded approach to differentiation ensure that student excitement and investment are poured into tasks that have meaning and purpose. In other words, differentiated tasks are both joyful *and* important.

3. Differentiating for all students within the classroom vs. sending students out of the classroom

As the term is used this book, *differentiation* is not synonymous with pulling students out for special programs, sending students to another teacher's classroom for one or more subjects, or regrouping students between classrooms for part of the day. Rather than describing *where* students learn, an upgraded conception of differentiation refers to *how* the classroom teacher makes important curricular goals accessible to all learners within the *same* classroom.

4. Recognizing *all* areas of strength and need vs. regarding reading level as an indicator of overall ability

Without question, a student's ability to decode and comprehend text serves as a requisite skill to completing many other tasks. It is *not*, however, synonymous with her or his intellectual capacity. Nor does a student's reading level reflect his or her competence in math, understanding of science, or familiarity with history, for example. Although reading skills are the most overt and frequently assessed or reported indicators of student achievement, they do not paint the whole picture of a child's ability. A student may struggle with reading but excel in math; conversely, a fluent and capable reader may struggle to make sense of numbers and mathematical relationships. A teacher using an upgraded approach to differentiation recognizes that each student possesses a *collection* of strengths and areas for growth—and adjusts instruction accordingly.

5. Using flexible grouping vs. maintaining static groups

Small groups and small-group instruction are the norm in many K–5 classrooms. Most teachers would agree that breaking the class into partners, trios, or quads for certain tasks can make teaching more responsive and learning more efficient. But when groups are static—that is, when students are in the same groups with the same peers for weeks or months at a time—grouping can work against the goals of increasing student learning and motivation. A teacher with an upgraded understanding of grouping uses many different configurations *flexibly* to meet a range of student needs and to grant access to rich learning opportunities. In doing so, the teacher not only builds students' capacity to engage with differentiated tasks but also strengthens camaraderie and respect among learners.

● ● ● ●

Teachers may recognize one, several, or all of these ineffective practices in their own classroom or school. Each one can serve as a launching point for a "differentiation upgrade." In that spirit, the rest of this book provides comprehensive guidance, tools, and examples for teachers seeking to build on how they are already successfully uncovering and addressing student differences, while propelling their journey toward expertise.

What's Ahead

This book is organized around entry points for a differentiation upgrade that we have posed as questions for teachers to consider:

- How do I build a family of learners?
- How do I focus what I have to teach?
- How do I know what students already know?
- How do I get students engaged with the content and with one another?
- How do I know if students are getting it?
- What if students are in different places?
- How do I increase motivation and investment?
- How do I manage it all?
- How can I continue to upgrade?

The answers to these questions form the backbone of this book, which aims to be a comprehensive guide to differentiation in the elementary grades. Teachers might choose to start with Chapter 1 or to begin with the chapter that most closely reflects their area of interest. Here's a brief look at what each chapter addresses:

Chapter 1 presents techniques for building a healthy community of learners in which students see *all* of their classmates as family members with important strengths to share and areas of growth to support.

Chapter 2 shows teachers how to prioritize, focus, and "translate" curriculum, texts, or programs into manageable and meaningful learning goals that are fit to be differentiated.

Chapter 3 offers guidelines on how best to gather information about what students already know, understand, and can do prior to beginning a unit or lesson.

Chapter 4 explains strategies for actively engaging *all* students in making sense of content and practicing skills through interaction and discussion.

Chapter 5 provides strategies and prompts for gauging the progress of student learning—both during the course of a lesson and at its completion—with the goal of using that information to inform future instructional decisions.

Chapter 6 focuses on approaches to adjusting content, process, and product for student readiness, with an emphasis on closely analyzing and planning instruction directly from formative assessment results.

Chapter 7 offers strategies for maintaining students' interest, enthusiasm, and investment throughout lesson and units, as well as techniques that provide students with varied avenues for taking in, processing, and demonstrating mastery of learning goals.

Chapter 8 offers practical tools for effectively managing a classroom that supports techniques described throughout this book.

The Conclusion provides encouragement and suggestions to help teachers continuously "upgrade" their practice and make progress in their quest to create more responsive classrooms.

This book recognizes that the most powerful and efficient learning often happens by example. Accordingly, Part 2 of each chapter provides a plethora of tools and examples*spanning a range of grade levels and content areas that were developed *by, for,* or *with* real teachers. These can be used to support teacher growth in myriad contexts, including professional learning communities, department or team planning meetings, and instructional coaching relationships. In addition, each chapter closes with a "before" and "after" example of a teacher experimenting with the principles and practices of differentiation. Our intent is to illustrate the kind of process and thinking that all teachers undertake in their journeys toward expertise.

Used well, this book and its tools have the potential to elevate what happens in elementary classrooms and, ultimately, to improve the learning and the lives of both teachers and their students.

A Note to Primary-Grades Teachers

The primary-grades examples in this book are written so that *teachers* understand the process or task. Primary-grades teachers can use these examples as the basis for delivery that is most appropriate for the skills of their learners, many of whom are at different stages of development in learning to read and write.

---

*For added utility, select forms and templates from this book can be downloaded at http://www.ascd.org/ASCD/pdf/books/Doubet2017forms.pdf. Use the password "Doubet201711 7014" to unlock the PDF. In addition, a study guide for this book can be found at http://www.ascd.org/books/An-ASCD-Study-Guide-for-Differentiation-in-the-Elementary-Grades providing questions and prompts for use in professional development and PLCs.

1 Building a Healthy Classroom Community

Part 1:

How Do I Build a Family of Learners?

Members of every family, regardless of how large or how small, share important commonalities and exhibit unique traits. The health of a family is often influenced by the extent to which its members acknowledge and even celebrate both their individual identities and their collective identity.

A classroom family operates in the same fashion. Teachers in differentiated classrooms, in particular, view each student as a family member. They seek out and celebrate students' common bonds while reveling in what makes each child an individual.

At first, students' differences may be more evident than their similarities. Although they are roughly the same biological age, students come to a classroom with distinct personalities and at different stages of development. They hail from different countries and represent a wide array of cultural and linguistic backgrounds. They span the spectrum of learning needs, strengths, and interests.

Yet within this vast assortment of characteristics, patterns emerge. Students share strengths with some classmates and weaknesses with others. Common interests —in sports, animals, art, or music, for example—can unite students who, on the surface, may appear to share very little. Although students come from different households, the classroom serves as a second home for *all* of them. It's where they spend the greatest portion of their weekdays; they are bonded by the culture of their classroom family.

Perhaps most important, every student in a teacher's charge shares a basic human need: the deep desire to be seen, known, and honored for who he or she is. Although some students are anxious to share everything about their personal lives and others are more reticent, *every* student in the classroom longs to be known and treasured.

As the "head" of this family, the teacher has three primary goals:

1. To celebrate individuals
2. To cultivate relationships

3. To send the message that all students are accepted exactly as they are—yet are also expected to grow

Celebrating Individuality

We cannot celebrate the unique qualities of each student unless we actively work to discover them. This endeavor begins by learning students' names and using them as often as possible in the first week of school. As Dale Carnegie rightly observed, "[A] person's name is to that person the sweetest and most important sound in any language" (1936, p. 79). This becomes even more important in a classroom family that boasts students from varied cultures whose names may sound different, even strange, to one another. When teachers call students by name in positive contexts and expect classmates to do the same, they are affirming who students are and where they come from.

But names are only the beginning. All students "come alive" somewhere in the world beyond school. Teachers can intentionally uncover students' passions by having them make pie charts or graphs of their interests (see p. 28) or asking Attendance Questions such as "When I call your name, tell me your favorite cartoon character" (see p. 19). Once such information becomes "public domain" in classroom conversation, teachers can reference it in examples, explanations, and assignment options. Such connections honor what individual students value and enhance their sense of belonging.

Cultivating Relationships

As the head of the classroom family, it is the teacher's job not only to connect with each student but also to connect students with one another. Because most students don't form bonds or reach out to their peers spontaneously or independently, teachers must lay a relational foundation from the first day of school and continue that work throughout the year. Surprisingly, using strategies that celebrate *individuality* can also build *community*. For example, when a teacher uses Attendance Questions, students discover things they have in common, and cries of "Me, too!" fill the room.

Community-building strategies like these can foster a sense of affirmation and plant the seeds of relationships because they help students to

- **Find common ground.** Once teachers have used Attendance Questions with the whole class, students can respond to "quick questions" before beginning partner work (e.g., "Cats or dogs?"). They may also use fist bumps, high fives, and catchphrases ("Pat your brain; you worked hard!") to begin and end activities with a personal touch. Alternatively, teachers can include a quick question at the top of any paper a student is to turn in (e.g., "How are you today?" or "Favorite ice cream flavor?"). This information gives teachers a window into children's lives as well as a means of connecting students (e.g., "We're going to form ice cream groups:

chocolate in this corner, cookie dough in that corner, strawberry near the door, and every other flavor in the front of the room").

- **Affirm one another.** Celebrating successes, both big and small, goes a long way toward building a culture of collaboration. When an individual, a small group, or the entire class does something worthy of praise, students can celebrate with an "alligator clap" (using their arms to clap like an alligator opening and closing its mouth) or, on cue, call out, "Whale done!" while using their hands to mimic the motion of a whale sounding in the ocean. To express agreement or celebration in a more subtle way, "silent applause" (waving hands in the air) or the "shrimp clap" (quickly opening and closing forefingers and thumbs) can serve the same purpose.

- **Manage the classroom together.** There are multiple points in a day when students must come together after working individually, in small groups, or at centers or stations. In a busy classroom, these transitions are best signaled with full-group responses. Giving students a say in developing these signals provides an opportunity for student buy-in and bonding. For example, students might assist the teacher in developing a few responsive clapping patterns. Teachers can use their students' favorite songs to signal a transition or to bring groups back together following an activity. Call-and-response phrases are another effective method for reconvening the class, especially if students help generate the phrases. For example, to signal students to await further instructions, a teacher may call out "SpongeBob!" to which the students respond in unison, "SquarePants!"

- **Build academic skills.** Teachers can use community-building activities to introduce strategies and skills that can be leveraged for academic purposes. For example, a teacher using the Matrix organizer (see p. 22) to help students find areas of commonality is also introducing the academic skills of comparing and contrasting, which students can eventually apply to characters, animals, community members, numbers, and so on. In other words, time spent helping students connect at the beginning of the year will pay off in multiple ways throughout the year.

Cultivating relationships is not an August-to-September "event"; rather, it is a process that continues until the last day of school. It establishes the expectation and the norm that students function as interdependent family members who work together to keep the classroom running smoothly.

Fostering Growth

As family head, the teacher is responsible not only for students' social and emotional well-being but also for each student's academic growth. While students need to feel accepted and valued for who they are right now, they also need to see themselves as dynamic individuals with much potential for academic growth. This belief is essential because, as Carol Dweck's (2006) work has revealed, students who believe their intelligence is malleable—that is, those who have a *growth mindset*—tend to persevere in the face of hardship. In contrast, students who believe their intelligence is static— that is, those who have a *fixed mindset*—tend to shut down in the face of challenge. This is true whether students see themselves as high achievers or low achievers.

Students will have the greatest chance for success if both they and their teacher view intelligence as a seed or a sapling, ripe for growth. Both the teacher and the student are responsible for nurturing that plant—the student by bathing it in the sunlight of concentrated effort and the teacher by watering it with appropriate feedback and instruction. The bottom line is that both the learner and the teacher *expect* to see growth; if they don't, they adjust, tending and pruning as needed until the roots grow down and the shoots grow up. This cycle fosters hope and persistence, two key indicators of a family's health and well-being.

It's also important to introduce the idea of differentiation as a method for promoting growth. If students recognize that each classmate is a unique individual with varying strengths and needs, then it will make sense that different students require different kinds of tending and pruning. Addressing this reality early in the school year invites students to adopt the expectation that different learners will need different tools and tasks to grow.

Strengthening Family Bonds Through Grouping

In any classroom, grouping can be either a catalyst for strengthening family bonds or a force that tears those bonds apart. Grouping is a means to an end, and no single grouping configuration is inherently better than another. More important than the grouping itself is the "fit" between the teacher's instructional purpose and the makeup or composition of the group. For example, a teacher might use a whole-group format to introduce concepts, model or reinforce processes, share work, or bring closure to a lesson or unit. That same teacher may use partners for practice or sense-making activities, and small groups for discussion or working on interdependent tasks.

Over time, a teacher's grouping decisions send powerful messages to students about their roles in and value to the classroom family. When they are put into a group, students begin to size up the learning situation (*Who's in my group? Who's in that group? What are we doing? What are they doing?*). They are conducting a kind of status check, gathering clues about what the teacher believes about the capacity of every student in the room. When groups are static—when they don't change often or in response to task purpose and evidence of student readiness, interest, or learning profile—students are likely to make inaccurate inferences about themselves and their peers.

To ensure that all students are valued and contributing family members, a teacher in a differentiated classroom groups flexibly. *Flexible grouping* is the means through which teachers can elevate the status of—and develop a growth mindset in—all students. When teachers group flexibly, they organize students intentionally and fluidly for different learning experiences by making a series of deliberate and purposeful decisions about the size of the group, who belongs in the group, and how the groups will be formed.

Practiced well, flexible grouping can

- **Bring students together (versus keeping them apart).** By nature and necessity, breaking the class into groups separates members of the classroom family. With flexible grouping, this separation is temporary. Over the course of days, weeks, and months, students are working with a wide variety of peers. Fresh and varied groupings bring students together in new ways that continuous whole-group work, independent work, or interaction in a static group would prevent.

- **Foster genuine relationships (versus making superficial connections).** Simply plopping students next to a variety of partners or placing them in new literature circles every week doesn't automatically create close or instant friendships. Genuine relationships are formed over the course of the year and require that the teacher plan multiple opportunities for students to work with all peers, driven by authentic purposes, for both longer and shorter time frames.

- **Expose students to new and divergent perspectives (versus keeping them "stuck" with the same bunch).** Much like adults, children of all ages gravitate toward people who are like them—who share their points of view, have similar experiences and interests, and seem to value the same things. Wanting to stick with one's "buddies" is understandable, and sometimes beneficial, but students can also get *too* comfortable or even stuck in a rut working with the same peers day in and day out. Flexible grouping pushes students out of their comfort zones and into interactions with peers they might not otherwise choose or get a chance to learn from.

Flexible grouping is the mechanism through which teachers build bonds among members of the classroom family. The *ultimate* purpose for using different grouping configurations is to grant students access to rich learning opportunities, both common and differentiated.

We Are Family

Just as with actual families, no classroom family is "perfect." But by celebrating students' unique qualities, cultivating relationships, and fostering a growth mindset as well as grouping flexibly to strengthen these pursuits, teachers can sustain the health of the classroom community. Part 2 of this chapter outlines specific strategies to support this endeavor.

> **Examples of Before and After "Upgrades"**
> To illustrate what this book's principles and strategies look like in action, Part 1 of each chapter closes with an exploration of how one teacher has upgraded his or her approach to more closely adhere to the chapter's principles. These before-and-after examples are designed to demonstrate a continuum of growth.

A Community-Building Upgrade

Nicole King loved to welcome her new 1st graders to her room each year. Because her established routine worked well, she tended to focus her professional goals on curriculum or instruction. But Nicole began to wonder if her opening-of-school activities could also use a "makeover."

Before Upgrade

Last year, Nicole spent many days preparing for students' arrival by setting up her room, complete with a "Welcome to Ms. King's Class" bulletin board on which she would post the photos she took of all her students on the first day of school. During week 1, Nicole conducted detailed assessments of students' reading levels and created a laminated grouping chart of the first quarter's reading groups. She flipped the light switch to signal when it was time to move to those reading groups. Most other groupings were selected by students, such as when they chose centers in the afternoon or did a "turn and talk" with the classmate they sat next to during circle time. She felt her classroom was a welcoming and collaborative space but recognized that, for the most part, students worked with the same peers from day to day.

After Upgrade

This year, Nicole decided that one of her professional growth goals would be to make sure that students knew and worked purposefully with all of their classmates. She started by giving her "Welcome" bulletin board a makeover. Rather than simply posting students' photos, Nicole implemented a project she called "Our 1st Grade Timelines." Each student received a one-by-three-foot piece of paper with a horizontal line across the middle. As a class, students talked about how they might be feeling about starting 2nd grade the following year. Then, after Nicole took each student's photo, students pasted their pictures as the first event on their timeline, labeled the event, and added a descriptive word or phrase to represent their emotions.

Throughout the year, students selected five to seven significant moments from home or school to add to their timelines, each accompanied by a photo or student illustration and a short description. Periodically, Nicole gathered the class members to ask one another questions about their events, celebrate their peers' successes, and encourage one another in their struggles. When she formed new groups, Nicole used the timelines as fuel for an icebreaker prompt (e.g., "Before you get started on your task, take 30 seconds each to share one event from your timeline."). These routines made students more comfortable with one another.

Nicole's grouping practices were different this year, too. Instead of a laminated chart for reading groups, she posted a blank chart on the front whiteboard that she used for all kinds of grouping. The chart depicted the layout of her room, and students' names were on magnets, allowing her to quickly adjust the composition of the groups. She could fluidly adjust reading groups as well as form new groups for different subjects and purposes, such as interest-based tasks or station rotations. Nicole noticed how this frequent rearrangement kept students on their toes, ready to adjust and eager to work with new classmates. In fact, everything felt more interactive, including her signals for attention. Students even helped her develop two signals:

1. When Nicole rang a bell, students responded, "Brrrr!" while freezing in their positions.
2. Playing on her name (Ms. King), Nicole would proclaim, "Royal citizens!" to which students cried in unison, "Unite!"

Not only did these measures enliven the school day, but they also significantly enhanced the feeling among students that their class was, indeed, a family.

Part 2:

Tools and Strategies

Strategies for Building Family Ties

What They Are:

Proactive strategies to help the teacher get to know students, to help students get to know one another, and to establish the feeling of "family" that enhances the implementation of differentiated tasks.

How They Work:

The teacher chooses one or two of these student-involved activities to use at the beginning of the year to strategically discover students' backgrounds and interests and help them find areas of overlap with one another. The teacher should continue to implement a variety of strategies throughout the school year to reinforce the sense of connection and shared purpose.

What They're Good For:

- The primary purpose for using community-building strategies is to help the teacher get to know what makes students "tick" so that he or she can connect with students on a personal level, ensuring they feel known and cared for.
- The teacher can also use the information gleaned from these activities to target student interests in instruction (e.g., through interest-based tasks, word problems, writing prompts, or student groups).
- These strategies encourage students to take risks, build an atmosphere of collaboration and trust, and cultivate relationships among students.

Tips:

- Most strategies require a setup; the teacher should make the point of the exercise clear in its introduction.
- With the exception of Attendance Questions and Fold the Line, all strategies in this section require the teacher to debrief with students following the experience. A combination of class discussion and individual reflection works best.
- Most community-building strategies can be repurposed as instructional strategies to help students process content and skills. Five strategies provide specific academic connections.
- The strategies work best if the teacher models them first, sharing his or her own stories and interests.

Strategies for Discovering Interests and Fostering Connections

---

Attendance Questions

Purpose:

- To build the foundation for an interactive class by beginning the day with *every* student speaking and sharing
- To help students uncover connections with their classmates

Directions:

- At the beginning of the class period, pose a prompt (either aloud or on the board).
- Have students announce their attendance in class by stating their name and their answer to the prompt.
- Use a simple question for efficiency (e.g., *Dogs or cats? Ice cream or cake? TV or video games? Favorite food? Favorite game?*).
- Use a more complex question if it holds the potential to serve as a lesson "hook" (e.g., *Who's the person you most admire?* to introduce a discussion of heroes in stories).

Variations:

- **Greeting Graffiti.** Write or display an Attendance Question, prompt, or topic on the board. As students enter the room, they draw or write their responses on the board and sign them. Comment on ideas and patterns before erasing the board and starting class.
- **Goodbye Gabfest.** Students use the downtime before lunch or between cleanup and dismissal to write or draw answers to a quick Exit Question (similar to the quick prompts described above).

Me Shirts

Purpose:

- To give students a chance to represent themselves and share those representations with peers
- To reinforce the idea that each learner is unique in some way, and to introduce the idea that classmates have more in common with one another than they might think

Directions:

- Have students decorate their own personal jerseys (real shirts or paper cut-outs) with words or art depicting who they are (e.g., interests, favorites, family, friends, or descriptors). The decorations should convey students' strengths, weaknesses, likes, dislikes, and so on.
- Hang the shirts around the room or in the hall and challenge students to find any two shirts that are exactly the same. In all likelihood, no two shirts will be exactly the same, which leads to the discussion of difference—that it is reality and something to be celebrated.
- Use this activity to explain that you will honor difference rather than ignore it.

Variation:

Have students put their names on the fronts of their shirts and then decorate the backs with the "clues" about who they are. In the beginning weeks of school, hang the shirts around the room with only the backs showing. Featuring a few each day or week, have students guess which jersey belongs to whom. This variation encourages student engagement, as classmates spend extended time studying the shirts and making guesses about to whom each belongs.

Fold the Line

Purpose:

- To give students the opportunity to express their opinions, preferences, and experiences
- To give students the opportunity to discover their classmates' opinions, preferences, and experiences
- To vary grouping configurations so that students get used to working in different formations and to remove the stigma that the sole purpose of grouping is to address differing strengths and weaknesses

Directions:

- Ask all students in the class to line up across the front of the room in a designated order, such as by height (e.g., shortest to tallest); birthday (month and day only); or favorite color (in ROYGBIV order).
- Allow students to talk to one another as they order themselves, or increase the challenge by asking that they use only nonverbal means of communication. *Note:* Put a time limit on student movement and communicate a sense of urgency, or the activity can take up too much time.
- Once the line is formed, ask students to pair up with the person next to them or on the opposite side of the spectrum from them (i.e., to fold the line). Assist students as necessary.
- If there is an uneven number of students, have the middle three students work together.

Variations:

- Once the line is formed, students can state the reason for their placement in turn (e.g., when their birthday is, the TV show they most love or detest).
- After using the strategy once or twice, keep students on their toes by deciding in the moment whether to fold the line or whether to pair students with their neighbor in the line.

Strategies for Building Community *and* Academic Skills

The Matrix

Purpose:
- To help students discover unique and shared areas of interest
- To build scaffolding for students to discover unique and shared characteristics in academic settings
- To build skill in comparing and contrasting

Directions:
1. Put students in groups of three and give each group a 4x4 grid on paper. Instruct students to write their names across the top row and down the left-hand column, keeping the same order in each listing (see Figure 1.1). Then ask students to follow these steps:

   — Where a student's name intersects with itself, the student should write or draw one thing that is unique to him or her.

   — Where two students' names intersect, those two students should write or draw something that they have in common that the third student does not share.

   — In the upper left-hand corner space, record one thing that all three students share.

2. When students have finished, ask the groups to share any surprising connections they discovered.

Academic connections:
- After students have completed the Matrix as a community-building exercise, they can use it to compare and contrast content in many subject areas. Simply ask students to fill in the grid with content connections rather than their personal characteristics.
- Give all students the same categories to guide group discussions *or* vary those categories to provide scaffolding or challenge for students at varying readiness levels.

Example:

Figure 1.1 | Matrix Example

We All . . .	Ezekiel	Harley	Mason
Ezekiel	[Something unique to Ezekiel]	[Something Ezekiel and Harley share that Mason does not]	[Something Ezekiel and Mason share that Harley does not]
Harley	[Something else Harley and Ezekiel share that Mason does not]	[Something unique to Harley]	[Something Harley and Mason share that Ezekiel does not]
Mason	[Something else Mason and Ezekiel share that Harley does not]	[Something else Mason and Harley share that Ezekiel does not]	[Something unique to Mason]

Variations:

- Put older students in groups of four and give each group a 5x5 grid; put younger students in pairs and give them a two-circle Venn diagram to work with.
- Tell older students to avoid characteristics they can observe (e.g., "We both have black hair") or assume (e.g., "We are both in 4th grade").
- For all students, suggest and list on the board categories for comparison, such as siblings, pets, hobbies, or favorites (colors, foods, cartoons, parks, animals, and so on).

Star Student of the Day

Purpose:

- To build community by "spotlighting" a student each week
- Kimberly Laurance, a 1st grade teacher at Washington Elementary School in Berkeley, California, uses her version of this popular strategy to help students recognize and appreciate one another's commonalities and differences and to bridge her social studies and ELA curricula by encouraging questioning and inspiring and supporting student reading and writing (visit https://www.teachingchannel.org/videos/building-classroom-community to see her strategy in practice).

Directions:

1. Each day, select a "Star Student of the Day," making sure that every student gets the title at least once in the opening weeks of school.

2. Invite the Star Student to sit on a special chair at the front of the classroom and don any articles of clothing designated for the honor (e.g., a cape or crown) while the rest of the class, seated on the rug, cheers and applauds.

3. Classmates interview the Star Student to gather information about his or her favorite things, asking questions like *What is your favorite color? What is your favorite animal? What is your favorite food? What is your favorite drink?*

4. While the Star Student calls on classmates and answers their questions, record the information at the front of the room, using a repetitive sentence stem for support and drawing pictures above unfamiliar words to help students recognize them in future steps of the activity:

   — Isaraya's favorite color is pink.

   — Her favorite animal is the giraffe.

   — Her favorite food is soup.

   — Her favorite drink is apple juice.

5. After the interview is complete, as a class, read the finished article that students have "researched" and written about the Star Student. When students encounter a characteristic or favorite they share with the Star Student, they show their agreement using silent applause (waving their hands above their heads).

Follow-up (Primary-Grades ELA):

- The Star Student chooses one sentence from the article for classmates to copy and illustrate. Students may copy and illustrate additional "favorite" sentences if they wish.
- Some students may begin by including only illustrations with labels, working up to writing sentences as they become more familiar with the activity.

Brown-Bag Artifacts

Purpose:

- To allow students to share important information about their lives
- To connect to the concept of artifacts in social studies

Directions:

1. Ask students to bring three items or pictures from home that represent who or what is important to them. They may draw items or find digital images at school if they are unable to bring them from home.
2. Each student places his or her items in a brown paper bag and puts the bag in the middle of the carpet. Each student takes a bag that is not his or her own.
3. In turn, each student makes inferences about the meaning of the items in the bag he or she chose and guesses which classmate the bag belongs to.
4. After the "guesser" finishes, the owner of the objects explains which guesses were right and wrong and gives further insight into the significance of each artifact.

Follow-up:

Lead a discussion about how students in the class are both alike and unique, which introduces the idea of community from a social studies perspective.

Variations:

- Students collect artifacts or symbols of their evening or weekend activities (e.g., a movie ticket stub). Students trade bags and try to find out what their classmate did the previous evening or weekend based on the artifacts.
- You may also use this technique to introduce the concept of individual development and identity (National Council for the Social Studies [NCSS], 2010) or of using evidence to draw conclusions.

Timeline of the Year

Purpose:

- To give students a chance to share important moments from their lives with their classmates and to build authentic connections and enduring relationships
- To connect to the concept of time and change in social studies

Directions:

1. At the beginning of the year, give each student a one-by-three-foot piece of paper with a blank timeline drawn down the middle.
2. On Day 1 of school, lead a class discussion on how students are feeling about starting the new grade.
3. Take each child's photo and have students paste their pictures on their timelines as the first event, labeling it "First Day of ___ Grade" and adding a descriptive word or phrase to represent their emotions.
4. Throughout the year, have students select five to seven special or important moments from home or school to add to their timelines. Each event should be accompanied by a photo or student illustration and a short description.
5. Periodically, gather students around the timelines to ask one another questions about their events.

Follow-up:

- When forming new groups, use the timelines as fuel for an icebreaker prompt (e.g., "Before you get started on your task, take 30 seconds each to share one event from your timeline."). These routines can make students feel more comfortable with one another.
- Timelines can be part of what students share during student-led conferences.
- Use this technique to introduce the concepts of time, continuity, and change.

Pie Charts

Purpose:
- To discover student interests
- To review (or preview) representing numerical relationships in charts or graphs

Directions:
1. Distribute ready-drawn circles.
2. Tell students that the circle represents their interests and that they are to turn the circle into a pie chart that represents the things they are most interested in. Students' charts should include at least five sections whose dimensions reflect how interested students are in that topic or hobby (e.g., if soccer is Josh's chief passion, that section should be the largest).
3. Older students can also represent their interests as fractions or percentages, either in the pie chart itself or below it.

Follow-up:
- Students share their charts and discuss similarities and differences.
- Use the information from the charts throughout the year to form interest-based groups and to create intriguing word problems and prompts.

Strategies for Fostering a Growth Mindset and Introducing Differentiation

What They Are:

Proactive, concrete, student-involved strategies used to introduce the following ideas:

- Our brains can grow if we exercise them.
- Our mistakes help us get better.
- *Fair* means that everyone gets what he or she needs to grow, *not* that everyone gets the same thing.

How They Work:

The teacher chooses one or two strategies to use at the beginning of the year to introduce students to the ideas about intelligence and growth listed above. The teacher should debrief or discuss each strategy within the context of these three guiding ideas. The teacher can also use strategies throughout the school year to remind students of the "norm" of difference and the expectation of hard work.

What They're Good For:

- The primary purpose for using mindset-introduction strategies is to instill in students the expectation that they will experience challenge, as it is a necessary precursor to growth.
- The teacher can also use the information gleaned from these activities to reinforce the fact that students *do* have control over their learning. If students believe they can grow, they will.
- These strategies also present the teacher with the opportunity to redefine *fair* and to define *differentiation*. The more proactive teachers are about sending the message that difference is the norm, the less pushback they experience when students are assigned different tasks.

Tips:

- Unlike the community-building activities, most strategies in this section are *inductive* strategies and do not require a setup. In other words, students should not be let in on the "point" of each exercise until after it is completed.
- All strategies in this section require the teacher to debrief with students following the experience to expose its purpose. The teacher should not automatically assume that students got the point of the exercise. A combination of class discussion and individual reflection works best.

Graphing Me

Purpose:

- To introduce the idea that everyone has both strengths and weaknesses
- To establish the expectation that every student will grow, no matter where he or she starts

Directions:

1. Give each student an empty bar graph, with the y-axis marked as a scale with "beginner" at the bottom and "expert" at the top, and the x-axis depicting several performance-based items (see Figure 1.2).

    — Several of these items should be school-oriented and appropriate for that grade level (e.g., reading for information, reading for fun, writing stories, writing information, remembering addition facts, solving problems).

    —Several should be items that seem OK for students to struggle with (e.g., keeping their room clean, being nice to their younger siblings).

2. Leave at least two items as "student choices" that students fill in with activities they personally enjoy (e.g., drawing, playing soccer). Gather information on student interests through strategies like Attendance Questions, Star Student of the Day, and Me Shirts so that you're able to propose appropriate categories that will allow all students to come up with areas of strength.

3. Students graph themselves according to their self-assessed level of expertise in each of the areas listed on the x-axis.

Follow-up:

- Ask follow-up questions such as

    — "Does everyone have things they feel are strengths?"

    — "Does everyone have things that are struggles?"

    — "Does anyone's graph look *exactly* like a classmate's?"

- Share the point of the activity:

    — "Why should I assume that, just because you're in the same class, you share the same interests, strengths, and weaknesses?"

    — "I won't treat you all like the same person, but I *will* expect you all to move toward expertise, no matter where you start."

Examples:

Figure 1.2 | Graphing Me: Sample Student Graphs

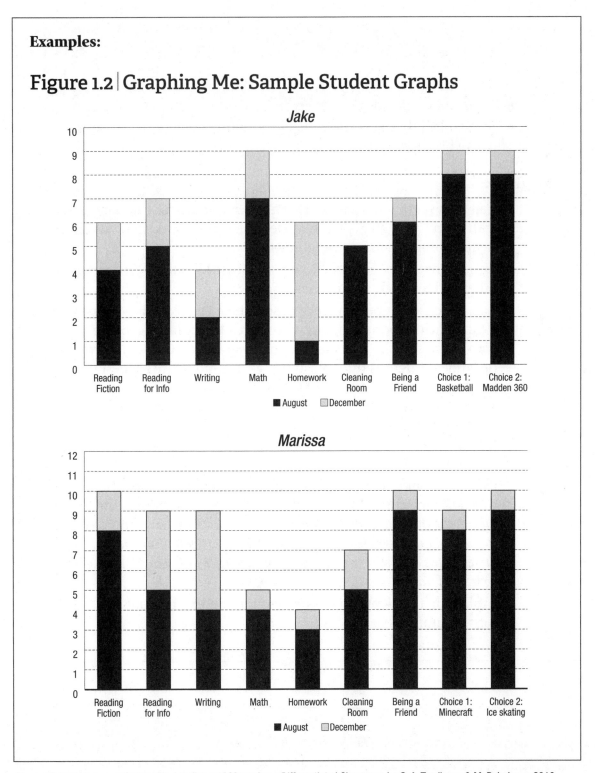

Source: This strategy was featured in *Leading and Managing a Differentiated Classroom,* by C. A. Tomlinson & M. B. Imbeau, 2010, Alexandria, VA: ASCD. Copyright 2010 by ASCD.

The Lineup

Purpose:

- To introduce the idea that everyone has both strengths and weaknesses
- To establish the expectation that every student will grow, no matter where he or she starts

Directions:

1. Call up a sampling of students (e.g., everyone whose last name begins with letters *A–K*, all September–December birthdays, students who are wearing blue) and have them line up.

2. Explain that one end of the line represents "I'm an expert," while the other end represents "I'm a beginner."

3. Call out different performance-based items (e.g., keeping your room clean, playing sports, singing, writing, reading, drawing, being patient with younger siblings, remembering song lyrics). Gather information on student interests through strategies like Attendance Questions, Star Student of the Day, and Me Shirts so that you're able to propose appropriate items that will keep all students moving up and down the spectrum.

4. For each item called out, students arrange themselves where they feel they belong on the continuum, determining their placement based on their personal level of expertise rather than by comparing themselves to others. To reinforce this, use a think-aloud to model for students (e.g., *One of the things I do best is sing; I sing at church and in others' weddings, so I will place myself near the expert end for that item. I will not compare myself with celebrities or even friends who sing; I just want to think about my own set of skills.*).

5. Explain that students do not need to remain in a line but can form "clumps."

Follow-up:

- Ask follow-up questions such as

  — "Did everyone have a chance to be on the 'expert' side of the line?"

  — "Did everyone have a chance to be on the 'beginner' side of the line?"

  — "Did everyone share the same strengths and weaknesses?"

- Share the point of the activity:

  — "Why should I assume that, just because you're in the same class, you share the same interests, strengths, and weaknesses?"

  — "I won't treat you all like the same person, but I *will* expect you all to move toward expertise, no matter where you start."

Shoe Race

Purpose:

- To establish the expectation that everyone will grow, no matter where he or she starts
- To provide an experience upon which the class can base a definition of *fair* that supports differentiation

Directions:

1. Call up two students with drastically different-sized shoes (do not call attention to this disparity).
2. Tell them they'll each have two "time trials" in which each will be racing against him- or herself to get his or her best time.
3. The first time, have each student in turn walk to and from a set point *in his or her own shoes*. Time each student, and record times on the board.
4. The second time, have each student *switch shoes with the other student* before walking in turn to and from the same set point. This twist should be a surprise; do not announce it ahead of time. Again, record their times on the board. In most cases, students' times increase.

Follow-up:

- Compare students' times in the first and second rounds and discuss the benefit of walking in shoes that fit.
- Explain that you'll be ensuring students' learning "fits," too, so that they will perform better and feel more comfortable. Sometimes they will receive work that's different from someone else's; this is because you are giving everyone a task that will ensure his or her growth in both skill and efficiency. Not everyone in the class "wears" the same-size task every day.

Source: Catherine Brighton, Curry School of Education, University of Virginia. Used with permission.

What Is *Fair*?

Purpose:

To provide an experience and concrete metaphor upon which the class can base a definition of *fair* that supports differentiation

Directions:

1. Ask students to define *fair* using synonyms; encourage them to go with their gut reactions. Most likely, they will propose synonyms like *same* or *equal.*
2. Write their responses on the board and explain that you are going to put these definitions to the test.
3. Call up two volunteers—one significantly shorter than the other (do not explain or call attention to the height differences).
4. Stand on a chair and hold a small "prize" (e.g., a dollar bill or a candy bar) just within reach of the taller person (i.e., he or she should have to stretch to grab it) but out of reach for the shorter person.
5. Explain that you will hold the prize at the same height and enforce the same rules for both of them: no jumping, no running starts, no standing on anything, no assistance from anyone or anything, no trickery.
6. Let the shorter volunteer try first (to no avail), and then let the taller person finish the trial successfully. Let the taller student keep the prize.
7. Ask students if the experience was fair. When they insist it was not, explain that the exercise upheld their definition of *fair*: the prize was held in the *same* place for both students, and the *same* rules were enforced for each attempt.

Variation:

When students define *fair* as "the same," ask everyone with glasses to take them off because it's "not fair" for some students to have glasses when not everyone else has them. Follow the same procedure for discussing and posting a revised classroom definition of *fair.*

Follow-up:

- Lead a discussion about what would have made the experience fair. Explain that lowering the prize is not an option because the prize represents your high expectations, which you will not lower for anyone. Write other solutions on the board (e.g., giving the shorter person a running start or something to stand on).

- Use the discussion to come up with a new class definition of *fair* (e.g., "*fair* = everyone getting what they need to stretch and succeed"), and post it in a prominent place in the room.

- Because the first round wasn't fair, give the shorter volunteer another chance to get the prize, this time using one of the modifications the class came up with.

Doctor Visit

Purpose:

To provide an experience and concrete metaphor upon which the class can base a definition of *fair* that supports differentiation

Directions:

1. Ask students to define *fair* using synonyms; encourage them to go with their gut reactions. Most likely, they will propose synonyms like *same* or *equal*.
2. Write their responses on the board and explain that you are going to put these definitions to the test.
3. Give each student an index card with the name of an ailment on it (e.g., a broken leg, a rash, a high fever, a sore throat, a bad cold). It's OK to give several students cards with the same ailment.
4. Ask students to spend a few minutes individually writing or drawing their ideas for how to treat their particular ailment.
5. Taking on the role of doctor, distribute a simple bandage to each student.
6. Tell students, "Raise your hand if this bandage will take care of your ailment."
7. The class observes the few raised hands and discusses why the class's original definition of *fair* might be inadequate.
8. Lead a discussion about what "fair treatment" means and how that might look in the classroom.

Variation:

Before debriefing the definition and concept of what *fair* means, put students in "like-ailment" groups and give them a few minutes to discuss what they might need to heal or get better. Write all of these treatments on the board to launch the discussion of what "fair treatment" means.

Source: This strategy was featured in *Leading and Managing a Differentiated Classroom,* by C. A. Tomlinson & M. B. Imbeau, 2010, Alexandria, VA: ASCD. Copyright 2010 by ASCD.

2 Articulating Learning Goals

Part 1:

How Do I Focus What I Have to Teach?

What to Teach

The standards. Unit 3 in the textbook. Problem solving. Plants. Charlotte's Web. *Fractions. Native Americans. Grade-level curriculum guide.* All of these are ways of talking about what students will learn and what teachers will teach. Each one *sounds* important and content-oriented and *seems* like something that students should be getting in school. But each one is only a snippet of what's truly important to consider when crafting curricular learning goals that empower students and lay a strong foundation for high-quality instruction and differentiation.

Planning a Unit, Planning a Trip

Imagine traveling by car from New York City to San Francisco. The destination of San Francisco is an analogy for teachers' intended destination for students: the knowledge, understanding, and skills that a student should "end up" with after a given amount of time. In today's elementary schools, there are numerous facets of the curriculum that can make the destination unclear or difficult to determine. Although they are *part* of curriculum, their role can be misunderstood. These include

- **Standards.** As important as local and national standards are, they are not curriculum. Grant Wiggins and Jay McTighe illustrate this point well with an analogy: "The Standards are like building code. Architects and builders must attend to them, but they are *not* the purpose of the design" (2012, p. 4). If curriculum is a house that teachers construct for (and with) their students, then that house can use many different designs as long as it meets "the code" (i.e., the standards). In the road trip metaphor, standards help teachers articulate what the destination should be.
- **Activities.** Teachers are rightly concerned with what students will "do" and produce during the course of a lesson or unit. But without careful attention to purpose and goals, such a focus can result in a string of fun

activities that keep students busy but take them "off-road" when it comes to providing evidence of what they have learned.

- **Pacing guides.** When a pacing guide or similar document is flexible and allows teachers to exercise sound professional judgment in response to student needs, it can be a helpful navigation tool. When such guidelines leave little to no room for detours or alternative routes, they restrict the teacher's ability to plan and differentiate thoughtfully.
- **Textbooks or packaged programs.** A well-designed textbook or packaged program can provide clarity, organization, and ideas that have been carefully curated by experts. It's akin to a comprehensive travel guide. But, rather than being *resources*, as they are intended to be, these materials too often become *the curriculum*. As a result, teachers shift to "autopilot," taking routes that miss the most important sites or lead to a different destination altogether.

None of these things—standards, activities, pacing guides, or packaged programs—is in itself an *obstacle* to focusing curricular goals. Rather, it is how schools and teachers treat them that can take curricular planning efforts off course.

Most teachers plan and implement grade-level content in subject-specific or interdisciplinary curricular units that span anywhere from two to six weeks, depending on scope. Typically, a *unit* includes a set of clearly articulated and closely connected learning goals, formative and summative assessment of those goals, and a sequence of learning experiences delivered through lessons that flow from the goals and equip students for the assessments (Wiggins & McTighe, 2005).

This chapter focuses on how best to determine and articulate the learning goals that make up the destination. Subsequent chapters focus on assessment of and instruction around those goals.

Using Concepts and Big Ideas to Articulate the "Worth" of a Destination

Planning a unit is much like planning a road trip. Deciding where to go is an obvious and critical first step, because, as Yogi Berra (2001) put it, "If you don't know where you're going, you might not get there." Wiggins and McTighe (2005) urge teachers to "begin with the end in mind" when designing units to ensure that goals, assessment, and instruction are aligned.

Let's return to San Francisco as the destination. There are many possible and worthy reasons for going to this city: taking a business trip, enjoying a vacation, visiting relatives, attending a conference, studying earthquake-resistant buildings, or sampling the cuisine, to name a few. When a friend asks, "Why are you going to San Francisco?" you wouldn't reply, "To go to San Francisco." Such a response would exasperate the friend and mask your real purpose for going!

Along the same lines, the reason for teaching something isn't the existence of the thing itself, whether it exists in the standards, in a packaged program, in a binder, or on a list. The contents of such documents are there because they have the potential to equip students with ideas, knowledge, and skills that can be used in and transferred to real-life situations.

One valuable and efficient way for teachers to articulate the worth and focus of a unit is to use *concepts*. Concepts are broad, abstract ideas—usually consisting of one to two words—that frame, unite, and organize the seemingly disparate chunks of information that are often presented as curriculum (Bransford, Brown, & Cocking, 2000). They connect topics, content, and skills to the essence of the discipline or subject area that is being studied.

Concepts are universal and timeless in their application and provide an integrated lens through which to examine a mountain of content and skills (Erickson, 2002). Various curricular topics and texts can fit under the umbrella of a single concept because they share common attributes. For example, in social studies, students could examine every conflict they study through the lens of *change*. A kindergarten teacher could unite her entire math curriculum around the concept of *patterns*.

There are two kinds of concepts: general and discipline-specific. General concepts are those that are organizers within and across multiple disciplines, such as *time, perspective, community*, or *conflict*. Discipline-specific concepts provide ways of classifying or categorizing topics and knowledge within a particular discipline, such as *symmetry* (mathematics), *needs and wants* (social studies), *habitat* (science), *fluency* (reading), *voice* (writing), *color* (art), or *fitness* (physical education). In this chapter, we have included a list of general and discipline-specific concepts for reference (see Figure 2.1, p. 44).

Carefully selected concepts provide openings through which students can tunnel their way into the core of a subject to discover its deep principles, issues, and controversies. For example, a teacher could organize a science unit around the concept of *interdependence* by consistently asking students to explore the ways in which changes to one part of a system (e.g., a plant, the human body, or the food chain) would affect all the other parts of that system. This type of concentration also invites interdisciplinary connections. For example, in social studies, the same teacher might focus on the interdependent nature of communities (e.g., members of a community have *needs and wants*, which are met by *goods and services*, which are bought and sold by *consumers and producers*).

Keep in mind that concepts do *not* trump or replace facts. Instead, they give students ways to *organize* facts and other knowledge so that they can retrieve them and apply what they learn to new situations as well as acquire new information (Bransford et al., 2000; Hattie, 2012).

Using concepts as an organizational tool makes even more sense in light of the ever-expanding body of knowledge in all subjects. For example, potential content for

Figure 2.1 | Concepts for Framing Lessons and Units

General
Altruism
Analysis
Approximation
Balance
Behavior
Beliefs
Bias
Bravery
Censorship
Change
Choice
Conflict
Commitment
Communication
Compromise
Continuity
Contribution
Conviction
Cooperation
Criticism
Cycles
Discovery
Diversity
Economy
Environment
Ethics
Evaluation
Evolution
Family
Fear
Habit
Hierarchy
Humanity
Humanness
Ideals
Identity
Independence
Interaction
Interdependence
Justice
Love
Memory
Moderation
Mortality and immortality
Organization
Patterns
Perseverance
Perspective
Philosophy
Power
Progress
Regulation
Relationships
Relativity
Revolution
Rules
Society
Stability
Symbol
System
Theory
Time
Transmutation
Values
Victim

Science
Adaptation
Conclusion
Conservation
Element
Energy
Equilibrium
Experiment
Force
Habitat
Hypothesis
Matter
Motion
Observation
Population
Principle
Sustainability
Taxonomy

Math
Algorithm
Correlation
Derivative
generalizations
Efficiency
Elegance
Equation
Factor
Formula
Function
Infinity
Label
Linearity
Measurement

Number
Operation
Permutation
Prediction
Prime/composite
Probability
Representations
Rules
Scale
Symmetry
Time
Variable

History/Social Science
Autonomy
Chronology
Citizenship
Community
Competition
Culture
Democracy
Demographics
Direction
Equality
Exploration
Fact/fiction
Freedom
Government
Globalization
Investment
Leadership
Location
Needs and wants
Patriotism
Place
Preservation
Production/consumption
Reform/reformation
Rights and responsibilities
Ritual
Subjugation
Supply/demand

English
Characterization
Composition
Conventions
Fate
Fluency
Genre
Heroism
Irony
Loyalty
Metaphor
Myth
Narrative
Persuasion
Roles
Rules
Story
Style
Symbol
Theme
Voice

Drama
Audience
Character
Delivery
Interpretation
Memorization
Mood
Performance
Presence
Rehearsal
Set
Stage/staging

World Language
Attitude
Code
Comprehension
Conjugation
Connotation/denotation
Context
Conventions
Custom
Delivery
Fluency
Interpretation
Language
Message
Pronunciation
Rules
Semantics
Structure
Translation

Music
Composition
Discipline
Dissonance
Harmony
Interpretation
Melody
Performance
Repetition
Rhythm
Technique
Tone

Art
Abstraction
Aesthetics
Color
Composition
Creativity
Expression
Form
Materials
Medium
Metaphor
Process
Representation

Physical Education
Competition
Discipline
Effort
Energy
Exercise
Fitness
Form
Leadership
Movement
Nutrition
Offense/defense
Position
Space
Strategy
Teamwork

Technology
Access
Algorithm
Efficiency
Hardware/software
Input/output
Interface
Storage
System
Tool
Universality
Utility

Source: From *Differentiation in Middle and High School: Strategies to Engage All Learners* (p. 36), by K. J. Doubet and J. A. Hockett, 2015, Alexandria, VA: ASCD. Copyright 2015 by ASCD.

history lessons is expanding every hour of every day! Information that decades ago was accessible only in print and to a privileged few can now be retrieved by billions of people in a matter of seconds. If units and lessons are to help students learn how to wade through and make sense of information, then concepts are key.

Getting from Topics to Concepts

So how can teachers go about efficiently identifying the uniting concepts for their disciplines, courses, units, and lessons? Silver and Perini (2010) offer a good first step in getting to the most powerful ideas: by taking the unit, lesson topic, focus, or text and considering what it is a "study" in, like this:

_____, a study in _____.
      (Topic/Focus/Text)   (Concept)

A unit on *insects*, for example, might be viewed as a study in *structure and function*. A unit on *the American Revolution* could be a study in *conflict over power*. *Addition and subtraction* might be a study in *balance*. A series of lessons on *opinion writing* could be a study in *perspective*. A look at the work of Mo Willems could be a study in *character* or *voice*.

Concepts are also useful for elevating the goals for teaching a particular story or text beyond skill practice. For example, *Frog and Toad Together* by Arnold Lobel is not a study in making inferences, but it could be a study in *relationships*. By studying the text through the lens of Frog and Toad's *relationship*, students will naturally engage in making inferences and finding evidence from the text, supported by rich questions.

This approach also helps teachers either move away from or upgrade units that focus on narrow topics with few or no transferable skills, powerful ideas, or connections to students' lives. *Native Americans* could be a study in *identity* and *survival*. *Rocks* are potentially a study in *change over time*. Sometimes, the topic itself needs to be broadened in order to make a conceptual connection. *Penguins* is a much more limited topic, for example, than *Arctic animals*, which could be a study in *habitats* or *survival*.

Although there's no special magic in a prompt like "_____, a study in _____"—and there are myriad other tools to help teachers consider a unit's purpose (see McTighe & Wiggins, 2004; Wiggins & McTighe, 2011)—it can be invaluable for quickly getting to the heart of what students should be studying.

Learning Goals: Getting Specific About the Destination

Concepts are only the *beginning* of unit and lesson design. They get students headed in a worthwhile direction, but they are not specific enough to constitute *learning goals*. In other words, saying, "I'm teaching about the structure and function of animal parts" is a good start, but teachers must also develop specific, assessable learning goals for the unit and for individual lessons and tasks.

There are three kinds of learning goals that every lesson and unit must articulate as the destination for students: *understanding goals, knowledge goals,* and *skill goals* (Tomlinson & McTighe, 2006; Wiggins & McTighe, 2005). These goals are distinct but interrelated, and they are all equally important.

Understanding Goals

Understanding goals (or *understandings*) are the principles, insights, essential truths, or "ahas!" that students should walk away with. They are the "so what?" of a unit. Another way of thinking about understanding goals is as overarching ideas that will last beyond a particular unit. They are written as complete sentences and often unpack or connect concepts. The following are examples of understanding goals:

- *Stories* in the same *genre* often follow a similar *pattern.*
- *Information* has the *power* to bring people together or keep them apart.
- Writing is a *process* that takes *time.*
- Maps and globes give different *perspectives* on where features, places, and things are *located.*
- People *migrate* to meet *needs* and fulfill *wants.*
- *Energy* in a *system* can be transferred or stored.
- The *relationship* between plants and animals is *interdependent.*
- An equal sign shows *balance* between the *values* on both sides of an equation.
- *Standard* units of measurement aid *communication.*

These examples use simple and direct language to make a statement about one or more concepts. Understanding goals can also be written in a more student-friendly voice and use language that *suggests* concepts. The latter is especially helpful in talking about more complex ideas with younger students, or in anticipating misconceptions. Here are some examples:

- People read (and reread) fiction to discover more about themselves, others, and the world around them.
- Writing begins in your brain. (It's first about thinking and ideas—not handwriting or spelling the words right!)
- Shapes can be combined to make larger shapes (composition) and divided to make smaller shapes (decomposition).
- When there isn't "enough" (scarcity) or there's "too much" (surplus), consumers and producers must make choices.

In the early grades, the most basic ideas can be understandings, especially when they are being introduced for the first time—for example, *A writer is someone who expresses ideas with written words* or *Everyone is a writer (including me!)* for kindergartners. Using "I" or "we" in an understanding goal can be helpful in personalizing the insight for younger children.

For teachers, another way of thinking about an understanding is as a possible answer to an *essential question* (McTighe & Wiggins, 2013). An essential question (EQ) is an ongoing, recursive inquiry that drives the study of a discipline, concept, or idea. The relationship between understandings and essential questions can be direct or implied, but their connection to each other should be obvious, as in the following examples:

- Stories in the same genre often follow a similar pattern. (EQ: How are stories the same?)
- Information has the power to bring people together or keep them apart. (EQ: What power does information hold?)
- Writing is a process that takes time. (EQ: How long does writing "take"?)
- Maps and globes give different perspectives on where features, places, and things are located. (EQ: What can a map show that a globe can't—and vice versa?)
- People migrate to meet needs and fulfill wants. (EQ: Why do people move?)
- Energy in a system can be transferred or stored. (EQ: Where does energy come from? Where does it go?)
- People read (and reread) fiction to discover more about themselves, others, and the world around them. (EQ: Why read?)
- When there isn't "enough" (scarcity) or there's "too much" (surplus), consumers and producers must make choices. (EQ: What happens when there isn't enough of something—or when there's too much?)

Additional points about and examples of essential questions are featured in Chapter 4.

Here's the most important point to keep in mind: understandings are revelations that the *students* arrive at through careful, ongoing study. They are not simply statements for the teacher to display and students to memorize. Students can't just spit out an understanding to convince the teacher that they "get it." For example, students who truly understand that *responsible citizens in a community carry out interdependent roles and responsibilities* are able to provide examples of how and when this is true; analyze situations in the classroom, school, and local community through this lens; predict and describe problems that can result when citizens fail to carry out their roles; and act as responsible citizens themselves. Understanding, then, is meant for the students to "uncover" using knowledge and skills (Wiggins & McTighe, 2005).

Knowledge Goals

Although concepts and understanding should be at the center of learning goals, there is no question that students need to acquire and retain facts as part of developing competency in a discipline. A key difference between experts and novices is that the expert has a deep well of factual knowledge from which he or she can draw (Bransford et al., 2000). But the expert understands those facts within the context of a bigger conceptual framework, not as disconnected pieces of information (Hattie, 2012).

Knowledge goals include the kind of discrete information that students can memorize or take notes on: facts, terms, dates, events, people, definitions, formulas, labels, categories, or rules. Knowledge is easy for students to forget—it is likely to fall out of their brains two minutes after a lesson—unless it is linked to a concept or related understanding. Knowledge goals can be written as short pieces of listed information, such as the following:

- Letters of the alphabet
- Characters, plot, and central message of *Sarah, Plain and Tall*
- Steps in the writing process: prewriting/planning, drafting, conferring, revising, editing, publishing
- Examples of two- and three-dimensional shapes
- Order of operations
- Different kinds of graphs (e.g., pie, bar, double-bar, or line)
- Types of maps
- Names and countries of "New World" explorers
- Events leading up to the American Revolution
- Parts of a plant (roots, stems, leaves, flowers, fruits)
- Differences among sedimentary, igneous, and metamorphic rocks
- Scientific vocabulary related to force and motion

Knowledge goals can also be conveyed as complete thoughts or sentences. Although this approach is more time-consuming, it is useful when crafting common curricular documents, designing lessons and units with colleagues, articulating vertical alignment across grade levels, or teaching something for the first time. Examples follow:

- Whole numbers can be written as fractions (e.g., $5 = 5/1$).
- Circles, rectangles, squares, and triangles are *two-dimensional figures*. Sphere, cubes, pyramids, and cones are *three-dimensional figures*.
- *Characters* are people, things, or animals in a story that interact with the conflict and move the plot forward through their thoughts and actions.
- The *author* is the person who writes the story. The *illustrator* is the person who produces the pictures in a story (i.e., the *illustrations*).

- A *nonrenewable resource* is a resource that is not naturally replenished in time for people to replace what they have used (e.g., fossil fuels or fissile materials). A *renewable resource* is a resource that is replaced naturally and can be used again (e.g., wind energy, water behind dams, or sunlight).
- *Wavelength* is the distance from peak to peak and trough to trough.
- The sun is the primary source of the Earth's energy.
- *Goods* are objects that can meet people's needs and wants (e.g., food, clothes, toys, or books). *Services* are acts that can meet people's needs and wants (e.g., babysitting, cutting hair, teaching a dance class, or washing cars).
- Barack Obama was the first African American U.S. president.

Phrasing knowledge goals as complete thoughts is also important for designing assessments, making it easier to ensure that prompts and items are aligned to the goals they are intended to assess.

Skill Goals

Skill goals represent the competencies that students will demonstrate as they apply what they know and understand. Examples include thinking skills, habits of mind, organizational skills, skills of a discipline (e.g., science, mathematics, geography, or music), or procedural skills. Skills do not describe or dictate production activities (e.g., filling out a worksheet or completing a Venn diagram); rather, they suggest intellectual avenues (e.g., comparing two texts that speak to the same central message or analyzing primary source documents). Skill goals begin with a powerful verb that describes what students do with or in their *heads*, not with their *hands*. Some examples follow:

- Gather and compare information from different sources on related topics.
- Investigate living things found in different places.
- Describe characters in terms of traits, motives, feelings, and actions.
- Compare two- and three-dimensional shapes in different sizes and orientations.
- Explain how environmental factors such as weather, people, and animals affect plants.
- Explain the difference between a rule and a law.
- Represent data in a graph.
- Measure length to the nearest foot.
- Distinguish living things from nonliving things.

There are many frameworks and schemas for thinking about and categorizing types of skills (e.g., Bloom's Revised Taxonomy, Webb's Depth of Knowledge, Wiggins & McTighe's Six Facets of Understanding). Regardless of approach, skill goals that guide instruction and assessment should require students to exercise higher-order thinking and suggest what students will "do" to grapple with the understandings and to apply knowledge.

The Connection Among Concepts, Understanding, Knowledge, and Skills

When concepts and understanding, knowledge, and skill goals come together, they lay out a clear, focused destination for students' learning. Figure 2.2 shows a full set of learning goals for 5th grade social studies. There is a topic (U.S. government) linked to a core concept (interdependence). The understanding goals are full-sentence insights, driven by essential questions, that students should gain about the interdependent system of U.S. government. Facts that students will use to "unpack" and show their understanding are listed in the knowledge goals. The skill goals articulate how students will demonstrate their understanding and knowledge.

Figure 2.2 | U.S. Government, a Study in Interdependence

Understanding Goals (Insights, bottom lines, principles, ideas)
- **U1:** The U.S. government is a system of three *interdependent* branches with different roles and responsibilities. (**EQ1:** How is the U.S. government "set up"? How are parts connected?)
- **U2:** The power of each branch of U.S. government is separated and "controlled" by an *interdependent* system of checks and balances. (**EQ2:** How is the power of each branch of government "controlled"?)

Knowledge Goals (Memorizable stuff, such as facts, terms, people, dates, events, or formulas)
- **K1:** The names, roles, responsibilities, and powers of the three branches of U.S. government
- **K2:** The "checks" that the branches of U.S. government have on one another

Skill Goals (Thinking skills, transfer skills, habits of mind, processes)
- **S1:** Explain the roles and importance of the branches of government.
- **S2:** Apply the powers of the branches of government to real-life situations.
- **S3:** Interpret the relationships among the branches of government.

It's important to keep in mind that understanding, knowledge, and skill goals form an interdependent relationship; they aren't a hierarchy of priorities. An insight from Henri Poincaré (1905), a well-known French mathematician and scientist, offers a useful way of thinking about the connection among these types of goals. He wrote, "Science is built up of facts, as a house is built of stones; but an accumulation of facts is no more a science than a heap of stones is a house" (p. 140). If student learning is a house, then knowledge is the bricks, understanding is the mortar, and skills are the building tools and methods. Just as it takes bricks *and* mortar *and* a process to build a house, so it takes knowledge *and* understanding *and* skill to construct student learning. Ultimately, we want students to *use* what they *know* and can *do* to show what they *understand*.

Communicating Learning Goals to Students

Once teachers have planned learning goals, when and how should they communicate those goals to students? Teachers differ in their methods and preferences for conveying these goals, and some schools and districts require teachers to display learning goals in a certain way, to recite learning goals to students, or to have students write or recite the learning goals themselves. Without question, students should have a clear sense of where units and lessons are headed, what progress they are making, and where they end up. Even more important is that the teacher keeps *all* learning goals (understanding, knowledge, and skill) at the forefront of his or her own planning and designs lessons that are aligned with those goals.

As they have been discussed in this chapter, concepts, essential questions, and understandings convey the direction and purpose of what students will be studying. Sharing what a unit will be "a study in" provides students with vision and purpose. Posing and returning to essential questions across multiple lessons helps students see connections. Displaying the understandings that students have uncovered and will revisit keeps meaning at the helm. These approaches keep students in the heart of the discipline they are studying.

Where Do Standards Fit?

National and state standards, along with the documents that accompany and explain them, can be useful starting points for developing robust learning goals. Many standards are written as broad or specific skill goals, beginning with a verb and describing what students should be able to do (and what they will be assessed on) by the end of a grade level. Examples from the Common Core standards (NGA Center & CCSSO, 2010a, 2010b) include "Quote accurately from a text when explaining what the text says and when drawing inferences from a text" (CCSS.ELA-LITERACY.RL.5.1) and "Compare two two-digit numbers based on meanings of the tens and ones digits, recording the results of comparisons with the symbols >, =, and <" (CCSS.MATH.1.NBT.3). These standards are skills and, depending on the focus of the unit or lesson, could be identified as skill goals. Like most standards, each includes or suggests knowledge of concepts, terms, or processes (e.g., quoting from a text, *inference, digit, place value, greater than, less than, equal to*). Standards often involve or imply multiple skills and need to be "broken apart" for purposes of targeting instruction and designing assessments that ensure students have mastered the standard by year's end.

Sometimes, standards articulate understanding goals; other times, they don't—even those standards that use the word *understand*. Take, for example, the 1st grade Common Core standard "Understand the meaning of the equal sign, and determine if equations involving addition and subtraction are true or false" (CCSS.MATH.1.OA.7). The standard doesn't communicate a full-sentence insight about the meaning of the equal sign; the teacher has to figure it out. One possible understanding is *The equal sign signifies that two sides of an equation have the same value; they are balanced.* With this articulated, the teacher can better ensure that students walk away from a lesson having gained this insight by "testing" whether addition and subtraction equations are true or false.

Another Common Core math standard, this one for 3rd grade, uses the word *understand* and includes an actual understanding goal (in italics): "Understand that *shapes in different categories (e.g., rhombuses, rectangles, and others) may share attributes (e.g., having four sides),* and that *the shared attributes can define a larger category (e.g., quadrilaterals)* (CCSS.MATH.3.GEO.1). A good clue that this is an understanding is the word *that*: the text that follows is a full-sentence insight about related concepts (in the example above, shapes and their attributes).

In general, it's neither efficient nor helpful to unpack standards into learning goals by focusing on one standard at a time and dissecting it in isolation from knowledge, understanding, and skills. A more useful approach is to group related standards together to figure out the goals that the standards explicitly state as well as those they imply.

Where Does Differentiation Fit?

Getting back to our metaphorical road trip from New York to San Francisco, we have learned that articulating a worthy destination requires a conceptual orientation to the content as well as specificity about the understanding, knowledge, and skills students will gain. This is not a "differentiation thing," but a part of designing clear and high-quality curriculum, assessment, and instruction in general.

Here's what *is* a differentiation thing: making that sure that *all students are working toward the same learning goals.* Different tasks aligned to different learning goals are not differentiated; they are simply different. All differentiated tasks should be centered on *shared* understandings, knowledge, and skills. Teachers are not trying to take students to two or three or four different destinations! Trying to do so not only is unmanageable but also erodes classroom community and hinders student mastery of important learning goals.

In subsequent chapters, we discuss exactly how to assess learning goals and use that assessment evidence to drive the creation of differentiated tasks—in other words, to design different routes to the same destination. This chapter is designed to help us make sure we are first clear about where we are heading. To scaffold that pursuit, Part 2 includes a Checklist for High-Quality Learning Goals (pp. 58–59) and Examples of Learning Goals Across the Curriculum (pp. 60–70).

A Learning Goals Upgrade

Without question, Lara Collins's favorite part of the year was the Butterfly unit. Her kindergartners loved the hands-on activities, books like *The Very Hungry Caterpillar* by

Eric Carle and *A Butterfly Is Patient* by Dianna Aston and Sylvia Long, and (of course) observing their own real caterpillars turn into butterflies. Their study coincided with a symmetry unit in math, allowing for natural interdisciplinary connections. Student excitement and parent feedback confirmed Lara's feeling that the unit was a high point for many of her students. Year after year, students who had moved on to other grades would stop by her classroom to reminisce about how much they had loved watching their caterpillars grow and change right before their eyes. One or two might add that they still wondered where their butterflies had gone after the release celebration.

Because of the way she and her students experienced the Butterfly unit, Lara had never written down explicit learning goals for it. During a professional development session at her school on curriculum design, Lara and her grade-level colleagues divided up their units to try their hands at framing goals. Lara took a stab at drafting some for the Butterfly unit in terms of conceptual focus, essential questions, and understanding, knowledge, and skill goals.

Before Upgrade

Figure 2.3 shows Lara's initial attempt at creating learning goals for the Butterfly unit.

Figure 2.3 | Learning Goals Before Upgrade

Butterflies, a Study in Stages

Essential Questions
- **EQ1:** What is a butterfly?
- **EQ2:** Why are butterflies important?
- **EQ3:** How does a larva become a butterfly?

Understanding Goal
- **U1:** The life cycle of a butterfly is egg, larva, pupa, and adult.

Knowledge Goal
- **K1:** Butterfly, moth, larva, pupa, metamorphosis

Skill Goals
- **S1:** Create a project that shows the life cycle of a butterfly.
- **S2:** Watch caterpillars grow into butterflies.
- **S3:** Write down observations.
- **S4:** Read books about butterflies.

Later that week, Lara sat down with her building-level coach, who had agreed to give Lara and the kindergarten team feedback on their goals. The team members received the following advice:

- "Stages" was not a robust concept; it had limited connections to other topics and to her students' lives. Through discussion, the team members identified several themes that were powerful conceptual vehicles: change, patterns, and cycles. Each of these concepts captured the essence of the butterfly study. In addition, patterns closely connected to the Symmetry math unit.

- Lara's draft essential questions were actually instructional questions; that is, students did need to be able to answer them, but they wouldn't necessarily pique students' interests, they weren't tied to concepts, and they lacked strong transfer power to other science units. A teammate also noted that essential questions should suggest the importance of learning something without having to "announce" it to students.

- The understanding statement, as written, was more about knowledge than about big ideas or transfer. The coach encouraged the team members to consider their concepts as they recrafted their understandings and to try "answering" the new essential questions in order to come up with the understanding goals. Lara observed that if she made "living things" the subject of the understandings, students could study *other* living things besides butterflies, both in this unit and in other science units.

- The "memorizable" information implied in Lara's initial essential questions and understanding goal became the new knowledge goals, along with additional facts and terms. The team members also came up with categories for some of this knowledge, which helped them organize and better "see" what they were asking students to recall.

- The skill goals that Lara had drafted read more like specific activities that students would complete than statements about proficiencies that students would attain through various activities. After reviewing the state science standards, the team constructed skill goals that centered on student *thinking* (versus just "doing") and invited students to demonstrate their learning in multiple ways.

After Upgrade

Figure 2.4 shows the revised learning goals for the unit.

Figure 2.4 | Learning Goals After Upgrade

Butterflies, a Study in Patterns: How Living Things Grow and Change Through Cycles

Understanding Goals and Essential Questions
- **U1:** All living things go through changes as they grow. (*But not all living things grow and change in the same ways.*) (**EQ1:** What happens to living things as they grow?)
- **U2:** All living things change through cycles. (**EQ2:** How do living things change?)
- **U3:** There are patterns in how living things change. (**EQ3:** What's predictable about how living things change?)

Knowledge Goals
- **K1:** Stages in the life cycle of a butterfly: egg, larva (caterpillar), pupa (chrysalis), adult (butterfly)
- **K2:** *Metamorphosis* is another word for the cycle that a butterfly goes through as it grows and changes from an egg into an adult.
- **K3:** Structure and function of butterfly parts
- **K4:** Types of butterflies native to the region
- **K5:** Differences between butterflies and moths

Skill Goals
- **S1:** Make, organize, and record observations about living things.
- **S2:** Observe, compare, and describe the changes in the structure and behavior of living things over time.
- **S3:** Represent and explain the life cycle of a butterfly.
- **S4:** Explain the differences between butterflies and moths.
- **S5:** Describe the characteristics of a favorite butterfly, including how to identify it.

To Lara's surprise, this collaborative exercise in articulating learning goals for a long-standing unit became a way of breathing new life into her team's approach to planning. The "upgraded" goals positioned the kindergarten team to make its Butterfly unit even more inviting and powerful than it had been in the past. In addition, the transferable ideas and skills reflected in the new goals inspired the creation of a RAFT assessment for the unit, which is featured in Chapter 7 (see pp. 282–288).

Part 2:

Tools and Strategies

Checklist for High-Quality Learning Goals

What It Is:

A tool to guide the articulation of learning goals for use in planning tasks, lessons, units, and assessments

How It Works:

Use the checklist on page 59 to guide the creation of learning goals and essential questions.

What It's Good For:

- Evaluating the power and efficiency of learning goals and essential questions
- Ensuring the alignment of learning goals for differentiated tasks

Classroom Examples:

See the Examples of Learning Goals Across the Curriculum (pp. 60–70) for examples of goals that are aligned with these criteria.

Understanding Goals

☐ Are written as complete sentences and phrased, "Students will understand *that . . . .*"

☐ Focus on a concept or big idea.

☐ Invite inquiry and require "uncoverage" (as opposed to *coverage*).

☐ Hold "transfer" power to self, world, discipline, and other disciplines.

☐ Are capable of being investigated on multiple levels or across lessons and units.

Essential Questions

☐ Are important to real people in the real world.

☐ Raise additional questions.

☐ Are worthy of discussion.

☐ Are provocative and debatable.

☐ Suggest more than one answer.

☐ Relate to or unpack the understanding goals.

Knowledge Goals

☐ Consist of information that can be memorized, such as facts, terms, definitions, formulas, algorithms, categories, and processes.

☐ Focus on *essentials* (as opposed to trivia or things that are "fun" to know).

☐ Are aligned with standards.

☐ Include prerequisite knowledge *if necessary.*

☐ Are related to the skills in which students will engage.

☐ Should be written in complete sentences if used for common planning or for planning assessments (e.g., "*Dynamic characters* grow and change throughout a story," NOT "the definition of *dynamic character*").

Skill Goals

☐ Focus on student *thinking* (what students do with their heads, not their hands).

☐ Begin with a powerful verb (see Bloom's taxonomy for suggestions).

☐ Incorporate higher-order thinking.

☐ Focus on a measurable verb.

☐ Avoid describing specific activities.

☐ Are aligned with but not limited by standards.

☐ Suggest what students will do to grapple with the essential questions and understanding goals and how they will apply the knowledge goals.

Source: Adapted from *Understanding by Design* (Expanded 2nd ed.), by G. Wiggins & J. McTighe, 2005, Alexandria, VA: ASCD. Copyright 2005 by ASCD.

Examples of Learning Goals Across the Curriculum

Primary-Grades Examples

Our Class, Our School, and Our City, a Study in Communities

Understanding Goals and Essential Questions

- **U1:** A *community* is a group of people who live and/or work interdependently. (**EQ1:** What makes a group a community?)
- **U2:** I am a member of many *communities* (e.g., family, classroom, city). (**EQ2:** What communities am I a part of? Where do I "belong"?)
- **U3:** Each member/citizen of a *community* has roles and responsibilities that help the *community* "work." (**EQ3:** What's my/our job in a community?)

Knowledge Goals

- **K1:** Key terms/concepts: *citizen, community member, interdependence, responsibility, role, rules*
- **K2:** Kinds of communities (classroom, school, religious, neighborhood, city)

Skill Goals

- **S1:** Explain how, why, and when interdependent communities function.
- **S2:** Identify and make connections among rules, roles, and responsibilities that are unique and common to different kinds of communities.
- **S3:** Propose solutions to community problems that are beneficial for individuals and the whole community.
- **S4:** Evaluate the benefits and drawbacks of different ways to make decisions as a community.

Source: Developed with teachers in Evanston/Skokie School District 65, Evanston, IL. Used with permission.

Sorting, Classifying, and Counting Objects, a Study in Attributes
(Based on Common Core Standards for Mathematical Practice, Kindergarten, K.MD.3)

Understanding Goals and Essential Question

EQ: How can we "see," count, and put objects in order?

- **U1:** Objects can have similar and different *attributes. Kidspeak:* Objects can look the same in some ways and different in other ways.
- **U2:** Objects can be sorted into categories that represent the *attributes* they share. *Kidspeak:* We can group objects together by the ways they look the same.
- **U3:** The number of objects in a category can be counted. The categories can be put in an order. *Kidspeak:* We can count how many objects there are of a kind and put them in order of how many there are of each one.

Knowledge Goals

- **K1:** Key terms/concepts: *attribute, category, order (least to greatest)*
- **K2:** Counting numbers 1–10

Skill Goals

- **S1**: Classify objects into given categories.
- **S2:** Count the number of objects in a category.
- **S3:** Sort categories of objects by count (i.e., the number of objects in the category).

Stories, a Study in Patterns

(Based on Common Core ELA Standards in Reading: Literature, Grade 1)

Understanding Goals and Essential Questions

EQs: What makes a story a story? How are stories alike?

- **U1:** Many stories follow a predictable *pattern* (e.g., beginning, middle, and end).
- **U2:** Stories have a sequence of events that happen in a certain time and place (*setting*).
- **U3:** Stories usually have a *problem* that characters are trying to solve.

Knowledge Goals

- **K1:** *Character*s are people, things, or animals that play a part in the story. Characters often face trouble or have problems to solve. Characters can be described in terms of how they look, think, feel, and act.
- **K2:** The *setting* is where and when the story takes place.
- **K3:** The *problem* in the story is the challenge or trouble faced by the main character(s) in the story.
- **K4:** The *solution* or resolution in a story is how the problem ends, or is solved or fixed.
- **K5:** An *event* is something that happened in a story. A *major event* in a story is an event that has a strong relationship to the problem.

Skill Goals

- **S1:** Ask and answer questions about key details in a text.
- **S2:** Retell familiar stories, including key details.
- **S3:** Identify characters, settings, and major events in a story.
- **S4:** Compare the adventures and experiences of characters in different stories.

I Am a Writer, a Study in Process

Understanding Goals and Essential Questions

- **U1:** I am a writer. (**EQ1:** Who is a writer?)
- **U2:** Writing is a *process* that takes time and practice. (**EQ2:** How does writing "happen"?)
- **U3:** The writing *process* begins in the brain/mind. *Kidspeak:* Writing is first about thinking and ideas—not handwriting, typing, or spelling words! (**EQ3:** Where does writing "begin"?)
- **U4:** Writers strengthen their writing by taking advice from "themselves" and from other people during the writing *process*. (**EQ4:** How do writers "get better"? How do they make their writing stronger?)

Knowledge Goals

- **K1:** Steps in the writing process: *prewriting/planning, drafting, conferring, revising, editing, publishing*
- **K2:** A *topic* is a person, place, thing, event, problem, or idea that the writer focuses on.
- **K3:** *Details* are pieces of information that can help make a piece of writing more interesting and descriptive.

Skill Goals (Based on Common Core ELA Standards in Writing, Production, and Distribution of Writing)

- **S1:** Use the writing process to produce and share a written piece.
- **S2:** Explore and use variety of digital tools to produce and publish writing, including in collaboration with peers.
- **S3:** Focus on a topic in writing.
- **S4:** Add details to strengthen writing as needed.
- **S5:** Respond to questions and suggestions from peers and/or adults about a piece of writing.

Plants and Animals, a Study in Structure and Function

(Based on the Next Generation Science Standards Performance Expectation "Design a solution to a human problem by mimicking how plants and/or animals use their external parts to help them survive, grow, and meet their needs.")

Understanding Goals and Essential Question

EQ: What do plants and animals have in common?
- **U1:** All plants and animals have parts that create *structure*.
- **U2:** Different plants and animals use the same *structures* for different *functions*.
- **U3:** Different plants and animals perform the same *function* with different *structures*.

Knowledge Goals
- **K1:** *Structure* is another way of talking about the parts of a living thing and how they are put together.
- **K2:** *Function* is another way of saying "job." All structures have "jobs"/functions.
- **K3:** External animal structures (e.g., eyes, ears, tails, nose, mouths, hands, feet)
- **K4:** External plant structures (e.g., roots, stems, leaves, flowers, fruits)
- **K5:** Ways that plants or animals use their parts: to see, hear, grasp objects, protect themselves, move from place to place, and seek, find, and take in food, water, and air

Skill Goals
- **S1:** Making observations about the natural world
- **S2:** Gathering and comparing information from different texts/sources on related topics
- **S3:** Comparing and contrasting the functions of similar plant and animal structures
- **S4:** Planning and collecting, discussing, and communicating findings from a scientific investigation

Source: Developed with teachers in Mannheim School District 83, Franklin Park, IL. Used with permission.

Upper-Elementary Examples

Creating and Interpreting Graphs from Data, a Study in Communication

Understanding Goals and Essential Questions
- **U1:** Graphs are visual representations that *communicate* relationships between data points. (**EQ1:** What's a graph and what does it "do"?)
- **U2:** In order to be useful, a graph must *communicate* information clearly. (**EQ2:** What makes a graph useful?)
- **U3:** Different types of graphs are "good for" *communicating* different information about data. (**EQ3:** Which kind of graph is "best"?)

Knowledge Goals
- **K1:** Parts and purposes of different kinds of graphs (bar graph, line graph, circle graph, type of vertical and horizontal bar graphs [side-by-side, stacked])
- **K2:** Benefits and limitations of different kinds of graphs

Skill Goals
- **S1:** Represent and interpret data using different kinds of graphs.
- **S2:** Evaluate the benefits and limitations of using different kinds of graphs in presenting a given data set.

Measurement Conversions, a Study in Equivalence
(Based on Common Core Standards for Mathematical Practice, Grade 4, 4MD.1-3)

Understanding Goals and Essential Questions
- **U1:** Measurements can be converted using mathematical operations to find *equivalence*. (**EQ1:** How can we change one measurement into another measurement?)
- **U2:** Changing one measurement into another measurement can affect precision. (**EQ2:** What can "happen" when we change one measurement into another?)
- **U3:** Using measurements that are *equivalent* can help solve real-world problems efficiently. (**EQ3:** When are equivalent measurements useful or necessary?)

Knowledge Goals
- **K1:** Units are *equivalent* when they represent the same measurement.
- **K2:** *Converting* measurements involves changing one kind of measurement to another kind of measurement.
- **K3:** Relative sizes of measurement units within one system of units including km, m, cm; kg, g; lb, oz.; l, ml; hr, min, sec.
- **K4:** Units of measurement for length and volume in U.S. customary and metric systems

Skill Goals
- **S1:** Rank units of measurement (e.g., least to greatest, greatest to least).
- **S2:** Convert measurements from one unit to another using appropriate mathematical operations.
- **S3:** Express measurements in a larger unit in terms of a smaller unit (and vice versa) within one system of measurement.
- **S4:** Use the four operations to solve problems involving measurement and conversion of measurement from a larger unit to a smaller unit.
- **S5:** Represent equivalent measurements in a chart or table.

Storytelling, a Study in Point of View
(Based on Common Core ELA Standards in Reading: Literature, Grade 3, 3.3, and 3.6)

Understanding Goals and Essential Questions

- **U1:** Stories are told through multiple *points of view* (e.g., author, narrator, characters). (**EQ1:** Who tells a story? In any story, who's talking when? How can the reader tell?)
- **U2:** The reader "tells" the story too—and has a *point of view* distinct from the author, narrator, and characters. (**EQ2:** How do I [the reader] "see" this story? What do I see that the narrator or characters don't or can't?)

Knowledge Goals

- **K1:** *Dialogue* is conversation between two or more people/characters in a story. In a (prose) narrative, dialogue is shown through quotation marks.
- **K2:** *Characters* can be described in terms of their traits, motives, feelings, and actions.
- **K3:** *Point of view* is how someone (the reader, the narrator, or a character) is "seeing" and understanding the events and characters of a story.

Skill Goals

- **S1:** Identify when and which characters are speaking.
- **S2:** Distinguish first-person point of view from third-person point of view.
- **S3:** Explain the difference between the author and the narrator in fiction.

Opinion Writing, a Study in Perspective
(Based on portions of Common Core ELA Standards in Writing, Grade 4)

Understanding Goals and Essential Questions
- **U1:** A writer's *perspective* is shaped by the writer's purpose, interests, beliefs, and experiences. (**EQ1:** What shapes a writer's perspective?)
- **U2:** A writer's opinion can change or influence other people's *perspectives*. (**EQ2:** What's the "power" of a writer's perspective?)
- **U3:** A writer can share his or her *perspective* by expressing a formal opinion. (**EQ3:** How can a writer convey his or her perspective?)

Knowledge Goals
- **K1:** *Opinion:* what someone thinks, prefers, or believes about something (e.g., a topic or a book). An opinion can be more or less persuasive (convincing) to other people.
- **K2:** *Reason:* an explanation for an opinion or a position. All reasons should be linked to the overall opinion and to one another.
- **K3:** The reasons in an opinion piece can be organized by order of importance (either *weakest to strongest* or *strongest to weakest*).
- **K4:** Specific linking words and transition phrases that show connections between reasons and evidence: *because, therefore, since, for example, on the other hand*
- **K5:** *Evidence:* facts/information that can be used to prove or disprove a reason or an opinion. Evidence can take many forms (e.g., examples, statistics, data, credible personal and expert opinions, or facts).

Skill Goals
- **S1:** Support an opinion with multiple reasons.
- **S2:** Develop reasons/evidence that include details (facts or examples) connected to the opinion.
- **S3:** Group reasons and support in a logical way.
- **S4:** Link opinion and reasons/evidence using words, phrases, and clauses.
- **S5:** Select an audience and an appropriate format for an opinion piece.

Westward Movement, a Study in Survival

Understanding Goals and Essential Questions
- **U1:** People migrated west to fulfill their needs and wants. Some people migrated west by choice, others by force. (**EQ1:** Why did people move west?)
- **U2:** The Westward Movement brought hardship and opportunity for different groups of people. (**EQ2:** How did Americans who moved—or were moved—*survive*? How did they adapt?)
- **U3:** Different groups of people might have seen Westward Movement as positive or negative, depending on what they gained or lost. (**EQ3:** Who gained something from the move west? Who lost something?)

Knowledge Goals
- **K1:** Key concepts/terms: *Manifest Destiny, pioneer, trail guide, territories, opportunity, terrain, landmark, risk versus reward*
- **K2:** People: Thomas Jefferson, Lewis and Clark, Sacajawea, Donner Party
- **K3:** Events/developments: Louisiana Purchase, Gold Rush, War of 1812, Oregon Trail, Transcontinental Railroad

Skill Goals
- **S1:** Explain what motivated people to move from one place (or geographic region) to another in the past.
- **S2:** Describe the risks and rewards people had to consider when making decisions about moving west.
- **S3:** Compare life before and after a significant historical event for different groups of people.

Source: Developed with teachers in Evanston/Skokie School District 65, Evanston, IL. Used with permission.

The Earth's Movements, a Study in Patterns

(Based on Next Generation Science Standards, Grade 5: Space Systems)

Understanding Goals and Essential Questions

EQs: How does the Earth move, and how can we tell? Why does the Earth move that way?

- **U1:** The Earth's rotation and revolution create *patterns*.
- **U2:** The Earth moves in predictable *patterns* that can be observed throughout the day, month, and year.

Knowledge Goals

- **K1:** The Earth has a *rotation* and a *revolution*.
- **K2:** The Earth's *rotation* is the spin on an axis between its North and South poles. The Earth completes one rotation in one day.
- **K3:** The Earth's *revolution* is its orbit around the sun. The Earth completes one revolution in one year.
- **K4:** Observable patterns caused by the Earth's and/or the moon's rotation and revolution: *day/night, daily changes in the length and direction of shadows, different positions of the sun, moon, and stars at different times of the day, month, and year*

Skill Goals

- **S1:** Distinguish between the Earth's rotation and revolution in terms of both mechanics and outcomes.
- **S2:** Describe the observable effects (for humans) of the Earth's rotation on its axis throughout the day.
- **S3:** Depict a timeline of the Earth's revolution around the sun.
- **S4:** Compare and contrast the observable effects on the Earth's rotation in the winter versus the summer.
- **S5:** Examine data to determine and describe patterns.

Source: Developed with teachers in Mannheim School District 83, Franklin Park, IL. Used with permission.

3

Constructing Useful Pre-Assessments

Part 1:

How Do I Know What Students Already Know?

Fortunately for teachers, no student comes to a concept, topic, or skill completely "empty" (Jensen, 2005). If students did, they would be vessels to fill rather than people to teach. All young minds are "under construction"—in a constant state of development, much of it not linear or predictable, along a route toward greater expertise.

In light of this reality, a teacher who wants to provide effective instruction must first uncover what students already know, understand, and can do. How well can students detect story elements? What do they think causes the seasons? Where do kindergartners' definitions of *community* come from? Are these 4th graders able to interpret and pose questions about data? The teacher's tool for opening up students' brains to find the answers to these questions—to ask, in effect, "What's going on in there?"—is pre-assessment.

What Is Pre-Assessment, and Why Use It?

Simply put, *pre-assessment* is the process of gathering evidence of where students are relative to learning goals *prior to* beginning a unit or series of related lessons, and then using that evidence to plan instruction that will better meet learners' needs.

No one would dream of traveling by car from New York to San Francisco without first scouting out road construction zones, "must-see" points of interest, and areas to skip because everyone taking the journey has already been there. Pre-assessment serves a similar purpose. It gives the teacher insights into student thinking, passions, learning preferences, and experiences—and even the content itself—that can be used to plot the instructional itinerary. Through pre-assessment, teachers can better foresee stretches of the journey where students might need more practice, more time to learn a concept or skill in a different way, or less time on something they already know. Metaphorically speaking, pre-assessment reveals which students aren't yet "in New York," which others are already "en route to San Francisco," and what might get all students excited about taking the journey in the first place.

Unfortunately, pre-assessment has earned a less-than-flattering reputation. In many cases, it is the *misuse,* not the use, of pre-assessment that has generated bad press. If its only purpose were to gather results to later compare with responses on a summative assessment, then pre-assessment probably *would* be little more than a thief of instructional time, a discouraging exercise for students, and a feel-good measure for educators. Hattie (2012) contends that students' normal development and simple exposure to material will naturally cause small jumps in achievement over time, regardless of instructional intervention. In other words, the traditional pre/post model may *reflect* that expected growth without having done much to *effect* change and significantly improve student achievement.

So why use pre-assessment? There are several reasons, each one linked to the benefits of using pre-assessment in instructional planning.

First, pre-assessment gives the teacher a more multidimensional perspective on where the class as a whole as well as individual learners are "located" relative to upcoming learning goals. It's all too easy to make assumptions about what students do or don't know without actually having gathered evidence to inform those conclusions. Using indicators like past performance, behavior, or general reading ability to decide whether students have high readiness or low readiness with respect to a particular concept or skill may lead to unwarranted (and ineffective) instructional decisions. Likewise, thinking, "I know my students," or "I've been teaching for a while . . . I get what 3rd graders need," is a less helpful stance than using pre-assessment to confirm long-standing insights and reveal new ones.

Second, unlike reports from standardized tests, pre-assessment yields current, classroom-level evidence of student thinking and skills that is relevant to what students are about to learn. The teacher knows not only what the questions were but also how each student responded. Armed with such information, the teacher can make timely and proactive decisions about what learners need to achieve mastery.

A third benefit of pre-assessment is its potential to give the teacher ideas for making a unit more focused, interesting, and worthwhile for all students. Items that tap into student interests can inspire inviting lesson hooks or reflection prompts while gauging conceptual understanding. For example, a teacher creating an ecosystems pre-assessment might include the item "Describe an important system at work in your life. How do the parts work together?" Students' explanations of video games, their lunchroom tables, a recess activity, or their family's rotating chore schedule can provide ideas for comparisons and metaphors that both clarify complex ideas and get students interested in the content.

Designing a Pre-Assessment

A pre-assessment doesn't need to be long or complicated. In fact, the best pre-assessments are often short and to the point. More important is that the questions or prompts "wake up" students' minds and prod them to provide information about what they know, understand, and can do (versus what they don't know or understand or can't do). Although there's no formula for designing a pre-assessment, the process follows some general principles. We advise teachers to

- **Begin by clearly articulating the goals of the unit or series of lessons.** Recall from Chapter 2 that high-quality learning goals are framed conceptually, driven by essential questions, and clearly articulated as understandings, knowledge, and skills. Without that compass, pre-assessment design is truly a shot in the dark—as is everything else in the unit! It's probably not necessary to pre-assess *all* goals in a unit. Instead, select goals for which there is little to no existing evidence of student readiness.

- **Consider prerequisites.** What background knowledge and skills should students have to be able to meet the requirements of the unit without pointless struggle? For example, a pre-assessment for a unit on fractions would probably include items that ask students to "place" fractions on the number line; add, subtract, multiply, and divide whole numbers; and "read" groups of items as parts of a whole (e.g., three of four cupcakes have white frosting).

- **Design questions and prompts that focus on measuring student understanding in addition to knowledge and skills.** Frameworks like the Six Facets of Understanding, Bloom's Revised Taxonomy, and Webb's Depth of Knowledge (see Chapter 4) provide useful schemas and stems for crafting powerful pre-assessment items. Some teachers also find it helpful to indicate the unit goal being measured next to each potential item. This process can be simplified by "coding" each learning goal (e.g., U1, K2, D1, D4). This makes it easier to "see" the balance among assessing understandings, knowledge, skills, and prerequisites. The Pre-Assessment Planning Template (p. 87) in Part 2 of this chapter can help structure this process.

- **Include items with good "discrimination" potential.** In assessment terms, this means including items that distinguish students who truly understand something from those who don't. Consider what a teacher could discern about student understanding from asking the following question on a pre-assessment: *Name four numbers less than –2 and greater than –1.* This question would elicit a range of responses revealing both misconceptions (e.g., zero isn't a number) and a grasp of the concept (e.g., fractions are numbers between –1 and 0 and 1 and 1).

- **Create relevance through conceptual connections.** The ideal pre-assessment gets students excited about what they will be studying. Start by identifying the underlying concept—maybe it's *interdependence, conflict, change,* or *perspective.* Write an item that invites students to consider the connection between the concept and their lives outside the classroom, such as *How could you use one or more math operations to show a change in your own life?* Students might mention adding pets to the family, subtracting siblings who have moved out, multiplying the number of baskets they made in a basketball game by the number of points earned, or dividing treats among friends at a birthday party.
- **Use items with potential instructional implications.** Asking students about narrow bands of dates, names, or definitions can squander valuable pre-assessment opportunities: such foundational information will most likely be included in the lessons regardless of student answers. Further, students' factual knowledge—or lack thereof—does not usually provide enough information to guide decisions on how to challenge and support students' processing of complex content. It may distinguish who has had the most enriching experiences without identifying who truly understands the content.
- **Arrange items in a logical progression.** The order in which students encounter pre-assessment prompts matters. As a general rule, begin with the most "invitational," most accessible, or simplest items and move toward more complex items. The idea is to ease students into the questions and give their minds a chance to engage with the content in a way that seems doable or is familiar.

The ultimate test of an effective pre-assessment is whether it gives the teacher information that he or she can act on. As with formative and summative assessment, it's only when the results come back that the designer can see how powerful an item was (or wasn't). With practice and feedback gleaned from students' responses as well as from colleagues, all elementary teachers can hone their pre-assessment design skills.

Pre-Assessment and Differentiation

What does pre-assessment have to do with differentiation? Because pre-assessment shows where students are starting from, it can help teachers determine when individual or groups of students need different things to make progress. As Tomlinson and Moon (2013) point out, "Pre-assessment helps the teacher locate the 'area of the pool' appropriate for each student as a unit of study is about to begin" (p. 28).

However, because pre-assessment cannot predict student growth over time, it should not be used to make judgments about students for the duration of a unit (e.g., placing them in static groupings). During the instructional sequence, teachers must continually check in to see how students' learning is progressing, where students are stuck, what they need to take the next step, and so on. These *formative assessment* checks have the power to reflect what has happened with student learning since the administration of the pre-assessment. Such information not only guides the general course of instruction but also informs *specific* decisions about differentiation. (See Chapters 5 and 6 for more on this.) In other words, pre-assessment is a *starting point*, not a definitive sorting tool.

Part 2 of this chapter contains several tools to help teachers plan pre-assessments. The Pre-Assessment Planning Template (p. 87) guides teachers as they think through what they want to pre-assess and why, and how they'll do it. The list of Sample Pre-Assessment Prompts by Type (pp. 88–89) can be used in tandem with the template to generate questions aligned with desired outcomes. Finally, the Pre-Assessment Examples (pp. 90–101), arranged by content area, can provide both inspiration and clarification during the design process.

Frequently Asked Questions About Pre-Assessment

In this section, we address common concerns among teachers and administrators about pre-assessments, our responses stemming from research and practice.

Do I pre-assess for every unit in every subject?

No! Most elementary teachers teach multiple subjects (reading, writing, math, science, and social studies). Embedded in each of those content areas are six to eight different units, so the idea of *formally* pre-assessing each unit is overwhelming. Wise teachers informally gather information from students before each unit to gauge experience, readiness, or interest but are strategic about when to use formal pre-assessment.

If I take the time to pre-assess, how will I get through the curriculum?

Discerning use of pre-assessment can actually *save* time by informing decisions about content that can be streamlined or skipped altogether. There's no sense either in lingering on what most students already know or in glossing over something they don't. Although pre-assessment can reveal significant gaps that take time to address, in the end, pre-assessment still helps the teacher make the best possible use of time.

Remember: there's no need to pre-assess everything. Even a more comprehensive pre-assessment doesn't need to be given all at once. It's OK to administer a longer pre-assessment in stages or parts (e.g., as exit slips), as the information is needed (Tomlinson & Moon, 2013).

It is also possible to use recent *summative* assessment results as pre-assessment results when they relate to the goals for an upcoming unit or set of lessons. The previous unit's summative assessment can capture information about the knowledge and skills necessary for beginning the new unit.

Should I use an end-of-unit test from a textbook or program as a pre-assessment?

Such tests are usually designed to gauge factual knowledge, not conceptual understanding, so they don't distinguish between students who have solid understanding and students who have truly advanced understanding—which is also why they might not make good summative assessments without substantial revision. These assessments also tend to rely on question formats that fail to capture students' reasoning or that allow students to answer correctly simply by guessing. In other words, they're not helpful for revealing misconceptions unless students are prompted to explain, defend, or justify their choices.

What do I do when students take the pre-assessment too seriously—or not seriously enough?

Often, when students are nervous about pre-assessment or don't take it seriously, it's because they think the teacher is trying to tell the "smart kids" from the "dumb kids." When pre-assessment is followed by forms of differentiation that create a status hierarchy or static groupings—or results in some students engaging in respectful tasks while others work on low-level tasks—that concern is well founded. Designing an invitational pre-assessment with well-worded prompts and item formats can also go a long way toward making pre-assessment feel low-stakes.

Won't pre-assessment scare my students or make them feel bad?

Talk with students about what pre-assessment is and why and how you will use it. Emphasize that it is not graded or scored but used solely for your planning and their learning. Students are more likely to believe you if they experience success through the lessons and tasks you design from the results. Depending on the age of your students, this might involve explaining throughout the unit how and where you've used pre-assessment results to design learning experiences.

Also, it's not always necessary to tell students that they are being pre-assessed. Using pre-assessment items on exit slips, as journal prompts, or as classroom activities—or just plain calling pre-assessment something else (e.g., *Gettin' Ready!*)—are "backdoor" approaches to pre-assessment that can reduce potential stress.

If I don't grade, score, or give credit for the pre-assessment, how will I get students to invest?

Experts (e.g., Guskey, 2003; O'Connor, 2010; Stiggins & Chappuis, 2011; Tomlinson & Moon, 2013) agree that grades do not have the extrinsically motivational value we think they do, except perhaps for students who have always earned high grades. If it seems students will engage in or complete tasks only when those tasks are linked to a grade, they have likely learned it from teachers using grades as motivators.

Frequent use of pre-assessment can actually be a good strategy for helping students become more intrinsically motivated. Most students can understand the rationale behind not being graded on something that the teacher hasn't taught yet.

What students *do* want—and need—is to get feedback on their responses. This doesn't mean simply marking answers on the pre-assessment as right or wrong and returning it to students. It *can* mean using individual or class responses in lessons (e.g., as hooks or in learning activities) or giving the pre-assessment back to students after certain lessons or at the end of the unit and prompting them to revisit or reflect on their original responses.

What about pre-assessing students who don't yet read or write?

Students don't need to be able to read and write fluently (or at all) to be pre-assessed. The exception is when reading and writing are the *focus* of pre-assessment. Perhaps even more than other students, children who are still learning how to express themselves verbally and in writing, or whose reading skills create a barrier to pre-assessment, need to be assessed with items that are jargon-free and give them the best possible opportunity to show what they *do* know and *can* do.

The following are some approaches to pre-assessment that ease the burden of the written word.

The teacher delivers by . . .

- Reading aloud written or displayed prompts.
- Using a one-on-one interview format.
- Showing and explaining images and words.

Students respond by . . .

- Speaking (e.g., to the teacher or into a recording device).
- Drawing (with or without oral explanation).
- Completing a hands-on/minds-on task (e.g., cutting, arranging, sorting, or matching).
- Performing (e.g., using movement or acting something out).
- Selecting from choices.

The teacher documents evidence by . . .

- Putting sticky notes in a file folder.
- Using a recording device.
- Taking pictures.

Part 2 of this chapter includes examples of pre-assessments for grades K–2, many of which assume that some or all students are not able to read and respond in writing.

What if there is no chance that students know anything about this content?

As mentioned at the beginning of this chapter, one of the biggest challenges in teaching is that students already know (or think they know) some stuff. Tapping into students' preconceptions prior to the start of a unit or focus can help the teacher anticipate roadblocks. Often, students have experiences with aspects of the content that the teacher isn't aware of. An extracurricular activity, a special interest, or a favorite movie may give some students more knowledge than the teacher is assuming.

If you have reason to believe that the content is brand-new, then pre-assess the prerequisite ideas and skills that the content assumes students have. Does the story students are about to read assume some familiarity with Greek mythology? Pre-assess that. Or start the unit without pre-assessing, but use formative assessment soon after students have had some exposure to preliminary or foundational concepts and skills.

There's also value in "priming the pump" prior to pre-assessment. For example, one kindergarten teacher wanted to gauge whether her students could distinguish symmetrical shapes from asymmetrical shapes. She first modeled symmetry using examples and nonexamples, without actually defining the term ("This shape has symmetry; this shape does not."). Next, each student sorted a baggie of shapes into *yes* and *no* piles based on their understanding of symmetry from the models. The teacher then interviewed the students about their decisions, documenting their accuracy and level of understanding. In this case, the modeling gave students a chance to engage in the thinking around the concept before the teacher gauged their readiness for it.

I gave a pre-assessment, but it didn't tell me anything I couldn't have guessed myself.

The culprit of a pre-assessment that doesn't challenge or inform teacher thinking is more often than not a problem with the pre-assessment items. Ask yourself,

- Is each item truly aligned with unit goals?

- Are there items that gauge *understanding,* or do they all measure only knowledge or skill?
- Are there items that have good "discrimination" (i.e., that have the potential to reveal even the subtlest differences in student readiness)?
- How clear is the language in each item? Does the language present a barrier to students showing what they know?

I pre-assessed and found out the kids are all over the place. Now I feel like I need 30 different lesson plans!

No teacher needs 30 different lesson plans! Look for *patterns* across students' responses rather than distinctions among their responses. Some of these patterns may suggest the need to create differentiated tasks; others may simply inform the design of whole-class activities. Pre-assessment isn't just a "differentiation thing" or a way of sorting students into groups. It's a way of beginning the journey with an informed view of your route.

A Pre-Assessment Upgrade

Fifth grade teacher Eric McLaughlin was less than pleased with the results from the pre-assessment he had given the previous year on the American Revolution. He didn't glean much that he couldn't have guessed or inferred without the assessment: students knew very little about the American Revolution other than scattered facts— and myths—about George Washington.

Before Upgrade

Eric's initial pre-assessment looked like this:

American Revolution Pre-Assessment

1. What year did the Revolutionary War begin?
2. What countries fought in the Revolutionary War?
3. Identify the following people: *George Washington, Thomas Jefferson, Samuel Adams, Betsy Ross, Paul Revere.*
4. Write what you know about these events: *Stamp Act, Boston Tea Party, Boston Massacre, Midnight Ride of Paul Revere, Battle of Bunker Hill, Battle at Yorktown.*
5. Who won the Revolutionary War?
6. What was one effect of the Revolutionary War?

Upon reflection, Eric realized that his pre-assessment included only questions that asked students to recall (or guess) factual information. For this reason, he couldn't envision meaningful or specific instructional adjustments that he might make in response to patterns in students' responses.

After Upgrade

After reviewing the understanding, knowledge, and skill goals for the unit, Eric took another stab at a pre-assessment. This one provided students with a preview of the unit's core concepts (*independence, conflict,* and *power*) and gave them a "fighting chance" to demonstrate their readiness for the content and skills. Eric also surveyed students about their learning preferences for potential unit activities (item 6). Here is Eric's revised pre-assessment:

American Revolution Pre-Assessment

1. What does it mean to "declare independence" from something or someone?
2. Give an example of a time in your life when *you* "declared independence." Include an explanation of whom or what you declared independence from, *how* you declared your independence, and *why*.
3. Which countries were involved in the American Revolution?
4. What people and events do you think of when you hear "the Revolutionary War"? List them below.
5. The cartoon below was published in a newspaper during the time of the American Revolution and is now very famous. It depicts a snake cut into pieces, each of which is labeled with the abbreviation of a colony. What do you think it means? Think about the picture *and* the slogan ("Join or Die").
6. Check all of the statements that apply to you.

   When we study the American Revolution, I hope we . . .
   _____ Read documents from the time of the Revolution.
   _____ Read from our textbook.
   _____ Watch videos.
   _____ Do a project. For example:_____
   _____ Write something creative.
   _____ I'm also hoping that . . ._____

Eric used students' responses to plan and focus the unit in multiple ways:

- Responses to items 1–2 served as "hook" material for the unit; as Eric shared the students' definitions and examples, he made specific connections to the Colonists' feelings and actions. He continued to do this at critical points throughout the unit.
- Most students knew that the United States and Great Britain fought each other (item 3), but not that other countries such as France, Germany, and Spain had some level of involvement as well. Further, the people and events that students associated with the Revolutionary War (item 4) were mostly on target, if somewhat limited. Using ideas from item 6, Eric created Learning Stations (see p. 326) and a Choice Board (see p. 298)— supported by a range of print-based and electronic primary and secondary sources—to reinforce and expand students' perspective on familiar content and to introduce new ideas.
- Students' interpretations of the "Join or Die" cartoon (item 5) were more thoughtful than Eric had anticipated. To support key skills goals around historical thinking, he created a series of tiered questions (see p. 208) to guide student analysis of both the "Join or Die" cartoon and other images from the period.

At the end of the American Revolution study, Eric returned students' pre-assessments and asked them to revise their responses based on what they had learned and to reflect on their growth.

Part 2:

Tools and Strategies

Pre-Assessment

What It Is:

The process of gathering evidence of students' readiness, interests, and learning preferences *prior to* beginning a unit or series of related lessons, and then using that evidence to plan instruction that will better meet learners' needs

How It Works:

Shortly before a unit of study (early enough to provide time to analyze results but close enough to instruction to provide the most recent data), the teacher

1. Articulates the goals of the unit or lessons in terms of what all students should know, understand, and be able to do, along with any crucial prerequisite knowledge and skills.
2. Designs prompts to assess each of these kinds of learning goals (especially understanding) as well as to uncover students' interests or learning preferences, if warranted.
3. Administers the pre-assessment and analyzes results for overarching patterns.
4. Uses the results to inform general, upfront planning for the unit.

What It's Good For:

- Directing the focus in a unit more precisely on what's essential for students to learn or master, given what they do or don't already know
- Alerting the teacher to potential trouble spots (common misconceptions or gaps in understanding) in a unit
- Revealing which students already know a great deal about the topic—and *what* they know
- Providing ideas for hooks, prompts, lessons, and activities aligned to student interests

Tips:

- Include just a few key questions that will provide useful information.
- Align questions with key lesson or unit goals (facts, skills, and understandings) as well as with prerequisite knowledge.
- Gauge students' understanding *in addition to* their knowledge and skill.
- Aim to discover what students *do* know, not just to confirm what they *don't* know.
- Include questions that are sensitive to and can reveal even subtle differences in student readiness, especially among higher-readiness students.
- Give students different and multiple ways to show what they know.
- Incorporate questions that reveal connections between students and the content.
- Make sure the pre-assessment is accessible to *all* students—not just to those with enriching backgrounds—so that it serves as an invitation, not a barrier.

Pre-Assessment Planning Template

Use your unit learning goals as a starting point for pre-assessment prompt ideas. Think through your ideas using this table.

Pre-assessment prompt	Goals or prerequisites assessed (use coding as discussed on p. 75)	What will this prompt help me discover? (Why am I asking this? What am I trying to find out?)	What is the "ideal" or most advanced response to this prompt?	What other kinds of responses am I anticipating or looking for?

Source: Adapted from *Professional Development for Differentiating Instruction: An ASCD Action Tool,* by C. A. Strickland, 2009, Alexandria, VA: ASCD. Copyright 2009 by ASCD.

Sample Pre-Assessment Prompts by Type

Pre-Assessing Readiness

- Read the passage and explain what the author's purpose was for writing it.
- Write a sentence that uses words to show the reader what your favorite shirt looks like.
- Make $0.50 in two different ways using the coins provided.
- Look at this student's work from a few years ago. What did she do well in setting up the problem and solving it? What advice would you give to help improve the clarity and accuracy of her work?
- Imagine that you are designing an experiment to test or find out how light affects color. Write a question that could guide your experiment.
- Do you see a pattern [in the shapes, in the numbers, in the data]? Describe it.
- What is the president's job? What is he or she responsible for?
- How can someone tell if a website is credible?
- Where and when was this photo taken? Why do you say so?

Pre-Assessing Experience

- What experience do you have with this topic/skill? When have you done or seen this before?
- What activities have you been involved in, in or out of school, that connect to this topic/skill?
- Briefly describe a project, performance, or game you have completed or participated in related to this topic/skill that you are proud of.
- Using the smiley face scale, rate how "good" you think you are in this topic/skill. Explain why you circled the face you did.
- In your experience with this topic/skill, what have you found to be the most important or helpful "rules" to remember or practice?
- Where do you use or hear about this topic/skill in your daily life?

Pre-Assessing Interest

- List three goals you hope to reach in this grade level/subject/unit of study. How will you know if you've reached these goals? How will your teacher know?
- Here are some topics we will be studying soon. Which ones sound most interesting to you? Rank your top three, and provide an explanation for why you chose each one.
- Which interest do you spend the most time on outside school? How might that interest connect to what we will be studying?
- Create a bar graph or pie chart to show what you are interested in.

Pre-Assessing Learning Preference

- What do you do when you have to memorize something (e.g., phone numbers, vocabulary, facts, or rules)?
- So far this year, we've used the strategies listed below. Which one have you liked best, and why?
- Use words and pictures to show what your "dream" version of this classroom would look like. Be ready to explain it to someone else.
- Most of the time, do you prefer to
  - » Work alone?
  - » Work with a partner?
  - » Work in a group?
- When you're learning about people and events from the past, do you prefer to
  - » Listen to a real person/teacher talk about it?
  - » Watch a video about it?
  - » Read about it?
  - Other: _____
- When you're learning a new program or tool, do you tend to
  - » Read directions before or as you begin?
  - » Dive right in and learn by doing?
  - Other: _____

Pre-Assessment Examples

Primary-Grades Examples

Retelling (Oral Prompt)

- Think about a story you know. It could be from a picture book, a movie, a TV cartoon, or somewhere else.
- Tell the story (orally or through words or pictures) to your teacher.
- Be sure to include where the story takes place, important characters or people in the story, and the important things that happen.
- If you like, you can begin your story with "Once upon a time, . . ."

Fiction and Nonfiction (Protocol)

The teacher provides students with 6–10 picture books, both fiction and nonfiction (including biographies), prior to lessons that define fiction and nonfiction. Some nonfiction texts should include drawn pictures, and some fiction texts should include photographs.

- Look at each book in the stack provided and decide whether it belongs in the pile marked "Real" or in the pile marked "Imagined/made-up."
- If you're not sure, leave the book "in between" or name a new pile.

After the activity, the teacher interviews students to capture their reasoning.

Analyzing an Image from the Past (Oral Prompts)

The teacher displays an image from the past (e.g., a photograph of an event or a place with people in it).

1. What is happening in this picture? Why do you say so?
2. When was the picture taken? (Last week? Before you were born? When your parents were little?) What makes you think so?
3. What time of year is it? How do you know?
4. Who is in the picture? How old are they? Why do you think so?
5. Where might this picture have been taken? What clues tell you that?

Community	
Words I think of	*Pictures in my mind*

1. Our classroom is one example of a community. What are some other examples of communities?
2. What do you think makes a community "work" or run smoothly?
3. What do all communities have in common?
4. What are some people or groups that are important to our community?
5. Choose *one* of these people or groups. Why is that person or group important to our community?
6. Think about that same person or group. What might happen if the person or group were *not* a part of our community?

Source: Developed with teachers at Temple Beth Am Day School, Pinecrest, FL. Used with permission.

Geometry (Shapes) Protocol with Oral Prompts
(Aligned with CCSS-M K.G.1-6)

1. *The teacher assembles paper cutouts of two-dimensional (2D) shapes (square, triangle, rectangle, circle, and hexagon) and representations of three-dimensional (3D) shapes (cone, cube, and sphere) and asks the student(s),*
   — What are these?
   — Are all of these the same? How so? How are they the same? How are they different?
   — Do you know some of the names for these?
   — Compare these two groups [of 2D and 3D shapes]. How are they the same? How are they different?

2. *The teacher shows the student different shapes (a shape or two is fine) and says,*
   — Pretend that I can't see this shape. How would you describe to me what it looks like?

3. *The teacher tells the student to use the room he or she is in for this next question and asks,*
   — What shapes do you see around the room? [Alternative: Do you see any of these shapes in front of you in this room? Where? Do you see any other shapes?]
   — Choose one shape that you see. Where is it? What is it next to?
   — Compare that shape with another shape you see. Is it bigger? Smaller? How do you know? Does it have more sides? Fewer sides?

4. *The teacher provides the student with paper, a writing utensil, and scissors and says,*
   — Make your favorite shape *other than a circle*. What other shapes can you make out of this shape? You can use whatever tools you need.

5. *The teacher shows the student a series of two different sizes of the same shapes to identify and asks,*
   — Are these shapes [e.g., a skinny triangle and a fat triangle] the same? How can you tell?
   — Place the shapes [e.g., two rectangles] in different positions/orientations. Are these both [rectangles]? How do you know?
   — How big can a [circle] be? How small can a [circle] be? Does the size of a [circle] matter? Is it still a [circle]?

6. *The teacher gives the student an assortment of pattern blocks and asks,*
   — Can you take a few shapes and make a new shape?
   — What shape did you just make?

7. *The teacher lets the student know that he or she has two final questions and asks,*
   — How do people use shapes?
   — How do you use shapes?

Source: Developed with Elaine Dekin, Sunset Ridge School District 29, Northfield, IL. Used with permission.

Measurement

The teacher inserts two appropriate images for each item.

1. Circle the _____ that is *longer.*
2. Circle the _____ that is *shorter.*
3. Circle the _____ that is *wider.*
4. Circle the _____ that is *heavier.*
5. Circle the thermometer that shows the temperature of the ice cream in the picture.
6. Circle the thermometer that shows the temperature of the hot chocolate in the picture.
7. Measure each line below and write down its length. You can use any tool you would like to measure the lines (e.g., a ruler, the cubes, your finger).
8. Why did you choose this tool?

Living Things

1. What's the difference between living and nonliving things? Use words or pictures to show the difference in the boxes below. In the *Not Alive* box, think about things that were *never* alive and will never be alive.

Alive	Not Alive

2. Choose any living thing. Name or draw it here:
3. What does this living thing need to stay alive? List or draw as many things as you can think of.
4. Is a rock a living thing? Explain why it is or is not.

Source: Adapted from *Tools for High-Quality Differentiated Instruction,* by C. A. Strickland, 2007, Alexandria, VA: ASCD. Copyright 2007 by ASCD.

Upper-Elementary Examples

Plant and Animal Parts

1. What do plants and animals have in common?
2. Name one plant part: _____
3. Describe that plant part's "job." What does that part do to help the plant?
4. Pick an animal and name one of its parts: _____
5. Describe that animal part's "job." What does that part do to help the animal?
6. Look at the photograph of a bee on a flower.
   — What do you notice about the bee? The flower?
   — How do the bee and the flower seem to be helping each other? How are they working together?

Reading Informational Text

Read the article on [topic].
1. What is the central idea of the article? (What does the author most want the reader to understand after reading this article?)
2. Write two questions that this article answers.
3. Answer those questions.
4. Write one question that *you* have after reading this article. This should be a question that the article content makes you wonder or think about, but does not answer.

Writing and Analyzing Opinions

This pre-assessment is designed to be administered in stages.

Part A

1. What is an opinion?
2. How is an opinion different from a fact? Give an example.
3. What makes an opinion *persuasive* or convincing?
4. What's *one* thing that you can do as a writer to persuade a reader that your opinion is the "right" opinion?
5. Use the one thing you described above to write a paragraph that expresses your opinion about whether teachers should assign homework.

Part B

1. Read the short opinion article provided and answer the following questions:
   — What is the writer's opinion? Say it in a sentence: *The writer thinks that* . . . .
   — Do you agree with the writer? Did the writer persuade you? Why or why not?

2. Which of the opinion-based topics listed below are most interesting to you? (In other words, which ones seem "worth" writing about?) Choose your top two.
3. List one or two other opinion-based topics you would be interested in reading about, writing about, or discussing.

Point of View and Close Reading

1. Think about the story we finished studying last week. From what or whose point of view was the story told? Explain why you think so.

2. What is the difference between the narrator of a story and the author of a story? Are they the same? Different? Use the story we finished studying last week or another story to explain your thinking.

3. The passage below [the first paragraph in the novel *Bud, Not Buddy* by Christopher Paul Curtis] is a scene from the story we will be reading next. Read it and answer the questions that follow.

> *HERE WE GO AGAIN.* We were all standing in line waiting for breakfast when one of the caseworkers came in and *tap-tap-tapped* down the line. Uh-oh, this meant bad news, either they'd found a foster home for somebody or somebody was about to get paddled. All the kids watched the woman as she moved along the line, her high-heeled shoes sounding like little firecrackers going off on the wooden floor.

   — Where do you think this scene is taking place? Be as specific as possible, and support your answer with evidence from the text.
   — Is the narrator in this scene an adult or a child? Why do you say so? Again, support your answer with evidence from the text.
   — Why do you think the first sentence is in italics?

Westward Movement

1. Have you ever moved, or have you always lived in one place?
   — If you've moved, what's hard about moving?
   — If you've never moved, what's hard about living in one place for a long time?

2. What are some reasons that people move from one place to another?

3. Name some people or groups of people who move from one place to another a lot. These could be people or groups you know personally or people or groups you know about from now or in the past.

4. Go to http://web.stanford.edu/group/ruralwest/cgi-bin/drupal/visualizations/vis-demographics and examine the maps of the United States from 1850, 1860, 1870, 1880, and 1890.
   — What change(s) do these maps show?
   — Think about what you've learned about U.S. history so far. Give one possible reason for the change(s) that you identified.

Using Search Engines to Conduct Research

1. How many times a week do you think you use the Internet to find out information? (Take your best guess!) _____

2. What kinds of information do you typically use the Internet to find?

3. Imagine that you want to use the Internet to find out something about _____ that other people might not know. How would you start your search?

4. Type _____ into two different search engines of your choice. Compare the results. How are they similar? How are they different?

5. Imagine that your family is planning a summer vacation. You have always wanted to go to [insert your dream destination here!]. Find *one thing* that you think will convince your family to go there. Then answer the following questions:
   — How did you find this? (What did you *do* to find this?) Be specific!
   — Why do you think this will convince your family to go to your dream destination?

Source: Developed with Eileen Goodspeed and Jeffrey Weir at The Skokie School, Winnetka, IL. Used with permission.

Estimation

1. Complete the table below. Explain your thinking.

How tall is the tree outside our window?	How did you figure out your answer?
How many kids go to our school?	How did you figure out your answer?
How much does your desk weigh?	How did you figure out your answer?
What is the population of the United States?	How did you figure out your answer?
How tall is the person sitting closest to your right side?	How did you figure out your answer?
How many books do we have in our classroom library?	How did you figure out your answer?

2. Choose *one* question from the left-hand column above. Circle that question.
3. When would someone need to know an exact answer to this question?
4. When would it be OK for someone to estimate the answer to this question? In other words, when would it be OK to *not* have or know the exact answer?

Source: Developed with Kelly DeRosa, Tom Erf, & Donna Sokolowski, Evanston/Skokie School District 65, Evanston, IL. Used with permission.

Positive and Negative Numbers (Integers)

1. Draw a number line from –5 to 5. Label each whole number on that line.	2. What does a number's sign (e.g., +/–) mean or show?

3. What temperature is it on the thermometer below? _____ °F

```
20 ⎓      ⎓ °F
          ⎓
10 ⎓      ⎓
          ⎓
 0 ⎓      ⎓
          ⎓
-10⎓      
```

4. Which is warmer, –9.4°C or –11.2°C?

_____

Which is colder, 9.4°C or 11.2°C? _____

Now, list the temperatures above in order from coldest to warmest.

_____, _____, _____, _____

5. Name four numbers less than 2 and greater than –1.

_____

_____

_____

6. Name four numbers greater than –8 and less than –5.

_____

_____

_____

7. Solve.
   a. 7 + 10 = _____
   b. 7 + –10 = _____
   c. –5 + –6 = _____
   d. –5 + 6 = _____

8. Susie owes her sister $7. Her aunt pays her $5 to walk her dog. Then she earns $4 babysitting and pays her sister back.

Number model:
How much money does Susie have now?

9. Write a brief explanation or "story" for each number model below.
   8 + (–3) = 5

   –1 – 9 = –10

Graphing Data

Shirt Colors of Girls and Boys in Ms. Smith's Class Last Friday

Shirt Color	Girls	Boys
Blue	5	1
Red	3	3
Yellow	0	2
Green	2	4
Black	3	2

1. Use your choice of the materials provided to create two different kinds of graphs that represent the data in the table above. There are many possibilities! Label all the parts of each graph so that someone else can understand what the graph shows.
2. What are the names of the two kinds of graphs you used?
3. Why did you choose to use each graph?
4. Write a question that someone could answer using each of your graphs.

Examples of Pre-Assessment in Music

Readiness Self-Evaluation

When I play my instrument, the tone is
- — Sweet.
- — Really decent.
- — Tolerable.
- — Not so good.
- — Awful—insert earplugs!

The best description of my playing ability is:
- — Take it on the road!
- — OK for the local crowd.
- — Only my parents would buy a ticket.
- — My dog outplays me.

I practice
- — Daily.
- — 5–6 times per week.
- — 3–4 times per week.
- — 1–2 times per week.
- — Never—what's practice?

Knowledge/Understanding Readiness

1. Write 4 measures of rhythm. Stay on the same line or space with the noteheads. Add bar lines where needed. [5-line staff is provided here]
2. Tell about the rhythm you wrote.
3. What do you know about rhythm in general? What does it "do"?

Rhythmic Notation	
Definition	Rules
Examples (draw notes)	Purpose of rhythm

Music Interest Survey

My favorite style of music is . . .
My favorite musical performer is . . .
My favorite classical composer is . . .
My favorite movie music is . . .
My favorite TV show theme is . . .
My favorite song is . . .

The teacher provides an extensive list of music styles. Rate your interest in the various music styles (10 = high interest, 0 = no interest). Use *U* for *unknown* if you don't know the style.

Learning Profile/Preference

Rank the following from 1 to 5, with 1 being your favorite and 5 being your least favorite.
- — Large-group rehearsal
- — Sectional
- — Individual lesson at school
- — Private lesson with instructor outside school
- — Individual practice

Where else do you like to learn about and practice your instrument?

Beginning-of-Class Interest Survey

What type of music do you listen to?
What type of music would you like to play in our class/group?
Why did you sign up for this class/group?
What activities would make this class/group more fun?
Name something that a music teacher could do to make you more excited about music.

Source: Jim Bawden, Fine Arts Curriculum Specialist (retired), Davenport Community School District, Davenport, IA. Used with permission.

4 Providing Interactive Learning Experiences

Part 1:

How Do I Get Students Engaged with the Content and with One Another?

Returning to our road trip metaphor, a thoughtful teacher begins planning a learning journey by articulating learning goals and then uses pre-assessment to uncover information about students' readiness and willingness to take that journey. The next step is to plot out the course of a worthwhile journey.

In today's elementary classrooms, that's a tall order—even for the most skilled educators. Elementary teachers face the challenge of addressing an enormous amount of material from multiple subject areas in a short amount of time. They also need to make sure that students are engaged, invested, and making progress toward important goals.

With these pressures, the temptation to teach by "covering" the curriculum is understandably strong. But racing through content and skills at top speed and hitting the brakes only to ask students to regurgitate their learning covers *the teacher* more than it results in actual student learning. Surface-level tours of facts and skills might get everyone through the scope and sequence of the curriculum, but at a great cost. As Howard Gardner put it, "The greatest enemy of understanding is coverage" (quoted in Brandt, 1993, p. 7).

As trip planner, then, the teacher must plot an efficient, rigorous, and fascinating course that gives students time to engage both intellectually and affectively with what they are studying.

What "Hooks" Students into Learning?

All children are naturally curious about the world around them, but that doesn't mean they come to class each day bursting with excitement about every curricular topic. A big part of the teacher's job is to convince students that "what's ahead" is worth studying and will improve their lives and empower them as people, both now and in the future. This task involves *hooking* students into learning and *holding* them there, even when the road gets rough. Teachers can glean ideas for powerful hooks from many sources, including pre-assessment results and what they already know about the experiences and interests of children of a certain age. Regardless of the means, the goal for teachers is to help students see what educator Steven Levy (1996) calls "the genius of the topic." In the following sections, we discuss three avenues for hooking and holding students into the genius of a topic: fostering relevance, presenting a puzzle, and incorporating novelty.

Fostering Relevant Connections

Brain research (Jensen, 2005; Willis, 2006) reveals that students perform better when they can connect content to themselves or the world around them. Reluctant learners, especially, are concerned with seeing the relevance of material to their personal lives. Finding ways to build such connections gives teachers a better chance of harnessing student attention and investment.

Essential questions are a powerful way to form relevant connections. In Chapter 2, we discussed using essential questions to generate understanding goals. Here, we consider their potential for issuing "invitations to learn" (Tomlinson, 2002).

Essential questions are provocative questions with the potential to foster inquiry, understanding, and transfer of learning. Unlike typical instructional questions, they give life—and language—to what learners are *really* wondering, even if they don't know it yet. Six-year-olds, for instance, see and hear about money in their everyday lives. The question "Where does money come from, and where does it go?" in a beginning economics unit speaks to what some students have already been pondering and awakens the idea in the rest.

A rich essential question has the potential to engage the youngest child and the expert alike. For example, "How do living things stay alive?" might focus a primary-grades science unit on the basic needs of living things. "What effect does power have on decision making?" could drive an ongoing inquiry in literature and social studies. Essential questions pique even the most reluctant learners' curiosity and beg to be discussed, debated, and explored.

Teachers can use strong essential questions as hooks simply by posing them. Using at least one essential question to guide learning throughout a unit of study helps hold student interest and keep learning focused on "arriving" at the goal of understanding. Figure 4.1 shows examples of essential questions across the content areas. Although there is no formula for writing an essential question, the generic frames in Figure 4.2 can provide a starting point.

Figure 4.1 | Examples of Essential Questions

Social Studies
- Where are we (in the world, in the country, in this city)?
- What are the rules—and who says so?
- How do communities solve problems?
- Where does government's power begin and end?

Reading and Writing
- What do skilled readers do when the reading gets tough?
- Must a story have a beginning, a middle, and an end?
- How can a reader get inside the author's mind?
- Spoken language versus written language—what's the difference?
- How do I know when to speak and when to listen (in a discussion)?

Mathematics and Science
- Can everything be counted?
- How are positive numbers related to negative numbers?
- What power do humans have over the environment?
- When does scientific truth or fact change?
- Why do objects move the way they do?

Figure 4.2 | Essential Question Frames

- What's _____ worth?
- How exact/precise does _____ need to be?
- Which _____ is "right"?
- When is _____ better than _____?
- Why does _____ change?
- Do all _____ have _____?
- Whose/what _____ matter? Under what circumstances?
- How powerful is _____?

Presenting a Puzzle

Cognitive psychologist Daniel Willingham (2009) maintains that student motivation is not dependent on intrinsic interest in the content: "We've all attended a lecture or watched a TV show (perhaps against our will) about a subject we thought we weren't interested in, only to find ourselves fascinated" (p. 7). Willingham believes that regardless of the topic, students will invest effort when they are presented with a *puzzle* that appears within reach but requires a "stretch."

Tea Party (pp. 120–121) is a strategy that asks students to solve a puzzle about content before they encounter it. In a Tea Party, the teacher presents students with "pieces" of any text—literary or informational—that they try to fit together like a puzzle in order to make inferences about events or meaning. *Concept Attainment* (pp. 122–123), another strategy that calls for student "puzzling," asks students to examine multiple examples and nonexamples of a concept to figure out what that concept means.

Incorporating Novelty

Brain research (Perry, 2000; Willis, 2007) reveals that *novelty* plays an important role in attention and motivation. As Wolfe (2001) explains, "Novelty is an innate attention-getter. . . . Our brains are programmed to pay attention to the unusual" (p. 82). Introducing or addressing a topic in unique ways can "perk up" students' minds. As a result, they may pay attention and remember more than they otherwise would have. *Shake 'n' Share* (pp. 124–125), which engages learners in quick conversation around different aspects of a topic, is a good way to do this. Its novelty springs both from its structure (students face one another in rotating parallel lines) and from its topics (unusual prompts around a concept or topic).

A connection. A puzzle. A surprise. These elements draw students into learning, but they are not likely to be found in the standards or in textbooks. As we explained in Chapter 2, the first step in crafting *any* meaningful learning experience—including a hook—is to examine and articulate the key concepts and learning goals. Teachers who take the time to study the meaning behind the content they teach can better see how they might use it to get students ready and willing to learn.

Sense Making: Teaching Actively and Interactively

We've reached the point in planning our road trip where students are packed and excited to take the journey. Now, how do we begin to guide them in their travels?

Surprisingly, the answer is not necessarily *Differentiate!* Although instruction in a differentiated classroom should always be *meaningful*, not every moment needs to be *differentiated*. More important, instruction in a differentiated classroom should be both *active* and *interactive*.

As cognitive science uncovers more about how the brain takes in, processes, stores, and retrieves information, it's clear that students acquire and retain more when they *analyze* and *restructure* information than when they simply *receive* or *consume* it (Jensen, 2005). In other words, pouring content into students' brains is not effective; requiring students to grapple and play with content is. Ensuring that learning is *intellectually active* is the first step of upgrading instruction for young learners.

Next, the teacher should strive to craft *interactive* learning experiences. In human relationships, the more we interact with people, the better we get to know them. Learning follows the same principle: we can learn only so much through observation. To truly understand content, students must interact both with the content and with one another around the content (Hattie, 2012). These interactions should be "visible" enough that the teacher can evaluate and facilitate student progress (Bransford et al., 2000).

Challenges to Incorporating Active and Interactive Learning

Learning actively and interactively in a room full of wiggly bodies can be difficult! There are many reasonable obstacles to this kind of learning. In the following sections, we examine a few of these obstacles and offer practical strategies to overcome them.

Challenge 1: Dealing with Limited Attention Spans

Anyone who has spent time with young learners knows that their attention spans are limited. After even a few moments on the carpet, students' eyes . . . and hands . . . and feet begin to wander. They raise their hands with what the teacher *hopes* is a contribution to the discussion, only to share that they got a pet rabbit over the weekend, that their head itches, or that their grandmother says, "Nobody looks good in yellow."

Research (Moore, 2008) suggests that attention spans for *all* age groups are shrinking to as low as five minutes or less. Imagine the implications of this figure for our youngest students! Such findings confirm the need for teachers to curtail the "passive delivery" model and give students more opportunities to interact with the content and one another. In short, if the teacher ignores the limits of students' attention spans, the students will likely ignore the teacher. The following strategies can help teachers capture—and maintain—student attention.

- **Narrated Wait Time.** Because of the waxing and waning nature of attention, some students may need to "reset" their brains to response mode before being able to answer a question the teacher asks. Others may simply need more time to process information to arrive at a conclusion. The teacher can meet all these needs by announcing that there will be *wait time* after each question he or she asks. Instead of answering immediately, students must first take time to consider their responses.

  Doug Lemov (2012) suggests that *narrated* wait time can be even more effective in guiding student thinking. During narrated wait time, the teacher interjects with prompts such as

  » "This is hard stuff. Take your time. No hands for five seconds."
  » "How can you connect your answer to what [a classmate] just said?"
  » "Take a chance! We learn by making mistakes."
  » "Why do you say that? Find something in the [story/problem/ numbers] to defend your answer."

Such prompts can help students' brains focus on the lesson topic rather than on the many other thoughts running through their heads.

Another useful prompt when students are stuck is to ask, "Do you need *time* or *help*?" Adapted from *The Daily 5* (Boushey & Moser, 2006), this question can be used in numerous subjects, including math. In a whole-group lesson, a student who selects "help" calls on a peer for assistance. The peer provides "coaching" via an explanatory answer or other hints. The receiving student then returns to the original question and responds using his or her own words. After the teacher has modeled this strategy and used it during whole-class instruction, students can use it with one another when working in small groups or pairs.

- **Agree or Disagree?** Rather than soliciting open-ended responses, teachers can ask students to agree or disagree with any number of statements or ideas. Examples include
  - » A solution to a math problem.
  - » A description of a character.
  - » A scientific hypothesis.
  - » A value or fact statement about an event in history.

  The teacher posts prompts on the board as statements that students must either support or contradict. Students can indicate their position by showing thumbs up or thumbs down when "polled," by raising color-coded response cards, or by moving to an area of the room to demonstrate their stance. In any case, students should be ready to support their answers with reasoning or evidence.

- **Think-Pair-Share.** This strategy (Kagan, 2008) works as a stand-alone technique or as a companion to the strategies above. In a Think-Pair-Share,
  - » The teacher forms student pairs, either by design or by convenience (e.g., seat proximity), and provides a prompt or question to the class.
  - » Students think silently and individually for up to two minutes, depending on the prompt.
  - » In their pairs, students compare answers, debate findings, or check solutions.

» Following the peer huddles, the teacher can call on *any* student, regardless of whether his or her hand is raised, with the understanding that the student can share his or her own response *or* his or her partner's.

This approach keeps the entire class on its toes, increasing attention and capitalizing on the opportunity for students to hear their peers' perspectives on the questions posed.

- **Popsicle Sticks** and **Talking Chips.** While using any of the strategies discussed above, the teacher calls on individual students to respond. Here are two ways to do this:
  » Write each student's name on a popsicle stick and place it in a cup. Rather than calling on volunteers, pull popsicle sticks to elicit responses at random. Because all students have already had a chance to process material collaboratively, they should be poised for success. The chosen student can share his or her own answer or one from a classmate. Be sure to put the stick back into the cup after a student has contributed. This keeps all students on the edge of their seats, knowing it could be their turn on the next draw, even if they already answered a question.
  » To manage the responses of student volunteers, give each student two to three talking chips (e.g., pennies, paper squares, Unifix cubes) and explain that they must use *some* of their chips but cannot speak once they have used *all* of them. It's also important to establish the expectation that if several students want to speak at once, they "yield" to the classmates who have the most talking chips left. This strategy encourages reluctant sharers to speak while reining in the "oversharers" in the group.

- **Logographic Cues.** Ideal for helping young learners maintain attention as they read, this strategy (see pp. 126–128 for a full discussion) asks students to generate and record visual symbols or codes to help them process a text.

Note that the effectiveness of these five strategies *decreases* as the duration of a teacher-led discussion *increases*. Teachers of lower-grades classrooms must strive to keep whole-class discussions short to meet the very real attention needs of the children in their charge.

Challenge 2: Decreasing Students' Dependence on the Teacher

Keeping whole-class discussions short makes sense given what we know about students' attention spans, but it also raises a follow-up question: "What do I do instead?" Teachers of young learners often wrestle with how to engage students in learning without delivering or directing it themselves.

This section describes several strategies for incorporating active, student-led learning experiences. Some of these keep students in whole-class configurations but put students at the helm rather than the teacher. Others divide students into smaller groups with specific instructions that lead to whole-class sharing at the end. Each of these strategies is designed to decrease the degree of student dependence on the teacher during the learning process. Note that we provide brief strategy descriptions here; more detailed instructions and examples follow in Part 2 of this chapter.

- **Looking/Listening Lenses** (pp. 129–131). A strategy for use with discussion, silent reading, videos, or read-alouds, Looking/Listening Lenses asks students to engage in an exercise that helps them focus and process the "text" at hand, such as searching for specific clues, adopting particular perspectives, or considering important questions. Teachers can assign lenses to students or allow them to choose.
- **Inside-Outside Circles** (pp. 132–134). In this modified Socratic Seminar, half of the class engages in a small-group discussion in the inside circle while the other half engages in a directed listening activity in the outside circle. Each student in the inside circle has a partner in the outside circle. During the discussion, the partners meet twice to "coach" or "debrief" with each other before switching positions (i.e., the partner in the outside circle moves to the inside circle and vice versa).
- **Discussion Duties** (pp. 135–137). Used alone or in conjunction with Inside-Outside Circles, Discussion Duties give students specific roles to fulfill, prompts to address, and questions to ask during large- or small-group discussions. As with Looking/Listening Lenses, teachers can assign roles to students or allow them to choose.
- **Jigsaw** (pp. 138–141). A method for "dividing and conquering" coverage of large amounts of content, this strategy encourages students to work in an interdependent, inquiry-driven fashion. Each student becomes an expert on one piece of a "puzzle" (e.g., an issue, a question, a method, or a perspective) and shares what he or she has learned with other students who studied different puzzle pieces; together, they complete a task that brings all the pieces together.

By using active discussion strategies like these, teachers put *students* in charge of classroom discourse. No longer can a few students dominate—or derail—the discussion; rather, every student must contribute to making the conversation successful.

With the teacher as the proverbial "guide on the side" rather than the "sage on the stage," the locus of learning is with the students.

Challenge 3: Providing Sense-Making Activities

It's not enough for teachers to introduce content and move on; rather, it's essential to give students opportunities to practice and process new information and skills through meaningful sense-making activities. To "digest" important ideas and skills, students need to "crunch on" them in active ways. If teaching is focused on high-quality learning goals, drill and worksheets won't be sufficient to develop expertise. Here we describe strategies that engage students in higher-order critical thinking to help them grapple with—and hang on to—what they've learned.

- **Quartet Quiz** (pp. 142–143). This technique offers the teacher a structured and collaborative method for checking for understanding. Quads of students create "we know" and "we wonder" statements based on what they discussed, viewed, or read. Implementing the Quartet Quiz at the close of whole-class activities puts students in charge of determining what they "got" and what remains fuzzy and positions the teacher to address misconceptions and use student-generated questions to drive further instruction.
- **Debate Team Carousel** (pp. 144–147). This flexible strategy is designed to help students process ideas and skills through the art of structured argument. Students must examine questions and responses from multiple perspectives and adopt several stances, supporting them with evidence.
- **Synectics** (pp. 148–150). A strategy for promoting critical thinking, Synectics works by *making the familiar strange* (getting a new perspective on learned or known information) and *making the strange familiar* (making sense of new ideas and information by associating them with something already known).
- **ThinkDots** (pp. 151–158). The teacher designs ThinkDots prompts to guide small-group processing of a concept, a text, or other lesson material. ThinkDots prompts can also be used to encourage exploration of a concept, a topic, an idea, or an issue from multiple perspectives.
- **The Matrix** (pp. 159–160). Introduced as a community builder in Chapter 1, this strategy engages students in structured analysis as they try to find common features among seemingly disparate people (or characters), places (e.g., ancient civilizations), things (e.g., shapes), or ideas (e.g., patterns).

For students to grow, they need time to think, discuss, debate, and practice—not just regurgitate what they heard. The teacher must spend as much time *listening* as he or she does *talking* (Hattie, 2012). Such a shift requires thoughtful planning and implementation of the strategies described above (and others like them). These practices can increase participation and achievement of all students (Marzano, Pickering, & Pollock, 2001).

Of course, reaping these benefits requires some investment up front. The strategies proposed above may *initially* take more time to implement than simply "covering" the content and skills. The good news is that this investment is worth it: students will actually walk away from learning experiences understanding and retaining the material, allowing the teacher to streamline instruction and spend less time on review (Guskey, 2007/2008).

Challenge 4: Moving Beyond Recall Questions

Every strategy discussed thus far relies on the quality of its driving *questions*. By their nature, questions can invite students to interact with content and with one another, both face-to-face and via technology. Although most teachers use questions instructionally, the *quality* of those questions varies. Plenty of questions do not foster engagement or elicit high-level thinking. Studies of classroom discourse (e.g., Hattie, 2012; Marzano et al., 2001) reveal that the majority of questions asked in a typical classroom require students simply to recall information, and to do so quickly with little feedback. When recall questions are the focus of any strategy, the power of the strategy plummets.

Methods for organizing and classifying questions abound. In Part 2 of this chapter, we present the following three frameworks accompanied by sample questions (see pp. 161–168):

1. Bloom's Revised Taxonomy (Anderson & Krathwohl, 2001)
2. Webb's Depth of Knowledge (DOK) (Webb, Alt, Ely, & Vesperman, 2005)
3. Six Facets of Understanding (Wiggins & McTighe, 2005)

Perhaps the best known of these is Bloom's taxonomy, which was revised and updated by Anderson and Krathwohl in 2001. This framework aims to encourage varied levels or types of thinking, ranging from *remembering* to *creating*. Although well known, Bloom's taxonomy is often misunderstood. Here are the two most important points of clarification:

1. *Bloom did not intend for the taxonomy to dictate the order in which students should engage in thinking* (Bransford et al., 2000). Unfortunately, many teachers believe that students must *remember* before they can accomplish anything else and therefore design the majority of instructional questions at the memory and comprehension levels. This limits opportunities for all students to engage in worthwhile discussions.
2. *Bloom did not assert that some students should participate in the lower levels of thinking while others engage in the higher levels.* Some teachers have been taught that Bloom's taxonomy is a framework for differentiating questions

and end up giving some students primarily recall-level questions and other students higher-order questions. In reality, Bloom designed his taxonomy to ensure that *all* students wrestle with a *variety* of cognitive demands. Exercising the higher levels helps strengthen the lower levels.

Teachers can avoid misusing Questioning Frameworks by keeping the following guidelines in mind:

- One level of thinking is not a barrier to the next; therefore, questions need not always build from "lowest" to "highest."
- Use a variety of question types throughout the course of a lesson; avoid overreliance on any one level of thinking.
- Plan questions in advance. Research (Marzano et al., 2001) indicates that teachers who don't plan in advance tend to pose mostly low-level questions, which are the easiest to generate on the fly. The level of thinking for all students in the classroom will increase when teachers have thought about "crunchy" questions ahead of time.

Regardless of the framework a teacher uses, good questions should form the heart of classroom instruction. Only in grappling with material will students truly comprehend it.

Teaching Actively and Interactively Versus Differentiating

This chapter's presentation of strategies has focused on increasing the quality of whole-class learning and teaching. From "hooking" students to facilitating student-led discussions to structuring rich sense-making activities to ratcheting up the level of questioning, each has the potential to improve student learning.

It is important to note that although these strategies may differ from the normal classroom fare, none is a strategy for differentiation unless the teacher uses it as such. For a task to be differentiated, some aspect of the content, process, or product must be adjusted for specific learner readiness, interest, or learning preference. Differentiated tasks aren't just "different"; they are aligned with and lead all students toward the same high-level learning goals.

Use of these strategies *can* set the stage for differentiation by helping students learn to work efficiently in collaborative settings. In addition, several strategies can be adjusted and used for differentiation, including Discussion Duties, Looking/Listening Lenses, Jigsaw, Debate Team Carousel, and ThinkDots. The "Tips" section of each strategy description in Part 2 offers suggestions for using these strategies to meet the wide range of student needs present in most elementary classrooms.

A Lesson Plan Upgrade

Fourth grade teacher Hannah Areda wanted to get her students more actively involved in the lesson that launched the class's Environmental Stewardship unit. Last year, students loved the book she used as a hook, but their attention and interest steadily declined as the lesson continued. Steps 2–4 were particularly difficult to manage, as so many students either tuned out or spoke out of turn.

Before Upgrade

Hannah's initial lesson plan looked like this:

1. *Read-aloud.* Read the book *Just a Dream* by Chris Van Allsburg, about Walter, an environmentally irresponsible boy who has a dream that takes him to the future and shows him some potential consequences of his careless behavior.
2. *Whole-group discussion.* After each page that shows a scene from the future, ask students how Walter's careless actions led to each consequence.
3. *Informational text.* Lead students in a round-robin reading of "Tiny Plastic, Big Problem" (https://www.commonlit.org/texts/tiny-plastic-big-problem). Tell them the text is about the problem of large amounts of plastic floating in the ocean.
4. *Processing the text.* Stop periodically to ask students questions about the article to make sure they are comprehending.
5. *Processing ideas.* Assign "Pollution Problems" worksheet that emphasizes key vocabulary and poses comprehension questions about recycling and pollution.
6. *Application.* Instruct students to draw a picture of themselves making a good decision to save the Earth. They can do this on the back of the worksheet.

As Hannah considered the lesson, it dawned on her that student attention waned the most during the whole-group activities. She realized that she needed to infuse more opportunities for active student processing. In addition, she felt she was missing some opportunities to integrate ELA standards into her science lesson. Informational texts were a statewide push this year, and she wanted to shake things up a bit with how she asked students to interact with those readings.

After Upgrade

Hannah decided to maintain the same texts from her initial lesson plan while adding strategies that would put her students in charge of making meaning and driving the discussion at every step of the lesson. Here is Hannah's revised lesson plan:

1. *Hook.* Ask students to free-write or sketch in response to the lesson's essential question: "How do our actions today affect our lives tomorrow? In the future?" Allow student volunteers to share examples from their personal lives and the world around them.

2. *Read-aloud.* Read the book *Just a Dream* to the class. Before reading, instruct students to choose one of the following Looking Lenses and gather evidence from the text accordingly:

   » *Fortune-teller*: Find examples of how Walter's behavior affects the future and hypothesize about other future consequences.

   » *Matchmaker*: Find connections between Walter's behavior and your own behavior. How are you alike and different in the decisions you make?

   » *Detective*: What does each of Walter's actions make you wonder about with regard to pollution and our future world? In other words, what needs to be investigated?

   Ask students to pause after each "consequence" page to discuss their findings and questions in "like lens" groups. Have each group share with the whole class in turn. Record responses.

3. *Informational text.* Instruct students to use the questions they generated in step 2 to guide their reading of the article "Tiny Plastic, Big Problem." Students will code their articles using Logographic Cues of their own design to (a) come up with answers to the class's questions, (b) generate additional questions, and (c) identify important vocabulary.

4. *Processing the text.* In quads composed of different Looking Lenses (step 2), instruct students to complete a Quartet Quiz about the article. As they present their "we know" and "we wonder" statements, their classmates will generate answers, responses, and more questions. These contributions will comprise the bulk of the class discussion; guide when necessary.

5. *Processing ideas.* Facilitate a Debate Team Carousel in new quads, where students argue for and against the statement "Can we as kids really do anything to help the Earth?" They should use evidence from both texts in their responses.

6. *Application.* Students write individual reflections about their personal role in stewarding the Earth's resources (written or drawn with annotations).

This lesson plan took more time to prepare than the previous lesson did, but as she implemented it, Hannah realized that the students were the ones doing the heavy lifting; she was facilitating discovery rather than dispensing information. For her students, the revised lesson paid off in higher engagement and deeper understanding. For Hannah, the payoff was a clear window into her students' thinking—and a fuller appreciation of their ideas.

Part 2:

Tools and Strategies

Tea Party

What It Is:

A prereading strategy developed by Kylene Beers (2003) that invites students to engage with short excerpts of a text they'll be reading and make predictions about the text

How It Works:

1. Each student receives a card with a different teacher-selected excerpt from the text the class will be reading (e.g., an informational text, a story, a poem, or a play). The excerpt can be anything from a single word to a sentence or two, or even a picture.
2. Students read their cards and imagine what the text might be about.
3. Students stand up and "Tea Party" with other students (i.e., circulate and chat with different classmates, one at a time) for a few minutes, sharing cards and trying to piece together ideas about the subject or theme of the larger text.
4. Students sit down when the teacher calls time and make one to three predictions in small groups or as a class.

What It's Good For:

Tea Party can be used as a prereading strategy with any text, but it is optimal for texts that are challenging or that at least some students might not be interested in reading. Consider using it when you announce the title or subject of a text and hear groans!

Tips:

- It's OK for more than one student to have the same excerpt—say, if there are 8 excerpts for 24 students. When a student encounters a classmate with the same excerpt, the pair can still talk about their interpretations and predictions. Alternatively, form three smaller groups and have each group mingle in its own Tea Party.
- Cards can be distributed randomly or intentionally (purposely assigning certain students certain cards).
- Use a bell or other signal to indicate when students should move on to someone else.
- Ask students to hold up their card or a hand as they move around the room to indicate that they are in search of a new partner.

Classroom Examples:

- Second grade teacher Mr. Rickert uses Tea Party to introduce his students to Gary Soto's poem "Eating While Reading." He puts single nouns (*bubble gum, candy, snow cone, book, syrup, slither, dance*), adjectives (*sweet, red, sticky*), and verbs (*pulls, yells*) on cards to prepare students for the surprising pairing of activities featured in the poem. He forms two groups of 10 and gives each one the same 10 cards for the Tea Party. He distributes the cards strategically to make sure students have words they're ready for.

- Fourth grade teacher Ms. Jackson uses Tea Party before her 24 students read informational texts with difficult vocabulary. Each student receives a card with one of eight new words from an upcoming article students will read. Because there are eight terms, she forms three groups of eight students. Students meet in trios with classmates who have the same term to study the meaning of the word, decide how to use it in a sentence, and develop a visual to put on their Tea Party cards. Then Ms. Jackson has each original group of eight engage in a Tea Party, making guesses as to what the article will be about. She finds that "frontloading" the vocabulary in this way makes the article more accessible *and* intriguing for students.

Concept Attainment

What It Is:

A strategy based on the work of Jerome Bruner and colleagues (1956), Concept Attainment leads students to deeper understanding of a concept by having them examine attributes of examples and nonexamples toward articulating, refining, and testing their definitions of the concept.

How It Works:

1. The teacher introduces students to examples and nonexamples of a concept, either in successive pairs or all at once. The categories for these examples and nonexamples can be labeled (e.g., *living things* and *nonliving things*) or unlabeled.
2. Working as a class, in groups or pairs, or individually, students examine the examples and nonexamples to induce what attributes the examples and nonexamples seem to share, respectively.
3. If the categories are unlabeled, students generate guesses about what the categories could be.
4. The teacher provides additional examples and nonexamples for students to categorize as examples or nonexamples, posing questions to challenge and guide their thinking.
5. The teacher confirms or challenges students' hypotheses, including the accuracy of their categories and the accuracy and depth and breadth of the attributes generated.
6. Students generate their own examples and nonexamples of the concept.
7. Class creates a final definition of the concept, list of attributes, and "best" examples and nonexamples.
8. *Optional:* Students apply their knowledge of the concept to a new task.

What It's Good For:

- Introducing students to a concept
- Extending, refining, and giving language to students' understanding of a concept
- Pre-assessing the depth and range of students' conceptual knowledge or understanding
- Providing collaborative sense-making opportunities

Tips:

- When selecting examples and nonexamples of a concept, make sure that the examples are clear representations of the concept under study. Just as important is that nonexamples are closely related to the examples such that they might be easily confused with the examples.

- Although the strategy is called *Concept* Attainment, the approach works well with anything that has a name, associated examples, and attributes (e.g., animals, heroic characters, or math facts that equal 20).
- For younger children, use the terms *yes* (instead of *example*) and *no* (instead of *nonexample*).
- Print initial or subsequent examples and nonexamples on paper and give them to students as a sorting activity. For example, give students printed pictures of living and nonliving things to discuss and categorize with a partner.
- Concept Attainment can be differentiated for readiness if different students or groups of students are working with examples and nonexamples that are more and less difficult to discern or distinguish. For a more advanced version of Concept Attainment, mix up the examples and nonexamples and have students sort or arrange them to induce possible categories.

Classroom Example:

Ms. Schwartz shows her 5th graders two lines from a poem about leaves: one line that is an example of a metaphor and one that is a description but not a metaphor. Without providing labels, she asks students to try to see the difference between the two lines. She then shows three more pairs of examples and nonexamples taken from various poems about nature.

Students generate lists of attributes that the examples share. Responses include "one thing is being compared to another," "two things that are alike but not the same," and "descriptions that paint a picture in your mind." Ms. Schwartz then gives each pair of students a plastic baggie of examples and nonexamples to classify. Students complete their sort, compare it with another pair's, draft their own definition of *metaphor*, and generate their own examples and nonexamples.

Ms. Schwartz then displays several dictionary definitions of *metaphor*, and several students note that the examples of metaphors are not all the same. Ms. Schwartz uses this opportunity to introduce the terms *simile, hyperbole,* and *personification* before having students further classify examples under these headings. For homework, students read a new poem and identify the metaphors in it as well as a phrase or line that is not a metaphor but might be confused for one.

Shake 'n' Share

What It Is:

A strategy for engaging learners in quick conversation around different aspects of a topic or concept

How It Works:

1. Students stand in two lines facing one another so that each person has a partner.
2. The teacher displays or calls out a discussion prompt or question for each pair to discuss.
3. After a minute or so, the teacher calls time, and one line moves down so that each person has a new partner. (The person at the end walks, skips, or dances down the middle to the other end.)
4. The teacher gives a new prompt for discussion.
5. The process continues for four to eight turns.

What It's Good For:

- Introducing a unit, topic, or concept
- Review (e.g., before a quiz or after a challenging lesson)
- Get-to-know-you or community-building time
- Reinvigorating a topic that has grown tired or exhausted (and, in the process, reenergizing students!)
- Engaging *all* students in discussion and accountable talk

Tips:

- Use a bell, music, or another loud noise to indicate the end of a turn.
- Have students shake hands with each new partner.
- Tell students who move down the middle to the other end to do something funny or silly as they walk—or to dance!
- When students return to their seats, give them a reflective prompt to think or write about that builds on or connects to what they discussed and heard in the Shake 'n' Share line (e.g., "What's the single most important piece of advice you could give someone about revising writing?").

Classroom Examples:

- Ms. Martinez uses Shake 'n' Share to review the social studies content she introduced the previous day. Students get into two lines facing each other and answer, in turn, the following six questions (based on Wiggins and McTighe's Six Facets of Understanding):
    1. *Explain it*: "What's the difference between a rule and a law?"
    2. *Interpret it*: "What does [this class rule] show about what we value?"

3. *Apply it*: "Where do we see laws in our community today?"
4. *Have perspective*: "Is it ever OK to break a rule? Why or why not?"
5. *Display empathy*: "One misunderstanding a new classmate might have about [this class rule] is _____."
6. *Self-reflect*: "What family rules are easy for me to follow? What family rules are hard for me to follow? Why?"

Following the Shake 'n' Share line, Ms. Martinez leads a whole-group discussion about rules and laws. Students are responsible for sharing ideas they heard from their classmates during the Shake 'n' Share activity.

- Ms. Rooney uses Shake 'n' Share to get her students talking about fractions in a non-threatening way. Drawing on the performance verbs she uses to create ThinkDots (see pp. 151–158), Ms. Rooney developed the following prompts:
  » *Describe it*: What is a fraction? What does it show?
  » *Analyze it*: Look at the number line at the front of the room. Where would you put 1/2? Where would you put 1/4?
  » *Compare it*: Think about these fractions: 1/3 and 1/6. Which one is the larger number (furthest from 0 on the number line)?
  » *Associate it*: Where do you see fractions used in real life?
  » *Apply it*: If you partitioned a pie into 8 equal parts and your big brother ate 2 of those parts, what fraction of the pie did he eat?
  » *Argue for or against it*: Saying "My brother ate 1/4 of the pie" is the same thing as saying "My brother ate 2/8 of the pie." Why or why not?

  Ms. Rooney made sure to have whiteboards available for students to use to figure out their answers and to illustrate their thinking when they talked to their partner.

- Shake 'n' Share is Ms. Hines's favorite way to build community throughout the course of the year. She especially likes using the following prompts to "get the juices flowing" on Mondays and to refocus fidgety students:
  » *Turn 1*: Choose one word to describe your weekend. Explain why you chose this word.
  » *Turn 2*: What's your favorite thing for breakfast? Why is it your favorite?
  » *Turn 3*: How is school like a video game? What else is it like?
  » *Turn 4*: I don't know how to _____, but I think it would be cool to learn because _____.
  » *Turn 5*: What two things do you wish you had known about [in last year's grade level] that you know now?
  » *Turn 6*: What's one "dream item" that you would add to our classroom? How would it make the classroom better?

Ms. Hines finds that using Shake 'n' Share as a community builder increases students' success when she uses the same strategy to review content later in the year.

Logographic Cues

What It Is:

A strategy developed by Kylene Beers (2003) in which students come up with or select visual symbols, or *logographs,* to serve as signposts in their reading that alert them to important aspects of the text or narrative

How It Works:

1. The teacher develops a series of ideas for students to note as they read (e.g., literary elements, literary devices, elements of historical analysis and interpretation).
2. Students devise or select a visual code, symbol, or emoji to represent each of these ideas.
3. As they read, students indicate the targeted ideas by jotting down the Logographic Cues in the margin of their text, on sticky notes, using the edit function of a PDF, or in some other way.

What It's Good For:

- Logographs help "cue" student attention during reading.
- Logographs help students reflect on important content after reading.
- Codes can direct students to important text to share during class discussions.
- Although it's best for students to develop their own codes, some codes can be developed by the class and used to flag important content in the teacher's lecture notes or in graphic organizers.

Tips:

- Develop long-term cues to use for concepts that reappear throughout the year or for ideas you want students to be in the habit of exploring.
- Encourage students to record logographs on bookmarks for easy access during coding.
- *For differentiation:* Using varied levels of text but the same cues allows for whole-group discussion.

Classroom Example:

Mr. Simpkins wanted his 5th grade science students to examine everything they read—the textbook, informational texts, websites, and so on—through the lens of the seven cross-cutting concepts outlined by the Next Generation Science Standards. During the course of the year, students would discuss the meaning and generate examples of five of those seven concepts. To guide their process, they developed Logographic Cues for each:

- Patterns: ❖
- Cause and effect: ↔
- Systems: ↻
- Structure and function: #
- Stability and change: ▲

Mr. Simpkins started with "Patterns" and added a new cue every two or three weeks. As the year progressed, the class compiled the Logographic Cues it developed on a poster. The cues supported students as they (1) noted the concepts in their readings and (2) used the concepts in discussions and investigations. (See Figure 4.3 on page 128 for more examples of Logographic Cues.)

Figure 4.3 | Logographic Cue Examples

General cues for informational text:

✔ = I knew that!

★ = Important information/statistic/quote

? = Debatable or questionable idea

! = Interesting . . . I want to explore this further

Reading reactions:

🙂 = This makes me happy.

🙁 = This makes me sad.

😐 = This makes me wonder.

😠 = This makes me angry.

😨 = This scares me.

Teachers can also let students create or select their own Logographic Cues to indicate all kinds of elements, such as different types of imagery, aspects of writing, and standards themes.

Imagery:

— *Sight:* Words that draw pictures in your mind—that help you *see* things.

— *Sound:* Words that portray things you can *hear*.

— *Smell:* Words that portray or remind you of *scents*.

— *Taste:* Words that depict *flavors*, *textures*, or *temperatures* in your mouth.

— *Touch:* Words that communicate *textures*, *temperatures*, or *pressure* on your skin.

Peer review cues (Spandel, 2012):

— *Ideas:* I can tell exactly what the writer wants me to understand.

— *Organization:* These key words help me see when the writer is changing ideas.

— *Voice:* The writer is using words to leave his or her "fingerprints" on the page.

— *Word choice:* The writer is "activating" my senses and helping me picture things in my head.

Social studies themes (adapted from NCSS, 2010):

— Culture

— Time and change

— Places and environment

— Identity

— Individuals and groups

— Power and government

— Producers and consumers

— Science and technology

Looking/Listening Lenses

What It Is:

A strategy for use with discussion, silent reading, videos, or read-alouds, Looking/ Listening Lenses gives each student a role to help him or her focus and process the "text" at hand, such as searching for specific clues, adopting particular perspectives, or considering important questions.

How It Works:

1. The teacher assigns Looking/Listening Lenses to students or lets them choose.
2. The teacher places students in groups of like or mixed lenses (Detective, Fortune-teller, Matchmaker, Defender).
3. The teacher provides the focus for each lens before students begin their engagement with the text.

What It's Good For:

Focusing and processing any "text"—be it in written, spoken, audio, or visual form— that students interact with before or during class

Tips:

- Introduce and model the lenses, or roles, to students one at a time with different readings so that they can learn what each lens entails.
- Choose only those roles that make sense for that particular reading or discussion. Not every lens is a good match for a given task.
- Display key discussion questions that link the reading focus for each lens (versus having students simply share what they read through their particular lens).
- Use the lenses in a Jigsaw fashion: have students meet and discuss the text in "like lens" groups before returning to their "mixed lens" groups to complete a new task or discuss a new question.
- Laminate the lens cards for easy use and reuse (see Figure 4.4 on page 131 for how these might look).
- *For differentiation:* Assign the lenses strategically or differentiate *within* lenses when necessary (e.g., not all Detectives need to have the same focusing prompt).

Classroom Example:

Ms. Saunders assigns Listening Lenses to her students to help focus them as she reads aloud the story *Mr. Popper's Penguins.* For the first few read-alouds, she gives every student the same lens. After every student has practiced with every lens, Ms. Saunders assigns the following Listening Lens prompts to students during a key chapter:

- *Fortune-teller:* Find hints of how Mr. Popper's decision about the "freezing plant" will affect the Popper household in the future.

- *Matchmaker*: Find connections between Bill's and Janie's thoughts and feelings and your own. How are you alike and different in the ways you think and feel?
- *Detective*: Capture the scenes, moments, passages, or dialogue that best help the reader understand Mr. Popper's worries.
- *Defender*: Decide whether you agree or disagree with this: "Admiral Drake made a poor decision when he sent Captain Cook to the Popper household." Gather evidence that would support your opinion.

When the read-aloud concludes, Ms. Saunders forms groups of like lenses to discuss and solidify their findings. Then she forms groups of mixed lenses where students can share their varied perspectives. To conclude, she poses the following prompt to the whole group for students to respond to in their journals: "Do you think the Poppers are better off or worse off since the arrival of the penguins? Why do you say so?"

Figure 4.4 | Looking/Listening Lens Cards

Fortune-Teller

Look for clues or hints that might help us make predictions about...

_____

_____

_____.

Detective

Capture the parts that best help us understand...

_____

_____

_____.

Matchmaker

Find connections between _____ and _____.

How are they alike and different?

_____.

Defender

Agree or disagree? _____

_____. Support your opinion with reasons.

Inside-Outside Circles

What It Is:

In this modified Socratic Seminar, half of the class engages in a small-group discussion in the inside circle while the other half engages in a directed listening activity in the outside circle.

How It Works:

1. The class forms two concentric circles with half of the students on the inside and half on the outside; each student in the inside circle has a partner in the outside circle. Students can sit at their desks or on the carpet.
2. The teacher poses an open-ended question or prompt.
3. Students in the inside circle begin discussing the prompt among themselves while their partners in the outside circle listen actively. The teacher changes prompts as needed. Students' specific duties are as follows:

    The inside partner
    » Participates orally in the discussion.
    » Takes notes on (a) points that have been made by others, labeled with 1 (agree), 2 (disagree), or 3 (in the middle) and (b) points or questions that he or she plans to raise in the discussion.

    The outside partner
    » Participates cognitively in the discussion but remains silent.
    » Takes notes on (a) points that have been made by others, labeled with 1 (agree), 2 (disagree), or 3 (in the middle) and (b) points or questions that he or she wants his or her partner to raise.

    In an online variation, the outside partner
    » Participates by commenting on a backchannel chat (e.g., TodaysMeet.com) with others in the outside circle.
    » Focuses on (a) points that have been made by those in the inside circle, labeled with 1 (agree), 2 (disagree), or 3 (in the middle) and (b) points or questions that he or she wants his or her fellow classmates in the outside circle to respond to *and* his or her own answers to points or questions raised in the outside circle.

4. Inside-circle and outside-circle partners meet twice to "coach" and "debrief" how the discussion is progressing thus far. This might involve offering feedback on what the partner is doing well, giving advice for what he or she might add, or suggesting questions that need to be raised before switching positions.

What It's Good For:

Helping students learn to engage in student-led discussions, listen to one another, and engage in productive debate

Tips:

- Stop discussion periodically for partners to confer (e.g., timeouts).
- Allow students to request a timeout (one allowed per pair per discussion).
- Have partners switch circles mid-discussion.
- Use Discussion Duties to prompt listening and speaking (see p. 135).
- Use talking chips (two to three per student) to limit or encourage participation (see p. 111 for more explanation of talking chips).

Classroom Example:

Ms. Davies uses Inside-Outside Circles to let students discuss the informational texts they read for social studies and science. She finds that the strategy leads them to invest more attention in their readings and to notice connections among different texts— both fiction and informational—as they progress through the year.

Early in the year, with Ms. Davies serving as a facilitator, the class had developed a list of "discussion norms" for Inside-Outside Circles talks. Ms. Davies had strategically allowed students to begin a discussion *without* norms so that they could experience the frustration that resulted from typical classroom behaviors, such as some students talking over one another while others remained silent. She stopped the discussion and asked students to reflect on how the discussion had felt thus far, recording their opinions on the board. The class collectively turned that list of reactions into the following discussion norms:

1. Listen actively.
2. Don't raise hands.
3. Make eye contact with classmates.
4. Monitor speaking time.
5. Yield the floor to classmates who have not yet spoken.
6. Always use evidence from the text in responses.
7. Use classmates' names in responses.
8. Use talking chips wisely.

Ms. Davies rotated between the traditional Inside-Outside Circles setup and a variation she called "the Huddle." In the Huddle, she formed trios instead of pairs so that fewer students were in the center at once. Inside-circle time was reduced for each group because trios had to rotate twice in order for everyone to be in the center. Still, the smaller discussion groups seemed to make it easier for all students to contribute.

See Figure 4.5 (p. 134) for diagrams of what Inside-Outside Circles and the Huddle look like.

Figure 4.5 | Inside-Outside Circles and the Huddle

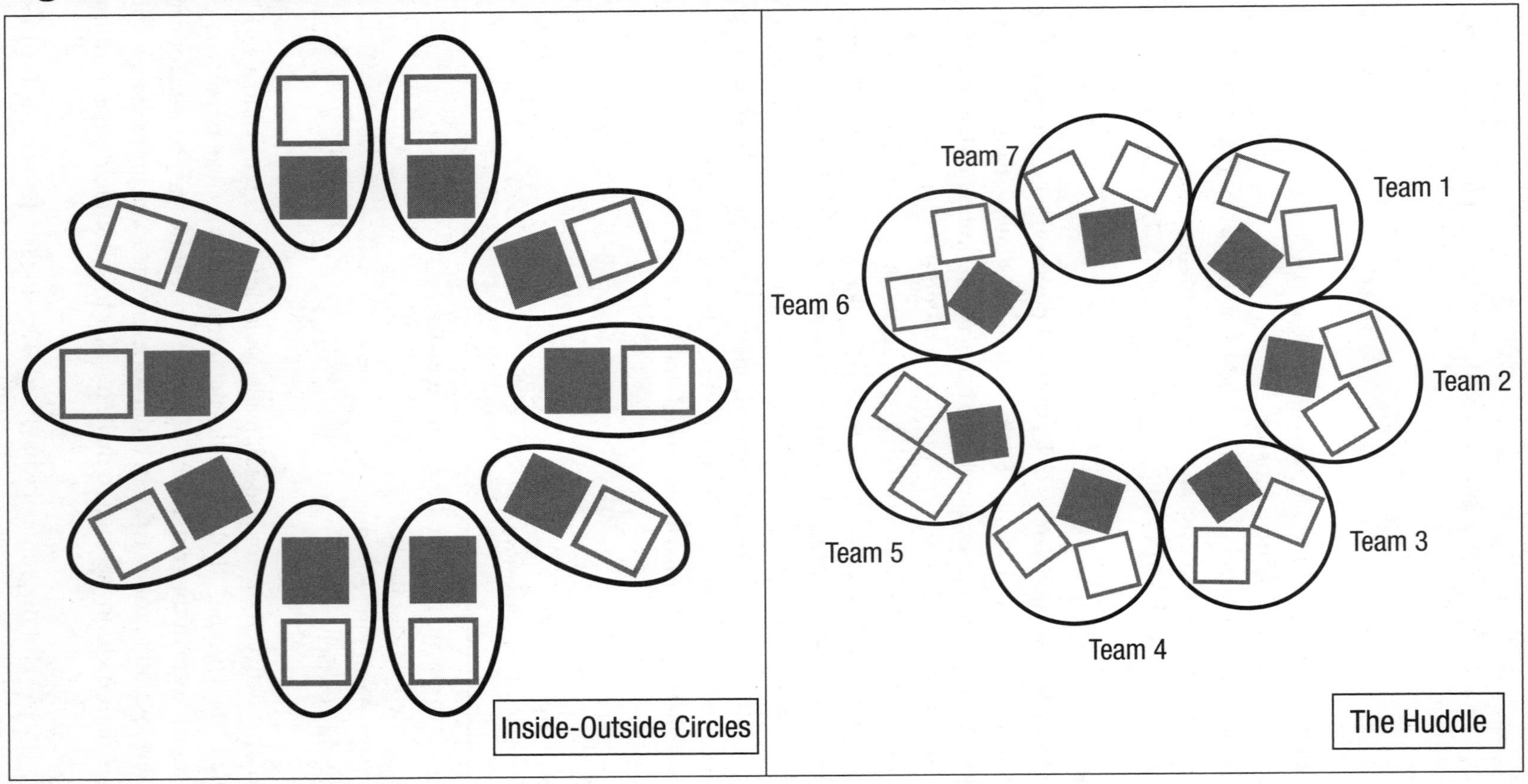

The Huddle

Inside-Outside Circles

Discussion Duties

What It Is:

A strategy used with individual or group tasks or in conjunction with discussion structures (e.g., Inside-Outside Circles) that gives students specific roles to fulfill, prompts to address, and questions to ask

How It Works:

1. Together, the teacher and students come up with a description of what a good group task or discussion looks like, sounds like, and feels like.
2. The teacher and the students devise roles students could play to help make sure the task or discussion flows in the manner described in step 1.
3. The teacher displays the roles prominently in the room.
4. The teacher and students generate "soundbites" that someone in each role might say.
5. The teacher puts these roles with their representative prompts or soundbites and accompanying icons on cards that can be reused for multiple tasks or discussions (see examples below).

What It's Good For:

Focusing student attention during tasks or discussions

Tips:

- Begin modeling with a few roles at a time.
- Debrief the process often and make adjustments where needed.
- Teachers can assign roles to students or allow them to choose.
- Primary-grades teachers can teach the roles and responsibilities using the icons only, and then post those icons in the room. During discussions, the teacher can distribute cards featuring the icon only (rather than the text associated with each).
- Explicitly model the use of Discussion Duties. This could involve using a "fishbowl" technique to demonstrate effective and ineffective conversations with the roles or holding a whole-group discussion with different students assuming different duties.

Examples:

Figures 4.6 (p. 136) and 4.7 (p. 137) offer examples of Discussion Duties for younger and older students.

Figure 4.6 | Discussion Duties—Younger Students

Bring Up Ideas

- "One thought I had was . . . ."
- "Another idea is . . . ."
- "What do you [the group] think about . . . ?"

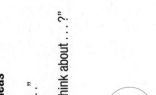

Listen Respectfully

- "I agree because . . . ."
- "I disagree because . . . ."
- "I heard you say _____. That connects to what _____ said because _____."

Stay on Topic

- "Does that relate to what we are discussing?"
- "I think we're off topic."
- "Let's get back to our point."

Ask for More Details

- "What do you mean by that?"
- "Could you give me another example?"
- "I think I see your point. Can you say more?"

Give Examples

- "On page ___, it says. . . . I think that shows . . . ."
- "What do you think the author means by . . . ?"
- "This part is powerful because . . . ."

Think About Our Understanding

- "Are we lost?"
- "Does this make sense to everyone?"
- "What questions do we have?"

Figure 4.7 | Discussion Duties—Older Students

Director

During Discussion:
- Begin the discussion. Use the questions that have been posted as a starting point.
- Make sure the discussion doesn't get off topic.
- Bring the discussion to a close when time is called.

Soundbites:
- "Let's start by . . . ."
- "Can we get back to . . . ?"
- "What about . . . ?"
- "Let's end by . . . ."

Includer

During Discussion:
Make sure that all group members contribute to the discussion and feel included.

Soundbites:
- "What do you think about that, _____?"
- "I agree/disagree with what you said, _____, because . . . ."
- "I want to hear what _____ thinks."
- "Wait, _____, I think you might have just interrupted _____."

Prober

During Discussion:
Make sure that all group members back up their opinions, ideas, feelings, and observations by giving details, examples, and explanations.

Soundbites:
- "Can you give an example?"
- "Do you remember where that is/was? Can you show us?"
- "How is that related to what we read?"
- "That's interesting! How did you figure that out?"
- "What part is that from/in?"

Pacer

During Discussion:
- Make sure that the discussion moves at a good pace.
- "Refresh" the discussion when you feel like it's lagging.

Soundbites:
- "We've talked a lot about _____. Can we also talk about . . . ?"
- "We have _____ more minutes, so let's also talk about . . . ."
- "I'm also wondering about . . . ."
- "Here's something else to think about . . . ."
- "It sounds like we agree/disagree about . . . ."

Jigsaw

What It Is:

> A cooperative learning strategy originally developed by Aronson (Aronson & Patnoe, 1997) in which each member of a small group becomes an expert on a different aspect of the content and shares his or her expertise with the other group members

How It Works:

1. Students meet in home groups for task introduction and division of labor. Each home group member selects or is assigned one "piece" of the larger task "puzzle" (e.g., a chapter, a perspective, or a subtopic).
2. Students reconfigure themselves into expert groups composed of students who share the same "puzzle piece."
3. Expert groups work to compile information on their chapter, perspective, or subtopic. The teacher provides guiding questions, resources, graphic organizers, and any other necessary supports to facilitate the process.
4. Expert groups disband, and members return to their home groups. In the home groups, each member shares his or her respective piece of the puzzle, providing information, examples, and insights. The teacher supplies a graphic organizer to facilitate this sharing process.
5. When all home group members have finished sharing, students engage in whole-class discussion to address questions, seeming contradictions, and interesting observations.
6. The teacher collects evidence of home group understanding (e.g., via a synthesis question on the back of groups' graphic organizers; one member from each group turns it in).
7. The teacher collects evidence of individual understanding (e.g., via an Exit Slip).

See Figure 4.8 for a diagram of the Jigsaw Format.

Figure 4.8 | Jigsaw Format

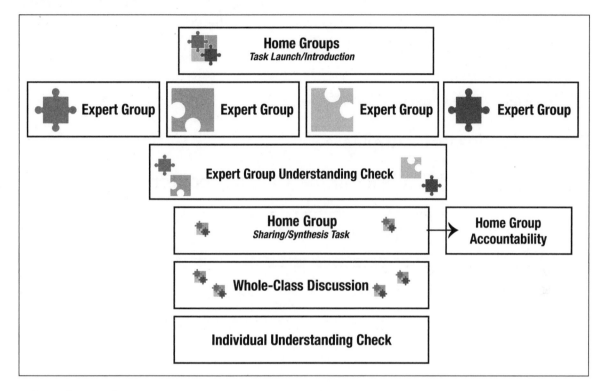

What It's Good For:
- Dealing with large amounts of information or varied perspectives
- Increasing student investment through choice of puzzle piece or increased accountability in home groups
- Designing and managing collaborative tasks

Tips:
- To prepare for Jigsaw, find and organize appropriate materials (e.g., readings, illustrations, websites) for each expert group. Develop appropriate guiding questions and organizers for both home groups and expert groups.
- Model the process students should follow in each grouping configuration.
- Circulate vigilantly to catch misconceptions during both expert and home group work.
- Set and enforce time limits for each phase.
- Be sure to conduct an understanding check of what students learned in their expert groups, so that they don't go to their home groups with misconceptions to pass on.
- Home-group tasks should go beyond reporting to one another for the purpose of completing a graphic organizer. Any information-gathering tool should serve as a support for completing a home-group task that requires students to bring information together and transfer what they've learned.

- *For differentiation*: It is possible to tailor expert-group materials and tasks to meet the specific readiness of students (e.g., strategic choices of reading levels, number of facets addressed, complexity of material). If this is the goal, *assign* students to expert groups rather than letting them choose.

Examples:

Figure 4.9 offers two examples of Jigsaws.

Figure 4.9 | Jigsaw Examples

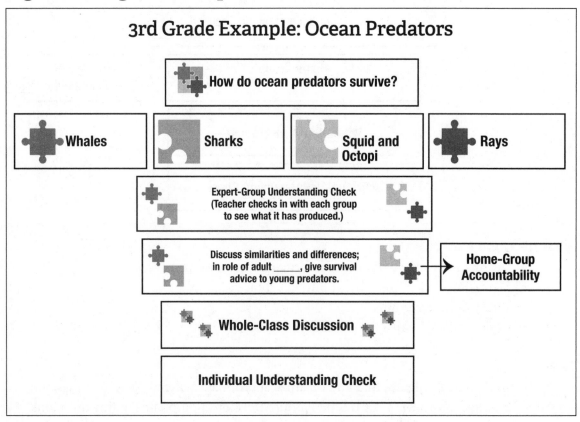

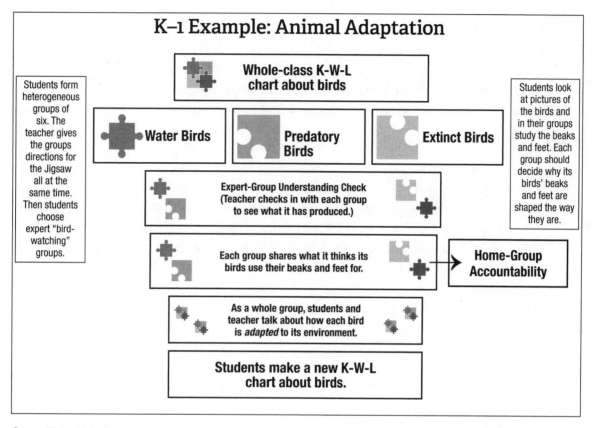

K–1 Example: Animal Adaptation

Whole-class K-W-L chart about birds

Water Birds

Predatory Birds

Extinct Birds

Students form heterogeneous groups of six. The teacher gives the groups directions for the Jigsaw all at the same time. Then students choose expert "bird-watching" groups.

Students look at pictures of the birds and in their groups study the beaks and feet. Each group should decide why its birds' beaks and feet are shaped the way they are.

Expert-Group Understanding Check (Teacher checks in with each group to see what it has produced.)

Each group shares what it thinks its birds use their beaks and feet for.

→ **Home-Group Accountability**

As a whole group, students and teacher talk about how each bird is *adapted* to its environment.

Students make a new K-W-L chart about birds.

Source: "Animal Adaptation" example by Catherine Brighton and Holly Hertberg. Adapted with permission.

Quartet Quiz

What It Is:

A technique developed by Carol Ann Tomlinson (2005) to check the understanding of the entire class while generating small- and large-group processing discussions and situating the teacher to address questions and misconceptions

How It Works:

1. The teacher poses a question about content from a lecture, a video, a text, or another medium.
2. Students individually prepare their responses to the question.
3. Students meet in quads to check and share their answers ("we know" statements) and develop questions about the content ("we wonder" statements).
4. The "summarizer" from each group reports "we know" and "we wonder" statements.
5. The teacher records student answers for the "we know" responses on the board, document camera, or other display, correcting misconceptions as they arise. The teacher continues rotating from group to group until all "we knows" have been recorded.
6. The teacher records student answers for the "we wonder" statements, placing them next to any "we know" items to which they might relate (if possible; there may be no relationship, and that's OK). The teacher continues rotating from group to group until all "we wonders" have been recorded.
7. The class discusses the "we wonder" statements, and the teacher ensures all questions are answered.
8. The class develops closure/clarification/summary statements.
9. The teacher can follow up with an exit question regarding how students' thinking has progressed since step 2, if desired.

What It's Good For:

- Checking in to see how students are grasping the lecture, video, text, or other content source
- "Catching" and redirecting misconceptions
- Picking up from a discussion begun the previous class
- Structuring the analysis of complex content

Tips:

- Use an open-ended Quartet Quiz question that is likely to yield multiple responses or "we know" statements. *What are the three branches of government?* is not a good Quartet Quiz question, whereas *Why do we have three branches of government?* is. The teacher can provide scaffolding in the form of prompts (e.g., "What were the Founding Fathers trying to avoid?") or key terms (e.g., "checks and balances").
- As an additional step, quartets can pass their synthesized we know/we wonder chart to another group for feedback. Groups can indicate agreement, pose and answer questions, or make suggestions.

Classroom Example:

Ms. Williams gave her students a Quartet Quiz (see Figure 4.10) after a series of lessons on how plants grow. She posed two questions: (1) "What have we learned from our study of how plants grow and change?" and (2) "What do we still wonder about?" Each quartet shared its "we knows" as Ms. Williams wrote them on the whiteboard. Then each group contributed its "we wonder" questions. Students' questions (and misconceptions) helped Ms. Williams figure out what to do next.

Figure 4.10 | Quartet Quiz on Plants

We Know	We Wonder
<ul><li>You have to plant a seed.</li><li>You have to water it and give it sun.</li><li>Don't give it too much sun. Give it some shade.</li><li>It can grow in soil or water.</li><li>We get oxygen from plants.</li><li>The oxygen comes out of the leaves.</li><li>When the leaves fall off the trees, they look sick. But not pine trees.</li><li>The plants change when their leaves change colors. Some bushes and flowers change colors, too.</li><li>Plants change by growing bigger and bigger over time.</li><li>Plants grow by sucking up all the water and delivering it [misconception].</li></ul>	<ul><li>Do plants have to be planted in the ground in order to grow? How do the roots grow if the seeds just land on the ground?</li><li>How can you tell what kind of tree will come from a seed that you see?</li><li>Can any plants grow in sand? What kind?</li><li>How do plants provide oxygen?</li><li>Do we get all our oxygen from plants and trees?</li><li>Where does oxygen come from in pine trees because their leaves are not really leaves?</li><li>Why are most leaves green?</li><li>Why do the leaves change color?</li><li>Do the roots grow down into the ground as far as the trunk and branches grow up into the air?</li></ul>

Debate Team Carousel

What It Is:

A strategy for conducting structured debate or discussion through writing (Himmele & Himmele, 2011)

How It Works:

Sitting in groups of four, each student receives either a template or a blank piece of paper (which students fold to create four boxes). The teacher poses a problem or challenge (e.g., "Was Alice's adventure in Wonderland a dream?"); an essential question (e.g., "Can everything be counted?"); or a challenging issue (e.g., "How do I know when to speak and when to listen in a discussion?"), and the carousel begins:

1. In box 1, students respond to the question with a claim or belief and provide their reasoning or evidence. They then pass their paper to a group member.
2. In box 2 of the paper they receive from their fellow group member, students write something to strengthen the argument in box 1, regardless of whether they agree with what was said, using reasoning or evidence. They then pass the paper to another group member.
3. Students read what was written in boxes 1 and 2 of the paper they receive from the second group member and make a counterclaim in box 3 with supporting reasoning or evidence. They then pass the paper to the last group member.
4. Students read what was written in boxes 1–3 and add their two cents in box 4.
5. Students return the papers to their original owners and read their classmates' responses to their own ideas.

What It's Good For:

- Introducing, exploring, synthesizing, or wrapping up an issue, concept, or topic
- Pre-assessing students' thinking and argument-writing skills or understanding of a concept
- Brainstorming or organizing ideas for argument-based writing
- Analyzing a piece of writing (e.g., best argument made, place where voice most emerges)
- For math: working through homework problems that students got wrong, reviewing for a test, or strengthening mathematical reasoning skills

Tips:

- Follow the carousel with whole-class, small-group, or partner discussion (e.g., offering opposing viewpoints, evaluating how one's thinking changed).
- Vary the prompts for each box to suit different needs or purposes (see Figure 4.11, p. 146).
- Post guiding questions or clarifying prompts for each box while students are working (these are included in *italics* in the problem/solution example on page 146).
- Have students initial each box they write in so that they (and you) know who wrote what.
- *For differentiation*:
  » Assign different groups prompts of varying complexity. Although the topics up for debate may differ to stretch or support student thinking, the analytical skills exercised in the activity are the same for all students.
  » For a more complex and advanced strategy for upper-elementary students that uses similar skills as Debate Team Carousel, try Structured Academic Controversy (Johnson & Johnson, n.d.). Directions and prompt ideas can be found at http://teachinghistory.org/teaching-materials/teaching-guides/21731.

Figure 4.11 | Debate Team Carousel Examples

Problem/Solution	
1. Say what you think and *why*. *"The biggest problem is. . . . Here's why: _____."*	**2. Add evidence to make the position in box 1 stronger, even if you don't agree.** *"Another reason this is a big problem is . . . ."* OR *"That's also true because . . . ."*
3. Offer a possible solution to the problem discussed in boxes 1 and 2. *"One strategy for overcoming this problem might be . . . ."*	**4. Make a comment about the solution in box 3 *or* offer another solution.** *"This solution would work well because . . . ."* OR *"Another solution might be . . . ."*

Giving an Opinion	
1. Say what you think and why.	**2. Make the argument in box 1 stronger.**
3. Give an opinion that's different from the opinion in boxes 1 and 2.	**4. Tell which opinion from boxes 1–3 has the strongest support and explain why.**

Math	
1. Solve the problem and show how you solved it.	**2. Check the solution.** Review the process and solution in box 1. Give two reasons why you think they are correct or incorrect.
3. Provide another way of solving the problem. Solve this problem in a way that's different from the process used in box 1.	**4. Find and correct errors.** Note any errors you see in boxes 1–3. If you don't see any, tell why you agree with your classmates' work.

Letter Sounds	
1. Draw something that begins with the letter *B*.	**2. Check the drawing in box 1**. If it begins with the letter *B*, draw a smiley face. If it does not, draw something else that begins with the letter *B*.
3. Draw something that begins with the letter *D*.	**4. Check the drawing in box 3.** If it begins with the letter *D*, draw a smiley face. If it does not, draw something else that begins with the letter *D*.

Synectics

What It Is:

A strategy for promoting creative thinking developed by Gordon (1961), Synectics is a series of metaphor- or analogy-based techniques for "making the familiar strange" and "making the strange familiar" (Prince, 1968, p. 4; Starko, 2013, p. 172). It can be used to inject interest into a tired topic or to push students to process information in new and deeper ways.

How It Works:

1. The teacher selects a topic or concept.
2. The teacher creates a series of direct analogies, personal analogies, or compressed conflicts. *Direct analogies* compel direct comparison of two seemingly unlike things, guided by the overarching question "How is one thing like another?" For example,
   » How is fog like a blanket?
   » What animal is like Dorothy in *The Wonderful Wizard of Oz*?
   » What can the human body be compared to?
   » What does community look like?

   Personal analogies invite students to "be" something through their imagination. The overarching question is "What would it be like to be [this thing]?" For example,
   » How would it feel to be a nimbus cloud?
   » What would life be like as a pyramid?
   » If you were a potato, what would you want to happen to you?
   » What couldn't you do if you were a fence?

   Compressed conflicts bring together diametrically opposed words and ideas. The underlying question is "How can two opposites come together?" For example,
   » Is there a difference between a "little" lie and a "big" lie?
   » What does someone who has divided loyalties sound like?
   » When is anxious patience possible?
   » Where do we see random patterns?

   In general, direct and personal analogies are well suited to grades K–5, whereas compressed conflicts are better suited to the upper-elementary grades.
3. The teacher uses all or a few selected prompts in whole-class, small-group, or individual activities.
4. Synectics analogies can also be used as a multistep process, like this one articulated by Catherine Brighton and Holly Hertberg-Davis (2008; used with permission):
   a. List characteristics/descriptors/associations with [topic/concept/thing].
   b. Brainstorm characteristics of a ["random" topic/concept/thing].
   c. What would it feel like to be a ["random" topic/concept/thing]?

d. What words in the list from step b seem to be opposites of each other? Brainstorm a list of "conflict pairs."

e. Which of these conflict pairs seem to be the most opposite/interesting/provocative?

f. What else could be described as [conflict pair]?

g. How is [original topic] like [thing from step f]?

What It's Good For:

- Introducing students to new material
- Extending or challenging student understanding
- Provoking fresh perspectives
- Facilitating sense-making activities
- Launching group discussions
- Instigating creative ideas and flexible thinking
- Generating project ideas or solutions to problems

Tips:

- When inviting and discussing responses to direct analogies, personal analogies, or compressed conflicts, take care to solicit a wide range of responses and to avoid suppressing or judging ideas. The best ideas may not be the first ideas, and students often build off one another as they hear more ideas from their peers.
- Teach students about the different kinds of analogies and have them generate their own prompts for individual or class use.
- Use Synectics-inspired analogies to plan prompts, questions, and tasks that can be "plugged in" to other strategies described in this book, such as Shake 'n' Share (pp. 124–125), Exit Slips (pp. 184–188), ThinkDots (pp. 151–158), and RAFT (pp. 282–288).

Classroom Examples:

- First grade teacher Ms. Haran uses several personal analogies prompts to ready her students for writing poems about the seasons from the point of view of a plant in that season:
  » Think about the season of [fall/winter/spring/summer]. How do you feel? What do you see? How do you feel during the day and at night?
  » Pretend you are a tree in [fall/winter/spring/summer]. What are you doing? How do you feel? What do you want most? What do you think will happen to you?

- Mr. Ellison's 3rd graders have learned something about Ruby Bridges every year since kindergarten. He uses the following Synectics process in small-group discussion to give students a new way of thinking about Ruby Bridges as a civil rights figure:

1. List all the facts you know about Ruby Bridges.
2. Brainstorm characteristics of an iceberg.
3. What would it feel like to be an iceberg?
4. What words in the list from step 2 seem to be opposites of each other? Brainstorm a list of "conflict pairs."
5. Which of these conflict pairs seem to be the most opposite/interesting?
6. What animal could be described as [selected conflict pair]?
7. How is Ruby Bridges like [animal from step 6]?

Source: Based on an idea from C. Brighton & H. Hertberg-Davis. Used with permission.

- Ms. Munoz, a 5th grade teacher, employs Synectics-type thinking with her students to create a class-generated chart of story starter ideas (see Figure 4.12). Students can refer to the chart for ideas during Writer's Workshop and are encouraged to add new possibilities throughout the year. They can also mix and match ideas for characters, places, flaws, strengths, and hopes—or come up with their own.

Figure 4.12 | Story Starter Ideas

Interesting Character	Interesting Place	Character Flaw	Secret Strength	Hope/Aspiration
Maddie	School playground on her 11th birthday	Bullies other kids	Solves math problems lightning-fast	Get invited to someone's house
Randy the raccoon	Alley dumpster	Wants to sleep at night	Sings like an angel	Learn to draw
Violet the mail carrier	Beach before sunrise	Doesn't trust anyone	Figure skates	Become a police officer
Coach Alex Stern	Frozen foods section at the grocery store	Smiles too much	Raps	Overcome fear of spiders
Polly the black Labrador	Busy airport	Lacks self-control	Has ESP	Taste chocolate, just once
A Granny Smith apple	Side of the road	Is extremely shy	Tells very funny jokes	Get back to the tree
Riley Foster, a curious child	In line at a theme park	Steals books from the library	Designs inventions	Make contact with alien life forms

ThinkDots

What It Is:

Conceived by Kay Brimijoin, ThinkDots is a versatile strategy for helping students think and talk about a concept, a topic, an idea, or an issue from multiple perspectives.

How It Works:

1. The teacher creates six ThinkDots cards, each with a number corresponding to one of the "dots" from a die on one side and a prompt or a question on the other side.
2. Students work in groups of two to six with one die and set of ThinkDots per group. Each student is responsible for one card's prompt or question.
3. There are three ways to conduct a ThinkDots activity:
   - » *Option 1:* Students take turns rolling the die, finding the card with the corresponding number of dots, and reading aloud and responding to the prompt.
   - » *Option 2:* Students roll the die to divide the cards. They silently read and respond to their prompts and then take turns sharing in numerical order.
   - » *Option 3:* Jigsaw-style, students form new groups with students from other home groups who have rolled the same number. Together, they discuss their prompt, jot down answers, and then return to their home groups to share those ideas.
4. For all three options, students should use tracking sheets to take notes on their conversation (see Figure 8.1, p. 314).

What It's Good For:

- Introducing a unit
- Processing a lesson or reading content
- Fueling general small-group discussion activities
- Reviewing content for a quiz or test

Tips:

- Use one of the frameworks in Figure 4.13 (p. 152) or from the Questioning Framework Examples table (see pp. 162–168) for brainstorming ThinkDots questions or prompts. (*Note:* If using Webb's DOK questions, include a combination of Level 2 and Level 3 questions for each set of six ThinkDots.)
- There are three different ways to display ThinkDots for students:
  1. *Screen:* Display the ThinkDots grid on the interactive whiteboard or screen. Give each group of students a die and allow them to roll to find their prompt numbers. Students will refer to prompts displayed on the screen during their discussion.

2. *Handout*: Provide each student with a full-page handout of the prompts. Give each group of students a die and allow them to roll to find their prompt numbers. Students will refer to their handouts during their discussion.

3. *Cards*: Cut the six prompts into six separate cards. Punch a hole in the cards and put them on a ring (see Figure 4.14). Give each group of students a set of cards and a die and allow them to roll to find their prompt numbers. Each student will take his or her card off the ring and refer to it during the discussion. This method works especially well for differentiation, as different-colored cards can help the teacher remember which version of the questions are which. It also works well if the ThinkDots discussion will be Jigsawed, as students can take their cards with them to their "number group's" discussion area.

- *For differentiation*: All groups of students can work with the same set of ThinkDots questions for different content at varying degrees of difficulty. Alternatively, the teacher can create different sets of questions (see tiered examples on pp. 208–209) that can be coded with different-colored dots—a form of "stealth" differentiation because students are usually unaware that different versions are being used.

Figure 4.13 | Frameworks for Brainstorming ThinkDots Prompts

Performance Verbs	Wiggins and McTighe's Six Facets of Understanding	Webb's Depth of Knowledge (DOK)		de Bono's (1999) Six Thinking Hats
		Level 2	Level 3	
• Describe it • Analyze it • Associate it • Compare it • Apply it • Argue for or against it	• Explain • Interpret • Apply • Have perspective on • Empathize with • Self-reflect on	• Categorize • Estimate • If/then • Organize • Predict • Find patterns	• Assess • Critique • Formulate • Hypothesize • Investigate • Revise	• Red Hat (emotions, feelings) • Purple Hat (drawbacks, critical) • Yellow Hat (benefits, positives) • White Hat (objective, data-driven) • Blue Hat (summarize, overview) • Green Hat (creativity, possibilities)

Source: From *Differentiation in Middle and High School: Strategies to Engage All Learners* (p. 138), by K. J. Doubet and J. A. Hockett, 2015, Alexandria, VA: ASCD. Copyright 2015 by ASCD.

Figure 4.14 | Sample ThinkDots Cards

Examples:

Figure 4.15 (pp. 154–158) includes a variety of ThinkDots examples across grade levels and content areas.

Figure 4.15 | ThinkDots Examples

Concept Review

Possible Applications: Processes (e.g., close reading, mathematical reasoning, historical thinking, the inquiry process) and topics (e.g., conflicts, fractions, leadership styles, energy).

Explain It	Interpret It	Apply It
How is _____ connected to _____? Give examples.	How would you explain _____ to an audience of _____?	Who uses _____? Why?

Have Perspective on It	Empathize with It	What Have You Learned About It?
Prove or provide evidence that _____.	What misunderstandings do people usually have about _____?	How has your understanding of _____ changed?

Observing with the Five Senses

Primary Science: To be used to process or discuss a nature walk.

Touch It!	Smell It!	See It!
What does it feel like? Is it rough? Is it smooth? Why does it feel the way it does?	Does it have a smell? What does it smell like? Does it smell good or bad to you? What do you think makes it smell?	How does it look? What colors does it have? What shape is it? What are the parts? What do you think the parts do?

Taste It!	Hear It!	Your Choice
Lick or taste it—only if your teacher says it's OK! What does it taste like? Is it sweet? Sour? Salty? Bitter? Does it smell like it tastes?	Does it make any noise by itself? What kind of noise? Make some noise with it! (Be careful not to break or hurt it!) What noise can you make? What causes the noise?	Describe how this looks, feels, tastes, smells, or sounds. Try not to use its name!

Source: Developed by Jessica Hockett for the Tennessee Department of Education. Copyright 2017 by the Tennessee Department of Education. Used with permission.

Six Thinking Hats (de Bono, 1999)

Possible Applications: Story analysis (e.g., theme); mathematical processes (e.g., classifying shapes); historical events (e.g., the Boston Tea Party); scientific issues (e.g., recycling).

Red Hat	Black Hat	Yellow Hat
What are my feelings and thoughts about _____? How would other people feel about _____? Why?	What problems do I see with _____? Why might I choose *not* to _____?	What good things can come from _____? What are some things that make _____ helpful?

White Hat	Blue Hat	Green Hat
What exactly *is* _____? What are the parts of _____? What questions do I still have about _____?	What is the whole "point" of _____? What can I (or we) do in order to better understand _____?	What are some new ways to think about _____? What might make _____ more exciting/useful?

Science: Energy Resources

Explain It	Interpret It	Apply It
Give specific examples of renewable resources. Give specific examples of nonrenewable resources.	How would you explain the difference between renewable and nonrenewable resources to a 1st grader?	Who uses renewable resources? Why? Who uses nonrenewable resources? Why?

Have Perspective	Empathize with It	What Have You Learned?
You are a beaver in your natural habitat. How might humans' search for renewable and nonrenewable resources affect you?	What misunderstanding might people have about how use of renewable and nonrenewable resources affects the environment?	How has your understanding changed of *all* the ways sunlight provides renewable energy?

Math

Applications: The teacher can use a dry-erase marker on these laminated cards to reuse in different lessons or units. Prompts can also be varied for student readiness.

Explain the mathematical reasoning involved in solving this problem:	Use pictures or objects to describe and depict the mathematical concept of _____ to an audience of _____.
	Come up with at least ____ different ways to solve the problem below. Then talk with your partner/group about which way you think is the "best" way.
Write a number model and number story for this problem:	Choose one problem from today's/tonight's homework and work through it with your partner. Talk about what you are doing and thinking as you work.
	Come up with a new problem that's like those you solved in today's/tonight's homework. Write it and solve it below:

Equations

- The teacher can write one problem on the board for everyone to use (undifferentiated).
- The teacher can give a different problem to each small group or write different problems on the back side of each card, differentiated for each group (differentiated for each student readiness).
- This strategy can be used for sense making after the introduction of a new concept or type of problem, as a review, or as part of a homework check.

Solve this problem. What was easy about it? Not so easy?	Create and solve a problem similar to this problem.
	What's one question someone should ask him- or herself when he or she first looks at this problem?
What's a mistake someone might make in trying to solve this problem? Why might he or she make that mistake?	What mathematical concepts or terms/vocabulary does this problem show? Be specific!
	Write a set of directions that tells someone who joined our class today how to solve this problem.

Character Study

For use in whole-class discussion and modeling or in guided and independent reading groups.

Physical Traits	Personality Traits
What does this character look like? Describe the appearance so that someone who can't see would get a clear picture in his or her mind.	Choose two or three words to describe this character's personality. Give examples from the words and pictures.
Problems	**A Good Friend?**
What problems or "trouble" does this character face? Are these big problems or little problems? Why do you say so?	If this character came to life, would he or she make a good friend? Why or why not? Use the words and pictures in the story to explain your thinking.
	Like and Dislikes
	List some things this character likes and dislikes. Be ready to explain how you know the character likes or dislikes these things.
	Lessons Learned
	What lessons does the character learn in this story? Were these easy lessons or hard lessons to learn? How so?

Language Arts: Word Choice

Directions: Each side of your die represents an overused word that needs to be spiced up. After you have rolled your word, use the dictionary and thesaurus (hard copy or electronic) to locate more descriptive synonyms. After you've recorded your ideas, rank the synonyms in order from what you believe is least to greatest amount of "flavor."

Say/Said	Go/Went	Do/Did
Mean	Nice	Angry

Continued

Figure 4.15 | ThinkDots Examples (continued)

Word Study (More Accessible)

When could using this word help someone? When could using this word get someone into trouble? (•)	Use this word correctly in a brief dialogue between two characters in a book or movie of your choice. (•••)	A car company wants to use this word as the name for its newest car. They've asked you to design the car. If this word were a car, what would it look like? Draw a picture and be ready to explain why you drew what you did. (••••)
Sketch a collection of three images that represent this word. Your images should represent what the word literally means and what it suggests or hints. (⁙)	Act out what you would do for this word in a game of charades. Then explain why you did what you did. (⁙)	Think of this word as a *color*, a *sound*, a *texture*, and a *taste* or *smell*. Use your above responses to compose a vivid, paragraph-long word description. (•••/•••)

Word Study (More Advanced)

In your opinion, is this word a "good" word or a "bad" word? Put another way, is this word useful? Does it do a job that no other word can do? (•)	What word is this word's "soulmate"? What word is this word's "worst enemy"? Provide a rationale for your choices. (•••)	Decide which of the following people would be most likely to use (or consider using) this word: • A children's book author • A musician • The U.S. president (••••)
Examine the picture provided. Come up with ways to describe this picture using your word. (You can use variations on your word, such as *beautiful* for *beautifully*). (⁙)	Create a concrete poem using this word as the poem's subject. (•••/•••)	Mark Twain said, "The difference between the almost right word and the right word is . . . the difference between the lightning bug and the lightning." When would this word be the "almost right" word and when would it be the "right" word? (•••/•••)

Analyzing an Opinion (More Accessible)

Opinion What does this author believe about [topic provided]? Why do you think so? (•)	**Reasons** What reasons does the author give to support what he or she believes? Do these reasons make sense to you? Why or why not? (••)	**Purpose** What does the author hope that *you*—the reader—will think or do? Why do you say so? (•••)
Details and Examples What details and examples does the author give to explain his or her reasons? Do those details and examples explain his or her reasons? (⁙)	**Believability** Can you believe what this author is saying? Why or why not? (⁙)	**Persuasiveness** Do you agree or disagree with the author? Explain why or why not. (It's OK to be unsure.) (•••/•••)

Analyzing an Opinion (More Advanced)

Opinion In your *own* words, what is this author's overall opinion? How do you know? (•)	**Reasons** How much sense do the author's reasons make? What problems in the author's thinking do you see? Why are those problems? (•••)	**Purpose** Why did the author write this opinion? What is the author hoping will or won't happen? (•••)
Details and Examples Does the author give enough details and examples to support the reasons for his or her opinion? Are the details and examples connected to the reasons? Why do you say so? (⁙)	**Believability** What is the author's job in real life? (It's OK to do a search!) Does that job make sense with the topic? Does it make the author easier to believe or harder to believe? (⁙)	**Persuasiveness** How persuasive or convincing is the author's opinion? What strategies does he or she use to persuade the reader? Do they work? (•••/•••)

Reading a Nonfiction Article (More Advanced)

Central Idea
What's *the* most important idea in the whole article? What does the writer want the reader to "get," no matter what? Why do you say so?

Structure/Organization
How does the writer organize information in this article? How can you tell?

Text Features
What text features does this article have? Which ones are the *most* helpful to the reader? How are they helpful?

Of Interest
What is the most interesting fact or piece of information in this article? Why do you say so?

Picture This
How do the pictures and words in this article "work together" to give the reader information? What's more important in this article: the words or the pictures?

Questions
What questions *doesn't* this article answer? Where might you find answers to those questions?

Historical Document Analysis

Origins
Who produced this document? When and where was it produced? What clues in or on the source tell you?

Purpose
Why was this document produced? What was the purpose? Can you tell for sure? Why or why not?

Time and Place
What does this document tell you about life in the time or place that it comes from? Identify and explain two or more things.

Proof
What does this document show or prove about this [event/person/idea]?

Comparison
Compare this document with this other document: _____. Make a simple Venn diagram to show the similarities and differences.

Missing Pieces
What are you wondering about after looking at this document? Write one or two questions that you have.

Reading a Nonfiction Article (More Accessible)

Central Idea
What is this article about, overall? What's the main topic or central idea? How do you know?

Structure/Organization
What does the writer write about first? Next? After that? Does this order make sense to you? Why or why not?

Text Features
The writer uses these text features: _____. Do these make the article easier or harder to follow? Why do you say so?

Of Interest
What is the most interesting fact or piece of information in this article? Why do you say so?

Picture This
What information do the pictures in this article give that the words don't? What information do the words give that the pictures don't?

Questions
Write one to three questions you have after reading this article. Where could you find answers to those questions?

Regions

Students work with sets of regional maps to answer questions on this set of cards. These questions could be adapted to *country* or *state*.

Geography
Describe this region in terms of its
- States.
- Major bodies of water.
- Landforms/features.
- Highest/lowest elevation points.

Resources
What resources does this region have that other regions don't? What do the resources in this region suggest about what kinds of jobs people in this region might have?

Inside Your Mind
What images come to your mind when you think of this region? Brainstorm a list or sketch pictures. Then compare your ideas with the info in the maps. Do they agree?

My Life in _____.
Based only on what you can tell from these maps, how might your life be different if you lived in one of the states in this region? Be ready to explain your thinking using one or more maps.

Google It
Use Google Earth to look at this region. Identify and be ready to share three to five things that you found out about this region that the other maps don't show.

Do You Know?
Come up with one or two interesting questions about this region for your group mates to answer using one or more of the maps. Be sure that *you* know the answer so that you can tell them if they are right!

Continued

Figure 4.15 | ThinkDots Examples (continued)

Music

Describe	Compare	Feelings About
Describe this song. Is it fast or slow? Is it smooth or choppy? Is it in a major or a minor key? Explain your choices.	Which of the other songs that we've listened to is this song most like? Explain how they are the same and how they are different.	How do you think the composer was feeling when he or she wrote this song? How does this song make *you* feel? Why?
Parts of	**Use of**	**Good and Bad Parts**
What instruments do you hear playing in this song? Think about strings, percussion, brass, woodwinds, and so on.	What if you could pick this song to use as a soundtrack for a movie, cartoon, or storybook? Which would you pick? What would it go well with? Why?	What in particular do you like about this song? What are its best qualities? Explain. What don't you like about this song? Why doesn't this appeal to you?

Drama

I'm Excited!	I'm Devastated!	This Is Hilarious!
Read this scene as if it's the best news you've ever received. Be very excited—make us feel your joy!	Read this scene as if it's the worst news you've ever received. Be really sad—cry if you want to!	Read this scene as if it's the funniest thing you've ever heard. It's OK if you have to take a break for a fit of laughter.
I'm Terrified!	**I'm Confused!**	**I'm Angry!**
Read this scene as if it's the scariest thing you've ever heard. Be sure to look around to make sure no one is after you!	Read this scene as if it makes no sense to you at all. Your brow might be wrinkled and your statements may sound more like questions . . . but that's OK, right?	Read this scene as if you are burning with rage. Shout if you want to. Make us want to run and hide from your anger.

The Matrix

What It Is:

> An organizer for discussing and visualizing relationships, including shared and unique aspects of people, topics, concepts, things, and so on

How It Works:

1. The teacher lists elements (people/topics/concepts/things) across the top row and down the left-hand column of a 4x4 or 5x5 table, keeping the same order in each listing.
2. The teacher writes a key question across the top to focus students' discussion of relationships and connections.
3. The box in the upper left-hand corner is reserved for a commonality among all elements being discussed.

Figure 4.16 shows an example of a Matrix for exploring genres.

Figure 4.16 | Genre Matrix

Question: What traits do these genres share? What makes each genre unique?			
	Mysteries	**Adventure Stories**	**Fantasy Stories**
Mysteries	[Something unique to mysteries]	[Something that mysteries and adventure stories have in common]	[Something that mysteries and fantasy stories have in common]
Adventure Stories	[Something else that adventure stories and mysteries have in common]	[Something unique to adventure stories]	[Something that adventure stories and fantasy stories have in common]
Fantasy Stories	[Something else that fantasy stories and mysteries have in common]	[Something else that fantasy stories and adventure stories have in common]	[Something unique to fantasy stories]

What It's Good For:

- Community-building activities (see pp. 18–28)
- Promoting small-group discussion
- Reviewing or synthesizing concepts, topics, or ideas
- Synthesizing in a Jigsaw task

Tips:

- The Matrix (and any graphic organizer) should be used as a means to an end, not as an end in itself.
- Limit the number of elements being explored to three or four.
- Be sure to frame the Matrix with a question so that the purpose of the tool and task is clear.
- Depending on the purpose, the guiding question may need to be specific about what kinds of relationships students should find and discuss. For example, there's a difference between saying, "How are these shapes similar and different?" and "How do these shapes compare in terms of their attributes?"
- The Matrix favors students who have strong visual-spatial orientation. Model its use with a document camera or projected computer screen using familiar content. It's also helpful for students to try out the Matrix for the first time in a "get-to-know you" way, free from discipline-based content.
- *For differentiation*: Because the same elements intersect with one another in two places on the Matrix, you can use those points of intersection strategically to increase the level of challenge. For example,
    » In the *characters* examples listed under Classroom Examples below, ask some students to list a shared positive trait of the characters in one square of intersection and to list a shared negative trait of the characters in the other square of intersection.
    » In the *regions* example listed under Classroom Examples below, ask some students to limit the shared traits of the intersecting regions to traits that the third region does not share (e.g., "Something that New England and the Mid-Atlantic have in common that is not true of the Midwest").

- *Variations*:
    » Students identify categories from a filled-in or partially filled-in organizer.
    » The teacher plans and completes an organizer, cuts it into cards, puts the cards into a baggie, and has students do an inductive sort (with or without categories provided).

Classroom Examples:

- *Arctic animals* (e.g., penguin, polar bear, and walrus)
- *Living systems* (e.g., populations, communities, and ecosystems)
- *Shapes* (e.g., rhombus, rectangle, and square)
- *Characters in the same work* (e.g., Charlotte, Wilbur, and Fern)
- *Characters by the same author in different works* (e.g., BFG, Charlie, and James)
- *Regions* (e.g., New England, Mid-Atlantic, and Midwest)
- *Explorers* (e.g., Christopher Columbus, Juan Ponce de León, and Jacques Cartier)
- *Artistic instruments* (e.g., paints, colored pencils, and markers)
- *Musical genres* (e.g., folk songs, spirituals, and nursery rhymes)

Questioning Frameworks

What They Are:

Three different frameworks for helping teachers plan questions that require students to process, organize, evaluate, and create knowledge rather than simply regurgitate it. Figure 4.17 (pp. 162–168) provides examples of questions across the content areas based on all three Questioning Frameworks.

How They Work:

1. *Bloom's Revised Taxonomy* (Anderson & Krathwohl, 2001). Teachers can pre-plan questions and activities at the higher levels of the taxonomy, knowing that students who are engaged in critical thinking are more likely to comprehend and remember knowledge than when asked to simply engage in lower-level exercises.

2. *Depth of Knowledge* (Webb et al., 2005). Norman Webb designed the Depth of Knowledge (DOK) framework as a tool for examining the alignment between the cognitive demand of standards and the cognitive demand of assessments measuring those standards. His framework can also be used to examine the match between learning objectives and the questions posed to unpack those objectives. For example, if a teacher's skill goal is written at the evaluation level, he or she should make sure lesson and assessment questions focus on evaluation as well. Webb's framework can help teachers ensure that the depth of their classroom questions— whether posed in discussion or in tasks and activities—is consistent with the depth of their instructional objectives and assessment items.

3. *Six Facets of Understanding* (Wiggins & McTighe, 2005). The Understanding by Design framework operates according to the principle that deep understanding— not just attainment of facts and skills—should be at the center of teaching and learning. Wiggins and McTighe contend that if someone truly understands something, he or she can explain it, apply it, interpret it, have perspective on it, show empathy with it, and reveal self-knowledge about it. These Six Facets of Understanding can be used to design questions and tasks that compel students to autonomously transfer and apply their knowledge and skills to authentic performances and situations.

What They're Good For:

Planning questions for a lesson, an assessment, or any of the other strategies discussed in this chapter

Tips:

- The upper levels of these frameworks can serve as Jigsaw prompts for longer-term investigations and as topics for discussion in Inside-Outside Circles and Debate Team Carousel activities.
- Use the Six Facets of Understanding as Looking Lens prompts, to structure Think-Dots discussions, or to drive a round of Shake 'n' Share.

Figure 4.17 | Questioning Framework Examples Across Grade Levels and Content Areas

Questions Based on Bloom's Revised Taxonomy (Anderson & Krathwohl, 2001)			
Question Type	**Nature of Question**	**Potential Stems**	**Sample Questions or Prompts**
Remembering	Recalling or recognizing information. Questions ask students to *define, name, recall, repeat,* or *state.*	The majority of "Remembering" questions begin with the word *who, what, when,* or *where.*	• What is a "stanza" in poetry? • When did the United States gain its independence? • What are the properties of a triangle? • Who invented the lightbulb?
Understanding* *This is *not* the deep and transferable "understanding" discussed in Chapter 2 (UBD).	Comprehending or grasping prior learning. Questions ask students to *describe, discuss, explain, paraphrase,* or *summarize.*	• Explain the process of ____. • Describe how to ____. • Summarize ____. • In your own words, tell ____	• Explain the conflict in the story you are reading. • Summarize the events that led up to the beginning of the Revolutionary War. • Describe the steps to follow when solving a long division problem. • How does an elephant stay cool?
Applying	Using information to solve a problem or complete a task. Questions ask students to *demonstrate, illustrate, interpret, solve,* or *use.*	• Demonstrate the process of ____. • Illustrate how ____ works. • Determine how ____. • Use ____ to solve this problem:	• How would you correct this flawed sentence? • Illustrate how one check or balance works in the branches of the U.S. government. • What are the errors in this solution to the problem? • How could the weaknesses in this experiment's design be improved?

Question Type	Nature of Question	Potential Stems	Sample Questions or Prompts
Analyzing	Breaking down material, examining organizational structure, finding patterns, or relating ideas. Questions ask students to *categorize, compare, contrast, discriminate,* or *distinguish.*	• ____ is an example of ____ because ____. • What are the similarities and differences between ____ and ____? • How does ____ affect ____? • ____ is/is not an example of ____ because ____.	• What internal conflict is the character in this story experiencing? How do you know? • How are the buildings of Ancient Rome and Greece similar? Different? • Is there another way that we could write the same equation to see if it would still work? • Is ____ an Arctic animal? Why or why not?
Evaluating	Appraising or critiquing based on specific standards or criteria. Questions ask students to *appraise, defend, judge, justify,* or *support.*	• How effective is ____? Why? • Which is better/stronger/more defensible: ____ or ____? Why? • Support the argument that ____. • Is ____ safe/helpful/ beneficial for ____? Explain. • Why might ____ agree/disagree with ____? Explain.	• How effective is the writer's use of imagery (ability to use words to paint pictures in your head)? Explain. • Why might some people have disagreed with the Boston Tea Party, and how would they defend their opinion? • How effective was [this former student] at solving this problem? • Will planting trees really help the environment? Why or why not?
Creating	Combining and integrating ideas and information into new schematics, products, plans, patterns, or structures. Questions ask students to *construct, design, develop, formulate,* or *propose.*	• Design a new way to ____. • Develop a theory about ____. • Propose a plan to ____. • Imagine a situation in which ____. • Formulate a new ____ using ____.	• Formulate a new story featuring the same characters facing a different conflict. • Propose a plan to help your classmates distinguish among the different regions. • What is another way to solve this problem, and how might it help people? • Imagine a world in which everyone sorts their trash and recycling. Develop a plan that would make that happen in real life.

Continued

Figure 4.17 | Questioning Framework Examples Across Grade Levels and Content Areas

(continued)

	Questions Based on Webb's DOK (Webb et al., 2005)		
Webb's Level	**Key Verbs**	**Potential Stems**	**Sample Questions or Prompts**
Level One: Recall *Who, what, when, where, why*	Arrange, calculate, define, identify, list, measure, recognize, recall, repeat, state, use	The majority of "Recall" questions begin with the word *who, what, when,* or *where.*	• When and where did the story of *Sarah, Plain and Tall* take place? • Where were the majority of the battles in this war fought? • What does it mean to say that two fractions are "equivalent"? • What kind of animal is a dolphin?
Level Two: Skill/Concept *Beyond recall; requires processing*	Categorize, estimate, identify patterns, organize, predict (if/then), separate, summarize	• If _____, then _____? • How would you organize _____ to show _____? • Illustrate how _____ works. • What do you think would happen if _____? Why? • Use _____ to solve this problem: _____.	• If the Grinch is motivated by greed, what do you think he will do next? • To which branch of government does [this power] "belong"? Why do you say so? • What angle measures would we get if we decomposed this angle into 3 smaller angles with equal measures? • Using what you know about the traits of mammals, categorize these animals into "mammals" and "nonmammals."

Webb's Level	Key Verbs	Potential Stems	Sample Questions or Prompts
Level Three: Strategic Thinking *Requires mental processing at a higher level*	Appraise, assess, compare, critique, formulate, hypothesize, investigate, revise	• How are ____ and ____ alike? How are they different? • Based on the data you've collected, what is your hypothesis about ____? • Use what you've learned about ____ to revise your thinking about ____ • How would you rate the ____ of ____? • Evaluate ____ based on the following criteria: ____.	• How does Steve Jenkins use illustrations in *What Do You Do with a Tail Like This?* How does this compare with how he uses illustrations in *Never Smile at a Monkey?* • Use what you've learned about a city community to evaluate our classroom community. • Use estimation strategies to assess the reasonableness of your answer to this story problem (CCSS4.0A.A.3). • Based on the data you've collected, what is your hypothesis about the temperature next week?
Level Four: Extended Thinking *Requires planning and developing; therefore, extended time is necessary.*	Apply concepts to, connect, create, critique (more factors), design, prove, synthesize	• Apply the concepts of ____ to creating a ____. • Plan and conduct an investigation to determine ____. • Critique this ____ in terms of ____, and ____. • Design an original application of ____ • Use ____ to prove ____.	• Create an original poem that reflects your favorite poem's theme. • Investigate the structures in our school to determine if they better represent Roman or Greek architecture. • Use what you know about area and volume to design a waterpark with 5 pools with the following dimensions: ____. • Plan and conduct an investigation to provide evidence of what plants need to live.

Continued

Figure 4.17 | Questioning Framework Examples Across Grade Levels and Content Areas

(continued)

	Questions Based on The Six Facets of Understanding (Wiggins & McTighe, 2006)		
Facet	Nature of Question/ Prompt	Potential Stems	Sample Questions or Prompts
Explain/ Explanation	Put information, ideas, principles, and processes into own words and explain thinking.	• What is the key idea in _____? • What caused _____? What are the effects of _____? • What are examples of _____? • How did _____ come about? • What might happen if _____? • What are some common misconceptions about _____? • What are some examples of _____? • How might we confirm/prove/justify _____? • How is _____ connected to _____?	• Draw and label a simple diagram that shows how plants "feed" themselves. Then explain what your diagram shows. • Think about a swimming pool. What is the difference among the *area* of the pool, the *perimeter* of the pool, and the *volume* of the pool? • What caused the American Revolution? • Circle the metaphor in the song/poem excerpt below. Then explain why you think this is a metaphor. • Give examples and nonexamples of symmetry.
Interpret/ Interpretation	Make sense of information, ideas, principles, and processes by creating comparisons, analogies, or stories.	• How is _____ like a _____? • What is the meaning of _____? • How does _____ relate to _____? • What are the implications of _____ for _____? • What does _____ reveal about _____? • What does _____ have to do with _____? • Explain _____ to an audience of _____.	• How is a plant like a human? • How does "manifest destiny" relate to us? • Write a story for this number model. • Use your own words to paraphrase this idea: • Explain to an audience of preschoolers why we *need* standard units of measurement. Be sure to use examples and analogies they would understand.

Facet	Nature of Question/ Prompt	Potential Stems	Sample Questions or Prompts
Apply/ Application	Use information, ideas, principles, and processes in new contexts and situations.	• How could someone use _____ to _____? • How is _____ applied in the larger world? • Where do we see _____ in the world today? • How could _____ help/benefit _____? • Solve _____. Name a real-life situation in which you might use _____. • Use _____ to create a _____ that shows _____.	• Create a table for these data that makes them easier to understand. • When would it be more appropriate to use the *mode* of a set of data rather than the *mean?* • Revise this paragraph for capitalization and punctuation. • Name three ways that someone could use fractions to plan a birthday party. • Choose your favorite symmetrical object in the classroom. Make a list of all the ways that this object's symmetry helps it do its "job."
Demonstrate/ Have perspective	Recognize and articulate the many possible different viewpoints regarding a situation.	• What are different points of view about _____? • How might _____ look from _____'s point of view? • What are the benefits and limitations of this _____? • How is _____ similar to/different from _____? • What are other possible reactions to _____? • What are the strengths and weaknesses of _____? • What are the limits of _____? • What's the evidence for _____? Is the evidence reliable? Sufficient? • Is it ever OK for _____? Why or why not?	• Analyze this student's work from a class several years ago. What did he or she do well? What did he or she not do well? • What are the benefits and limitations of using a bar graph to display these data? • How might the problem in the story look from [this character's] point of view? • Give the pros and cons of relying on GPS for directions. • Argue that a car is a *need.* Then argue that it's a *want.*

Continued

Figure 4.17 | Questioning Framework Examples Across Grade Levels and Content Areas

(continued)

Facet	Questions Based on The Six Facets of Understanding (Wiggins & McTighe, 2006)		
	Nature of Question/ Prompt	Potential Stems	Sample Questions or Prompts
Display empathy/ Empathize	Take on the viewpoint, concerns, or opinions of another and argue from that perspective.	• What would it be like to walk in the shoes of ____? • How might ____ feel/have felt about ____? • How can I reach a better understanding about ____? • What was ____ trying to make ____ feel or see [about ____]? • One misunderstanding someone might have about ____ is ____.	• What would it be like to walk in the shoes of a Native American child? • Respond to someone who might say that capitalizing doesn't matter. • Assume the role of the main character and explain why you made the choice you did in this chapter. • What is one misconception that someone might have about *scale?* What would you say (or do or show) to correct that misconception? • What did the author want you (the reader) to better understand after reading this story? How do you know?
Self-reflect	Reflect on one's own connection to, use of, and strengths and weaknesses with regard to the ideas and processes.	• How do I know ____? • What are the limits of my knowledge about ____? • How are my views about ____ shaped by my [experiences/habits/prejudices/styles]? • What are my "blind spots" about ____? (What *don't* I know?) • How can I best show ____? • What are my strengths and weaknesses in ____? • What is one question people should ask themselves when they ____? • What is a mistake that someone might make in trying to ____? Why might he or she make that mistake?	• What is a mistake someone might make when adding or subtracting fractions? Why might he or she make that mistake? • What don't you understand yet about using quotation marks? • How has your understanding of the writing process changed over the past month? • How can a person know when to use an estimate and when to use an exact measurement? • What should people be sure to do when working on the kind of problem we've been learning about this week? *They should be sure to . . . because. . . .*

5

Checking for Understanding Using Formative Assessment

Part 1:

How Do I Know If Students Are Getting It?

In her reflection at the end of Chapter 4, 4th grade teacher Hannah Areda noted that teaching in a more active and interactive fashion gave her a window into student thinking. In other words, she decided that the lesson was effective because she was able to determine how well students were processing the ideas.

This approach to lesson evaluation isn't typical. Usually, when gauging the effectiveness of a lesson, the teacher focuses on how it went for him or her as *the teacher*. That is, the lesson was "good" if most students were well behaved or seemed engaged, or if the activities flowed smoothly. In reality, such criteria set a low bar for success and fail to reach the heart of what matters most: *whether students are learning*.

The strategies presented in Chapter 4 provide opportunities to monitor whole-class progress and make on-the-fly adjustments for the larger group. But at the end of such a learning experience, the teacher can't gauge success according to his or her own impressions of how interactive or lively the lesson was. Instead, teachers should pointedly ask themselves, "Is my teaching working?" This question encourages teachers to shift from seeing themselves as managers of students or deliverers of content to seeing themselves as "evaluators of their effects on students" (Hattie, 2012, p. 14).

The evaluator-teacher wonders, "What are my learning goals? What am I hoping that students now know, understand, and are able to do better than they did before? Are students reaching those goals? Who is? Who isn't? Why?"

The best method for answering each of those questions is formative assessment.

What Is Formative Assessment?

Formative assessment is the ongoing process of taking regular and varied snapshots of students' learning during or after a lesson (or series of lessons) to inform next steps in instructional planning. Through formative assessment, teachers can peer into each student's brain to see if he or she "got it," uncover misconceptions and gaps in students' skills or knowledge, and gather evidence of advanced insights.

Again, consider the road trip analogy: the teacher has defined the learning destination by establishing clear and robust learning goals, administered and analyzed a pre-assessment of key goals to determine first steps, and planned active strategies for engagement and discussion to help students progress in their journey. In this analogy, formative assessment is the incessant question "Are we there yet?" that asks how far a student is from the learning destination. If a teacher waits until the end of the unit to find out that some students are back in Iowa while others arrived in San Francisco days ago, it's much too late to do anything about it, let alone make adjustments to the route. On a road trip, a GPS device can give the driver information about progress, time remaining, where the next rest area is, and points of interest along the way. This information is most beneficial when it is up-to-the-minute and accurate. For teachers, formative assessment serves the same purpose.

Is This Formative Assessment?

Certain practices are sometimes confused with formative assessment. One is "assessment by sampling" (Hockett, 2010). A teacher using this method may pose a few questions at the end of a lesson to see if everyone "got it." Two students respond with reasonable answers. The teacher decides that this sample is representative of all students' thinking, or that because all students have heard these responses, everyone now gets it. Although structured whole-group discussion can be a valuable tool (see Chapter 4), it is not a means for tapping into individual minds—and therefore is not assessment.

"Noticing" or monitoring what students do or say is also often mislabeled as formative assessment. All good teachers keep a close eye and ear on students as they work individually or in groups, and respond accordingly when they see students struggling, coasting, or getting off track. The best teachers go a step further and conduct close and careful analysis of student thinking. However, unless the teacher is *systematically observing* individual students' progress and *gathering or recording that information*, the chances that he or she is administering an assessment are slim.

Hannah's use of active learning strategies was an important part of the lesson launching her Environmental Stewardship unit, but her techniques did not meet the criteria for the best kind of formative assessment. Her use of Quartet Quiz and Debate Team Carousel came close, as small groups provided her with feedback on how they were processing information and what questions remained; however, they did not provide data on *individual students'* grasp of learning goals. She needed to collect more targeted information to inform strategic decisions about how to move each student forward in his or her learning during the next lesson.

Recall Hannah's "Application" task, which she envisioned as her formative assessment:

> Students write individual reflections about their personal role in stewarding the Earth's resources (written or drawn with annotations).

Although this task invited personal application, it did not provide guidelines for what students should include in their responses. Most students turned in illustrations of themselves depositing recycling into a labeled bin. This was a good start, but it didn't capture the important learning goals.

To implement a more strategic formative assessment, Hannah could tighten the assessment questions, like this:

> Please answer the following questions before we leave for recess:
>
> - Describe two things that *you* can do to care for the Earth.
> - Give one piece of advice to adults about how they can better care for the Earth.
>
> In your answers, use and <u>underline</u> at least three vocabulary words from the article "Tiny Plastic, Big Problem."

These exit questions would have revealed who firmly grasped the learning goals for the day (those who were able to provide multiple applications and use vocabulary effectively) and who struggled to meet the learning goals (those who misused terms, had misconceptions, or lacked the ability to transfer learning). In addition, Hannah would have noted which student responses showed unusual depth and specificity in their explanations and advice. She could have addressed these patterns proactively the next day before moving on to new material. This kind of targeted feedback could significantly improve her students' learning (Hattie, 2012).

Constructing Useful Formative Assessment Prompts

So how can teachers structure formative assessment prompts to glean information about student learning in a powerful but efficient way? The process is similar to the one for designing a pre-assessment, but it is narrower in scope. As with pre-assessment, the teacher starts by articulating what students should understand, know, and be able to do—but in terms of the learning goals for a *lesson* or short series of lessons rather than for the entire unit.

The next step is to design questions or prompts that would require students to demonstrate their grasp of key concepts or goals from the lesson. As with pre-assessment, there's no need to assess *every* single thing that has been taught; rather, the teacher should decide what the *pivotal* points of the lesson are. In other words, what must students really "get" before they can move forward in their learning? What misconceptions could prevent future learning from taking hold? Which skills must students demonstrate if they are to build on those skills with further steps? Determining these pivotal points helps make formative assessment more efficient.

Keep in mind that powerful formative assessment asks students to do more than simply regurgitate facts. Student responses on recall-based formative assessments have limited instructional implications. Although they can show what students have memorized, they cannot reveal whether students can *transfer* that knowledge, *how deeply* students understand it, or *why* students don't understand a concept.

Fact-based formative assessment reveals little evidence of students' expertise with the content and provides teachers with limited instructional implications. Fact-based assessment cannot reveal *why* students don't understand a concept or *how deeply* they understand it.

Assessment questions that require students to make connections and to use their knowledge in some way—in other words, to provide evidence that will "convict" students of learning (Wiggins & McTighe, 2005)—are the questions that give teachers the most bang for their buck. In sum, the most useful formative assessment prompts

- Are aligned with pivotal learning goals (understanding, knowledge, and skill goals).
- Are administered deliberately and intentionally (not off the cuff or as an afterthought).
- Are limited to a few key questions.
- Gauge *individual* student progress and learning needs.
- Invite application, synthesis, and transfer—not just regurgitation.
- Elicit responses that the teacher can evaluate and respond to in a timely manner.

One method teachers can use to arrive at such prompts is to consider, "If I asked students what the big idea or point of the lesson was, what would the ideal response sound like? Now, what would a prompt or question designed to elicit that response sound like?" Student answers to such questions enable the teacher to discern patterns in how well students grasped the learning goals and how to move the entire spectrum of learners forward.

In general, it's advisable to use varied questions and strategies for assessment over the course of a unit. Learners of all ages appreciate variety. It's also a good idea to walk through the potential range of student responses and consider what to do or plan as a result. If the students' responses don't matter or if there's only one right answer, the assessment isn't likely to yield useful information. Save formative assessment opportunities for those things that really matter. In other words, avoid giving an assessment just for the sake of giving an assessment.

Types of Prompts

Formative assessment prompts are useful for gauging student readiness to tackle the next phase of learning. Part 2 of this chapter includes multiple examples of *general readiness prompts* (p. 185) and *subject-specific prompts* (p. 186) to assist teachers in gathering evidence of student knowledge, understanding, and skills.

Although student readiness is the main target of formative assessment, determining other factors that influence readiness is equally important to instructional planning. Therefore, Part 2 includes examples of additional prompts that can help teachers gather other kinds of information that is relevant to the learning process:

- *Monitoring progress:* where students are with a task or process; work habits, attitudes, or dispositions relative to a task or topic (p. 187)
- *Interest/learning preference:* the level or nature of students' interest in what they are learning; how or under what conditions students prefer to learn (p. 188)

Uncovering different kinds of information related to student progress is important because it gives the teacher a more complete picture of what students are learning. In addition, it increases students' awareness of what they are learning and keeps them from becoming bored by responding to the same kind of prompt day after day.

Strategies for Formative Assessment

There are numerous strategies that teachers can use to check for understanding. These strategies vary in how much time they take to prepare and implement, and they can be used across content areas and grade levels.

Exit and Entry Slips

Exit and Entry Slips (pp. 184–188) are among the most commonly used methods of formative assessment in classrooms today. Teachers appreciate them for their flexible structure, their ease of administration, and their ability to be collected and analyzed efficiently. In general, Exit Slips (administered at the end of the lesson) have a greater effect on the teacher's decision-making process than do Entry Slips (administered at the beginning of the lesson). This is mostly because Exit Slips give the teacher time to read and digest the information and plan accordingly.

An exception is upper-elementary teachers using the "flipped" instructional model (Bergmann & Sams, 2012), who may rely more heavily on Entry Slips to discover how well students grasped the information they processed at home. Ideally, students would post these Entry Slip responses to a class blog or discussion board to give the teacher time to examine them before students come to class the next day.

Sticky Notes

Teachers and students alike can generate Sticky Notes (pp. 189–193) as a method of formative assessment. For teachers, Sticky Notes provide a method of tracking the progress of students, including nonwriters. Sticky Notes can be used to capture student learning in a variety of ways. For example, a teacher might close small-group time by quickly recording what individual students have grasped and what they are missing. These notes can then be stuck to students' file folders or running records. "Digital" Sticky Notes provide another option; the teacher can simply record voice memos at the end of a small-group meeting regarding each student's progress and use those reminders to plan future instruction.

Even very young children can use Sticky Notes to record evidence of what they've learned. For example, Ms. Roeschley asked her kindergartners to write a capital *B* and a lower-case *b* on a Sticky Note following her instruction on that letter (see Figure 5.9, p. 192). She then put each student's Sticky Note next to his or her name on a chart and was able to see all students' progress at a glance as she planned the next day's instruction.

Older children can independently compose formative assessment responses on Sticky Notes. For example, Ms. Ng posted a 5x5 square chart at the back of her room; each square had a student's assigned number on it. When Ms. Ng wanted to see where students were, individually, at the end of a lesson, she posed a question and had each student respond on a Sticky Note. Students stuck their notes to their square on the chart as they transitioned to the next activity or lesson (see Figure 5.10, p. 193). This gave Ms. Ng a quick read of where students were in their grasp of that lesson's learning goals.

Frayer Model

The Frayer model (pp. 194–198), named for Dorothy Frayer, is a four-square organizer that asks students to provide the *definition* of a concept, its *characteristics* or *attributes*, some crystallizing *examples*, and some *nonexamples* that may be frequently confused with examples. The categories of the original Frayer model are better suited to some concepts and topics than to others. A good test is whether myriad examples and nonexamples can "fit" under the concept. For some learning goals, the traditional categories are not the most efficient. In such instances, the categories of the diagram can be tweaked to better capture student thinking.

Using the Frayer diagram as a formative assessment measure has many benefits. It helps students organize their thinking, even as they share what they have learned. It allows young or reluctant writers to sketch or draw their understanding if the prompt is conducive to visual representations. Designing a Frayer also helps the teacher organize content in a clear fashion that may spill over into more organized instruction. Further, the organization of student responses in the diagram can make it easy to spot patterns in the results. Part 2 of this chapter includes examples of both traditional and modified Frayer diagrams to demonstrate how such an organizational structure can serve as a learning check for students and an instructional tool for teachers.

Is Formative Assessment Really Worth It? and Other Questions and Concerns

In recent years, research has revealed the power of formative assessment to improve student achievement (see Black & Wiliam, 1998; Hattie, 2009). Even more recently, however, the focus has turned to what teachers actually *do* with the information from formative assessment (see Guskey, 2007/2008; Hattie, 2012; Wiliam, 2012). James Popham (2006) asserts that assessment can be considered "formative" only if it is used "during the instructional segment in which the assessment occurred to adjust instruction with the intent of better meeting the needs of the students assessed" (p. 4). So collecting Exit Slips and tossing them in the recycling bin is not worth the time invested, whereas collecting Exit Slips, examining results, and shaping instruction accordingly can yield tremendous dividends.

Buying into formative assessment is one thing; putting it into practice is another. The prospect of looking through all those student responses and trying to manage the results amid the general day-to-day challenges of teaching can seem daunting. But the promise that formative assessment holds for improving instruction is unmistakable; it *is* worth trying.

What follow are common concerns among teachers and administrators about formative assessment, with responses stemming from research and practice.

How much time should this take?

There's no rule of thumb for how much time formative assessment should take. Much depends on such factors as the kind of evidence being collected, what has led up to the assessment, students' age, and the length of the lesson. A general guideline is to dedicate at least 10 percent of lesson time to administering formative assessment. Doing so helps students solidify their learning and enables the teacher to streamline instruction the following class period. Assessment is a part of teaching—you can't do one without the other—and lesson plans should reflect that synergy.

If I take the time to formatively assess every day, then I won't have time to teach everything.

Assessing *is* teaching if conducted in an informative manner. Saving a few minutes at the end of a lesson to administer a formative assessment helps students retain what they've learned because they have a chance to reflect on and process it in a new way (Jensen, 2005). In addition, regular use of formative assessment can make instruction more efficient: teachers can address misconceptions as they go rather than build new learning on the shaky foundation of partial or erroneous understanding. It takes more time to "undo" misconceptions at the end than it does to correct them along the way (Bransford et al., 2000).

It's a good idea to reserve chunks of instructional time to address formative assessment results. This may mean answering a few recurring questions, reteaching something everyone struggled with, or spending some time in small-group work (see Chapter 6). Adjusting to the habit of building that time into the lesson plan helps teachers naturally restructure the flow of their teaching activities.

Finally, remember that it's not necessary to assess every single learning goal. Plan formative assessment as an ongoing process rather than as an "event" to ensure that you focus on the goals that are crucial in determining whether students are ready to move forward.

What do I do with those few students who regularly "get" everything on my formative assessment questions?

Consider the quality of the questions. Are they truly "sticky" questions whose responses will reveal deep thinking? If they're not, revisit "Constructing Useful Formative Assessment Prompts" (pp. 173–174) and consult Part 2 of this chapter for examples. If they are, see Chapter 6 for ideas to help students go deeper in their thinking once they've mastered the initial learning goals.

What do I do with young students (or students who have language barriers or reading or writing disabilities)?

As with pre-assessment, there are multiple ways to gather formative assessment data. The following examples give an idea of the range of formative assessment options possible.

The teacher could deliver the assessment by

- Reading written or displayed prompts aloud.
- Using a one-on-one interview format.
- Showing and explaining images, pictures, or words.
- Using a technology program or app (e.g., Kahoot!).

Students could respond by

- Speaking (to the teacher or into a recording device).
- Drawing (with or without oral explanation).
- Completing a hand-on/minds-on task (e.g., cutting, arranging, sorting, or matching).
- Performing (e.g., using movement or acting something out).
- Selecting from choices.
- Responding (e.g., via response cards, clickers, or hand signals).

The teacher could document evidence by

- Placing sticky notes in a file folder.
- Using a recording device.
- Taking pictures.
- Saving electronic responses.

What about digital methods of formative assessment? How effective are they?

Technology provides many ways to check student progress throughout instruction. Plickers, Kahoot!, Socrative, GoFormative, and Padlet are just a few examples. Aside from Plickers, all of these methods require students to be able to access and use devices during instruction, which is becoming more commonplace. Still, *access* to digital learning checks does not ensure the *quality* of those learning checks. The tool must suit the purpose. For example, Plickers and Kahoot! invite closed-ended responses, which affords the teacher a quick check of the "weather" of the class, but not nuanced insights into individual student understanding. Used properly, Socrative, GoFormative, and Padlet can provide teachers with more detailed information about students' understanding, knowledge, and skills.

The bottom line is that collecting useful information with digital tools requires just as much thought and planning as does using traditional methods.

What about data from standardized assessments? Are they formative?

First, it's worth noting what standardized assessments—including state-mandated accountability tests, benchmark assessments, achievement tests, and district-developed common assessments—*can* do. Interpreted appropriately, they may

- Provide one of many data sources for district and school leaders to use in judging the effectiveness of programs and initiatives, especially over time.
- Reveal general patterns of strengths and weaknesses across a district, within a school, within a grade level, and so on.

- Provide a reference point that allows schools and educators to discern and report general patterns of student growth over time.
- Give individual teachers a sense of their own instructional strengths, tendencies, and areas of growth relative to goals measurable by the test design and item format and content.

On the other hand, standardized tests generally do *not*

- Allow teachers to see the actual test questions in a timely manner (that is, alongside student results).
- Provide individual student responses.
- Use item formats that will provide insight into a student's thinking (i.e., why the student chose or gave a certain response).
- Align with specific unit or lesson goals that the teacher aims to address in the classroom at a particular time.
- Provide the most recent information about individual student performance relative to learning goals.
- Reveal the instruction that students need in order to progress in their learning.

In other words, data from standardized tests can be used to paint, in broad strokes, an Impressionist's view of the learning landscape. But these data are not useful for the more exacting and immediate task of designing meaningful learning experiences for all students.

A Formative Assessment Upgrade

Third grade teacher Andrew Knox, a colleague of Hannah Areda's, observed her studying her Exit Slips before their PLC meeting. He liked the specificity of what Hannah could glean from the results and decided to try a similar technique with his students the following day.

Before Upgrade

Andrew presented Hannah with a draft of his Exit Slip (see Figure 5.1).

Figure 5.1 | Exit Slip Before Upgrade

- 3 things you learned about Ancient Rome's geography:
- 2 questions you have about Ancient Rome's geography:
- 1 thing about Ancient Rome you want to explore further:

Hannah affirmed her colleague's efforts, remarking that his last question was her favorite. It might give him ideas for future centers, lessons, or Anchor Activities for students to move to if they finished their work early (see Chapter 8).

She did wonder, however, if the first two prompts might be a bit too broad. Remembering her own students' vague drawings and references to recycling from her stewardship lesson, she suggested that Andrew restate those questions more specifically to make sure he would get the information he wanted from students. Andrew wanted to make sure that students could locate Rome on a map, describe its geography, and discuss the connection between geography and the other aspects of Roman life and civilization.

After Upgrade

After reworking his questions to reflect these learning goals, Andrew showed Hannah an "upgrade" the following day (see Figure 5.2).

Figure 5.2 | Exit Slip After Upgrade

Circle Rome on the map provided. Then share
- 3 words that describe Ancient Rome's geography:

- 2 ways Ancient Rome's geography affected citizens' lives:

- 1 thing about Ancient Rome you want to know more about:

p.s. Is there anything we discussed today about Ancient Rome that was "fuzzy" or confusing?

Hannah applauded these changes but noted that the Exit Slip seemed writing-heavy. Andrew had already thought of this and explained that he'd most likely need to pull a few students aside and let them either speak their answers to him or record their answers on the tablets he had checked out from the media center. Because he was reserving 15 minutes at the end of the lesson to collect this information, they felt sure he'd have enough time to rotate among those students who needed accommodations.

Before he gave students the Exit Slips, Andrew explained to the class that he wanted to know how well his teaching was working. The Exit Slips would show him what students had learned, but they would also reveal how well he had taught the lesson and what he could do better next time. He thanked his students ahead of time for helping him with his teaching. This seemed to calm their anxiety, and they readily invested in the assessment.

Part 2:

Tools and Strategies

Exit and Entry Slips

What It Is:

An efficient and simple method for formatively assessing students during the learning cycle. An Exit Slip is administered at the end of class, whereas an Entry Slip is administered at the beginning of class.

How It Works:

1. The teacher poses one to three prompts at the beginning or end of a lesson for students to answer on a half-sheet of paper or an index card, or via technology.
2. Prompts can be designed as assessments or self-assessments of
   » *Content/skill readiness:* what students understand, know, and can do relative to the learning goals.
   » *Progress:* where students are with a task or process; work habits, attitudes, or dispositions relative to a task or topic.
   » *Interest/motivation/preference:* the level or nature of students' interest in what they are learning; how or under what conditions students prefer to learn.
3. The teacher collects and analyzes individual responses, looking for patterns among students in the class.

What It's Good For:

Students' responses on Exit and Entry Slips can inform adjustments to whole-class instruction, guide plans for differentiation, provide ideas for lesson activities, inform grouping decisions, and help refine small-group work or individual conferences.

Tips:

- Avoid reducing Exit and Entry Slips to an everyday instructional routine (e.g., as a way to end or begin lessons); instead, use them to gather valuable evidence that students aren't otherwise generating.
- To avoid student fatigue and robotic responses—and to gain a more complete picture of what students are learning—vary the format and type of prompts in Exit and Entry Slips over time.
- Intermix use of Exit and Entry slips with use of Sticky Notes (pp. 189–193) and the Frayer model (pp. 194–198), and vary the medium (e.g., illustrated, spoken, or recorded versus handwritten) to give students a sense of variety. This will also support students who are acquiring English and those who are not yet reading independently.
- Refer to the Questioning Frameworks in Part 2 of Chapter 4 (pp. 161–168) as a resource for developing Exit and Entry Slip prompts.

Classroom Examples:

For clarity and readability, the following examples of Exit and Entry Slips are organized into four categories:

1. *General readiness prompts for all content areas:* Examples of prompts that can be used to gauge student understanding, knowledge, or skill across content areas and topics within a content area (see Figure 5.3)
2. *Subject-specific readiness:* Examples of content-based items related to specific topics, concepts, or skills in language arts, social studies, science, and math (see Figure 5.4, p. 186)
3. *Monitoring/reflecting on progress in all content areas:* Examples of student self-assessment of readiness, work habits, attitudes, or dispositions relative to a task, topic, or method of instruction, and individual or group progress toward a goal (see Figure 5.5, p. 187)
4. *Gauging interest/learning preference:* Examples of prompts for tapping into what students find motivating or intriguing during a unit of study, including the level or nature of students' interest in what they are learning and how or under what conditions students prefer to learn (see Figure 5.6, p. 188)

Figure 5.3 | General Readiness Prompts for All Content Areas

Don't Misunderstand Me . . .	**3-2-1**
• One misunderstanding someone might have about [*equivalent fractions*] is . . . . • Here's what I might say to that person to help him or her better understand the "truth":	• Three things I learned about [the topic] are . . . . • Two ways I contributed to class are . . . . • One thing I hope you'll explain better tomorrow is . . . .
Be Sure to . . .	**Important Things**
What should someone "be sure to do" when [*solving the kind of problem we have been working on this week*]? He or she should be sure to _____ because _____.	• Some important things about [*using verbs, the three branches of government, habitats*] are _____ and _____. • But the *most* important thing about [*using verbs, the three branches of government, habitats*] is _____ because _____.
Discussion Follow-Up	**Support It or Sink It**
1. What was the most convincing evidence you heard today on *both* sides of the discussion? 2. What next step would you take to investigate this issue further? What would you hope to find?	Select two ideas from the list: one that you can "support" and one that you want to "sink." • Idea I'll support: • Idea I'll sink: Use evidence from [*the text, the photos/sources/documents, this lab*] and your reasoning to explain and justify your thinking.

Figure 5.4 | Subject-Specific Readiness Prompts

Fictional Stories	**Descriptive Writing**
• What do you think [character] is trying to get [other character] to see, understand, or do in the part of the story we read for today? • How do you know? Cite specific examples and evidence from the text.	• Three *keys to success* when using adjectives are . . . . • Two *examples* of adjectives used powerfully in a sentence are . . . . • One *thing* about adjectives I'm hoping you will reteach in a different way is . . . .
Government	**Economic Choices**
A friend says to you at lunch, "I think the president is the most important branch of government." • What *two* misconceptions does your friend have? • What would you say to your friend to help him or her understand the branches of government and how they work?	Explain the "opportunity cost" of this choice: • What was given up? • What was gained? • In your opinion, was it "worth it"? Why or why not?
Resources	**Plants**
• Sketch two *nonrenewable* resources that you used in school or at home today. • What makes these resources nonrenewable? • Sketch two *renewable* resources that you used in school or at home today. • What makes these resources renewable?	• We have been learning about plants. Draw a picture of a plant, and label its parts. • Does every plant have these parts? Why or why not? • How does a plant stay healthy?

Show and Tell Math	**Fractions**
How many legs would there be if you had 5 horses? ——— 1 horse = 4 legs 2 horses = 8 legs 3 horses = 12 legs How did you figure this out? Show and tell using numbers, words, and pictures.	What fraction of this shape is shaded? How did you find your answer? What is another way to write this fraction? How do you know your answer is correct?

Figure 5.5 | Prompts for Monitoring/Reflecting on Progress in All Content Areas

Today & Tomorrow • Today I learned that . . . . • This is important [*to math, to my life*] because . . . . • *Tomorrow,* I think/hope we	**How's It Going?** Use the smiley-face scale to rate how comfortable you feel with the topic/skill we learned today: Explain why you circled the face you did:
Worked for Me! We used the following strategies this week: Which one(s) seemed to work best for you? Why?	**Pace Check** Today's lesson moved (circle one): • Too slowly for me. • At the right speed for me. • Too fast for me. Please explain your choice:
1-2-3 Summarizer After reading over my draft, • One thing I really like about it is . . . . • Two resources I can use to help me improve it are . . . . • Three revisions I plan to make are	**Group Work Evaluation** 1. How well did your group stay on task/use your time wisely? 2. Which role were you assigned for the group work? 3. Explain your greatest strength/best accomplishment in playing that role today. 4. Describe how you could have done a better job in that role. 5. Did your group encounter any conflicts? If so, how did you work around them?

Where Am I?
 	
1. What did I accomplish today? (Explain and attach evidence.)
2. What do I still have to do?
3. What's my plan of attack for tomorrow? (What are my next steps?)
	Where Were You?
	
	1. Check the station you visited today.
	    ____Station 1
	    ____Station 2
	    ____Station 3
	    ____Station 4
	2. Did the task at the station help your learning? Why or why not? (Be specific!)

Figure 5.6 | Prompts for Gauging Interest

Rank & Relate	**How Will You Learn Best?**
1. Rank the following [*topics, people, events*] that we've studied in order of how interesting they are to you. (5 = most interesting; 1 = least interesting) 2. How are the topics that you ranked #1 and #5 related or connected to each other?	As we continue our lesson tomorrow, would you rather learn about _____ by • Watching _____? • Reading _____? • Listening to _____?
This Just In!	**What's Making Things Click?**
1. Restate the most interesting thing you've learned this week as either a news headline or a billboard sign. 2. What made this interesting to you? Explain.	1. What happens in this class that helps you learn (strategies, the way ideas are presented, your grouping configurations, etc.)? 2. What's one thing I (your teacher) could do to improve [*this class, this unit, this topic*] for you?

Sticky Notes

What It Is:

A method for tracking the progress of students, including those who are just learning to write. Sticky Notes can be either teacher-generated or student-generated.

How It Works:

Teacher-Generated Sticky Notes (Two Approaches):

1. As the teacher circulates around the classroom during group or individual work, he or she makes notes about students' learning. These notes may keep track of
   » Student progress on a skill.
   » Where a student gets "stuck."
   » An approach or strategy that is particularly helpful for a student.
   » Classmates with whom a student seems to work particularly well (or *not* well).

   At the end of the day, the teacher can transfer the Sticky Notes to each student's running record file folder (see Figure 5.7, p. 191).

2. The teacher keeps a running record file folder for a particular skill or process (e.g., narrative writing; see Figure 5.8, p. 191). After a small-group session, the teacher
   » Makes notes on where each student is in relationship to the goals of that skill or process.
   » Makes notes about each student's progress or next steps.
   » Makes notes of student comments or questions that were particularly illuminating.

   The file folders can be reused with each new skill or process or kept to document student progress throughout the year.

Student-Generated Sticky Notes (Three Approaches):

1. Primary-grades teachers may ask students to record simple ideas (e.g., letters, numbers, or words) at the conclusion of small-group work. Placed on a chart or in a folder, these notes provide the teacher with an at-a-glance view of patterns in student progress (see Figure 5.9, p. 192).
2. Teachers of older students can create a chart for the room with a designated square for each student (see Figure 5.10, p. 193). These squares can be denoted with students' names or with student numbers, if the teacher wants to give students anonymity or reuse the chart for multiple classes. At the end of a lesson, students record their responses to the closing prompt on a Sticky Note and stick it to their square. The teacher should pose prompts that invite brief answers (e.g., an answer to a problem or an example of a poetic device) in order for student answers to fit in their squares.

3. Teachers may also use Sticky Notes to employ the "stoplight" method of formative assessment. For this strategy, the teacher posts a large paper stoplight in the room (see Figure 5.11, p. 193). Students write answers to one or more of the following prompts on Sticky Notes and stick them in the appropriate spot:
   » *Red*: "I got stuck (or stopped) in my learning today when . . . ."
   » *Yellow*: "I have a question about . . . ."
   » *Green*: "This [*idea/hint/strategy*] helped my learning 'take off'!"

Students can record multiple Sticky Notes for one or more colors. They must sign their names so that the teacher can attend to questions the next day. Visit the Teaching Channel (https://www.teachingchannel.org/videos/daily-lesson-assessment) to see English teacher Sarah Brown Wessling use a version of this strategy.

Alternatively, students can answer an exit prompt and place their Sticky Notes on the lights as follows:
   » *Red*: "I'm not at all sure of my answer."
   » *Yellow*: "I am a little unsure of my answer."
   » *Green*: "I am very sure my answer is correct."

What It's Good For:

- Generating quick responses from students
- Getting a "quick read" of where the class is as a whole, as well as what individual students need to move forward

Classroom Examples:

Figure 5.7 | Individual Student Running Record

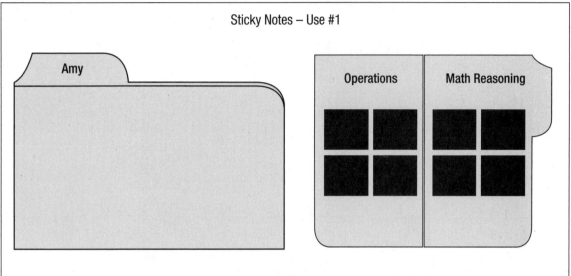

Each student has a folder to serve as a running record. The teacher records Sticky Notes both systematically (e.g., after small-group work) and incidentally (e.g., whenever Amy does something that gives the teacher an insight into her learning).

Figure 5.8 | Running Record for Particular Skill

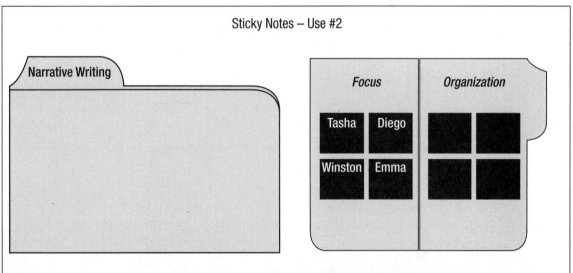

The teacher keeps a folder to serve as a running record for a given unit or grading period. The teacher records Sticky Notes both systematically (e.g., after small-group work) and incidentally (e.g., whenever a student does something that gives the teacher an insight into his or her learning).

Figure 5.9 | Primary Student–Generated Sticky Notes

Source: Lisa Roeschley, Mountain View Elementary School, Harrisonburg, VA. Used with permission.

Figure 5.10 | Sticky Note Chart

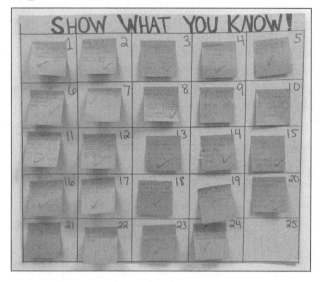

Figure 5.11 | Stoplight Sticky Note Chart

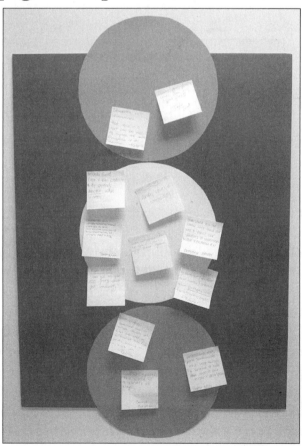

Frayer Model

What It Is:

A tool for probing and assessing the depth at which a student has mastered a concept (Frayer, Frederick, & Klausmeier, 1969)

How It Works:

The Frayer model (see Figure 5.12) asks students to provide the *definition* of a concept, its *characteristics* or *attributes*, some crystallizing *examples*, and some *nonexamples* that may be frequently confused with examples.

Figure 5.12 | Frayer Model

Concept	
Definition	Characteristics/Attributes
Examples	Nonexamples

What It's Good For:

- The Frayer model can be used either as an Exit or Entry Slip or as an in-class processing tool.
- The format of the Frayer model is also conducive to structuring whole- or small-group discussion and synthesis, depending on the concept being studied.
- If used as formative assessment, the Frayer model should be completed by *individual* students in the wake of *recent, lesson-level* learning experiences.
- The original Frayer model works particularly well with abstract concepts, overarching concepts in or across disciplines (e.g., *patterns, change, systems, perspective, proportion*), and topics or concepts that are often misunderstood or misapplied. It can also work as a vocabulary strategy for expanding or checking students' understanding of the connotations and denotations of a word or term. Events, people, and skills (e.g., acting or reading) are not the intended targets of the Frayer model.

Tips:

- Before students' first independent use, share a completed or partially completed Frayer model with them and allow them to talk through possible responses with a partner.
- Give learners the option of using a combination of words and illustrations to complete the Frayer. Students may also need to record their answers or speak them aloud to the teacher.
- The idea of listing "nonexamples" isn't intuitive for many students, so it's important to emphasize that a nonexample isn't just anything that is not an example of the concept; the goal is to list those things that may be "tricky," or commonly confused with examples.
- When adapting Frayer model prompts, no matter what the content is, maintain a focus on the intent of the original model: to gauge whether students have a deeper understanding of the concept that includes but goes beyond explaining what it is.
- Adapt prompts by regarding them as four "lenses" for viewing different layers of the concept.

Classroom Example:

Ms. Forbes used an adapted Frayer model as a formative assessment during a series of lessons on the concept of congruence (see the first example in Figure 5.13, p. 196). She rephrased "characteristics/attributes" as "What are some important clues that help us recognize congruence?" to better connect the assessment to the manner in which she taught the lesson. Although she specifically asked students to *draw* and *label* their examples and nonexamples, she let them know it was OK to use pictures and labels in the "clues" box, too. She also clarified that the nonexamples should be "so tricky that someone who wasn't in our class would get them confused with examples."

Examples:

Figure 5.13 shows some examples of how Frayer models can be used across the content areas.

Figure 5.13 | Frayer Model Examples

Congruence	
What does this word mean?	What are some important clues that help us recognize congruence?
Draw and label two examples.	Draw and label two nonexamples.

Mammals	
Describe a mammal (you may use words or pictures).	
Write or draw two examples of animals that are mammals.	Write or draw and label two nonexamples, or animals that are *not* mammals.

Rectangles	
What is a rectangle?	Give some important clues for recognizing or drawing a rectangle.
Draw and label two examples.	Draw and label two nonexamples.

Captions	
What is a caption? Where would you see one?	Why do writers use captions?
Create a clear and helpful caption for the picture on the board.	Create a confusing caption for the picture on the board. Then explain why it is confusing.

Continued

Figure 5.13 | Frayer Model Examples (continued)

Good Citizens in Our Classroom	
What might they say?	What might they do?
Draw a picture of you being a good citizen in our classroom. Use words and labels to explain your drawing.	

6 Differentiating According to Student Readiness

Part 1:

What If Students Are in Different Places?

Every day, elementary teachers are confronted with what educational change expert Michael Fullan and colleagues (Fullan, Hill, & Crevola, 2006) call "the inescapable dilemma" of classroom instruction: "One teacher and 30 students, all individuals with different motivations to learn, different starting points, different strengths on which to build, and different areas of weakness that inhibit learning" (p. 30). In such classrooms, making sure that all students grow from their respective "starting points" isn't easy. But it also isn't impossible. Recall that differentiation is *not* individualization; the teacher is *not* supposed to plan 30 routes from New York to San Francisco. Doing so would shortchange some travelers, keep the trip from being a communal experience, and be a waste of time for the trip planner!

Without question, *all* students deserve high-quality curriculum, engaging instruction, and rigorous tasks in the context of healthy classroom families. Sometimes, however, ongoing assessment results reveal that students are "all over the map" and will need to take different paths to arrive at or make progress toward the same end. Teachers who adjust students' learning routes to ensure that they receive the support and challenge they need are differentiating for student *readiness*.

Readiness: What It Is and Isn't

Many different terms can be used to describe a student's understanding, knowledge, and skill: *capability, potential, level, aptitude*. None, however, captures the spirit and precision of *readiness*.

Readiness refers to where a student is in his or her grasp of learning goals at a certain point in time. It is not the same thing as *ability*—a more static label that carries with it fixed ideas about who will succeed and who won't (Tomlinson, 2014a).

The term *readiness* reflects the realities of how people learn and the dynamic and fluid nature of intelligence. Readiness can vary from lesson to lesson or from skill to skill. Students can have higher readiness in writing fictional narratives and lower readiness in writing opinion pieces. They may initially struggle to master a math skill but catch on after much grappling or repeated practice. Or they may immediately comprehend a set of social studies content and then hit a roadblock and become stumped. *Ability*, by contrast, is a "proclamation" about a student's overall capacity as a learner or human being. It's often treated as fixed across subjects, skills, or time. People might say things like, "She's a high-ability learner," or "He has low math ability," implying that a child probably won't change or grow.

Students' *ability* is usually inferred from standardized test scores or grades and involves or implies comparisons to other students. *Readiness* is best discerned from classroom-level formative assessment designed by classroom teachers and analyzed relative to curricular learning goals. Teachers attending to student readiness avoid making assumptions about students who "get it" and students who "don't get it." Instead, they use formative assessment to discover exactly what each learner needs to propel him or her to the next step toward mastering the learning goals.

For all of these distinctions, does it *really* matter for teachers to think in terms of *readiness* rather than *ability*? Isn't it just semantics? The work of Claude Steele (2011) and Carol Dweck (2006), among others, has revealed that most students achieve only what they *believe* they are capable of achieving, and that teachers significantly—and often unconsciously—influence students' perceptions of what those capabilities are. To be effective, teachers must not only *believe* that all students can grow but also *communicate* that belief—both through the language they use in talking to or about students and in the approaches they take to designing tasks. Looking at each student through the fresh lens of up-to-the-minute evidence is the only way to challenge what labels, past experience, and standardized assessments would otherwise dictate students can and can't do.

Readiness: A Case in Point

Let's play out this idea with a 5th grade student named Damien. Last year, Damien's teacher characterized him as a "low reader," citing his standardized test scores and overall class performance. Damien was usually relegated to activities and practice with texts written for younger students that didn't challenge his thinking. This year, after looking at scores on a benchmark assessment, Damien's teacher wanted to better understand the nuances of his reading readiness within specific skills so that she could design targeted learning experiences to encourage his growth. Figure 6.1 shows her classroom-level assessment.

Figure 6.1 | Classroom-Level Formative Assessment

Read the article on giant squids.
1. What is the central idea of the article? (What does the author most want the reader to understand after reading this article?)
2. Write two questions that this article answers.
3. Answer those questions.
4. Write one question that *you* have after reading this article. (This should be a question that the article content makes you wonder but does not answer.)

Analyzing Damien's responses, his teacher noticed that he

- Identified an *important* idea in the article but not the *central* idea.
- Generated and answered two questions from the article. The questions were literal, with "right there" answers.
- Posed an insightful question that the article raised but didn't answer (*Why is it so rare to see a giant squid alive in the ocean?*).

This analysis of Damien's readiness moves beyond the generic description of "low reader" or "in the 45th percentile" to describe his readiness in much more specific terms. The teacher has language for talking about his readiness in multiple dimensions *and,* more important, can use the results to plan instruction that matches his needs.

Readiness Differentiation: A Way of Giving and Receiving Feedback

Few travelers would dispute that a GPS device is a handy tool on a road trip. It has the power both to confirm that the driver is headed in the right direction and to get the driver back on track when he or she veers from the route (by choice or by error). GPS tools are effective because they give timely and accurate *feedback* that encourages the driver either to keep going or to take a different way.

In John Hattie's (2012) meta-analysis of the effects of instructional interventions, *feedback* was noted as one of the practices with the strongest influence on student learning. Feedback doesn't mean making value judgments or giving praise; rather, it focuses on providing targeted information that will help students reach important goals (see, for example, Wiliam, 2011). Like a GPS device, teachers who are adept at providing feedback use what they know about the current "state" or status of a student's learning to change or affect the future state or status of what the student knows, understands, and can do.

Feedback can take many different forms, including a conversation, written comments and questions, or a list of steps to follow. Regardless of format, effective feedback requires more work from the *student* than it does from the teacher (Wiliam, 2012). The voice on a car's navigation system can tell the driver that he's off course, but the driver has to respond in order for that information to influence where the car is headed. Similarly, a teacher's feedback has to require the learner to think or do something differently in order for the learner to move forward.

Just as satellites provide a GPS device with information about the driver's position, ongoing assessment provides teachers with information about where students are in their learning. Of course, the teacher must *do* something with assessment results in time to affect student learning. Reading them isn't enough. Recording them isn't enough. Analyzing, interpreting, and *acting on* the results to make better instructional decisions is what makes evidence of learning truly formative and effective (Bransford et al., 2002; Wiliam, 2011).

Ideally, feedback that responds to student readiness gives each learner guidance that is "just in time" and tailored to his or her needs (Hattie, 2012). This is where readiness differentiation comes in. At some point in the instructional cycle, not every student in the room will require the same feedback. When, for instance, a teacher sees significant differences in students' understanding of fractions or their skill in crafting complete sentences, the solution isn't to teach the same lesson in a louder voice. Students need different kinds of feedback. One way this feedback can reach students is through differentiated tasks.

Finding and Responding to Patterns in Assessment Results

Providing feedback through tasks differentiated for readiness makes sense but can be overwhelming on a practical level. How can teachers efficiently give targeted information to 30 students in multiple subjects every week?

This is where teachers can focus on the *patterns* revealed by formative assessment. Keeping in mind what they have articulated as the "ideal responses" to their formative assessment prompts (see Chapter 5), teachers can literally sit and sort assessment results into piles of "like need."

Sometimes, those patterns are as simple as "got it" and "didn't get it." More often, the patterns reveal gradations of understanding (e.g., some students are ready for the next step; a few have some holes in their understanding that need to be patched before they move on; others need to start again from the beginning). At times, the patterns simply reveal different kinds of errors or misconceptions. In any case, the answer to the question "How do I sort my formative assessment results?"

lies in actually *analyzing the formative assessment results*. Students' responses often reveal exactly what they need to move forward.

Seeing patterns in student readiness primes teachers for what is perhaps the most challenging aspect of differentiation: deciding how to respond to the differences. Tasks designed to address student readiness should directly address the patterns revealed by formative assessment by (1) providing feedback that is linked to results, (2) helping students recognize and address mistakes or misconceptions, and (3) requiring all students to take a "next step" in their learning.

Let's return to Damien. Given the results of his assessment, his teacher decided that he would benefit from

- Practice distinguishing the central idea of a text from an important (but not central) idea.
- Prompts or reading lenses that push him to focus on the ideas in a text (versus just the facts) and to generate questions that those ideas address or answer.
- A chance to seek out answers to questions raised by a text (i.e., to conduct further research propelled by his own questions).

This level of analysis and planning may seem like a lot of work to put in for one student. But consider this: most likely, this pattern and its implications will apply to *many* students in the class, not just Damien. Often, by closely studying the readiness needs of specific students, teachers gain insights that improve instruction for many, if not all, students.

How to Move from Formative Assessment Results to Readiness Tasks

The protocol outlined in Figure 6.2 (p. 206) is useful for seeing and addressing patterns in readiness not just for one student but also for all students in a class, as revealed through formative assessment evidence.

This protocol may seem cumbersome; however, the more frequently a teacher engages in it, the more familiar and efficient it becomes. Remember, too, that *some* variance in student responses and thinking during a unit is natural. Slight differences in understanding don't necessarily require differentiating lessons and tasks for readiness. If the assessment results reveal minor questions or bumps in the road that can be addressed with the full class, a brief discussion or clarifying example will probably suffice. Reserve higher-prep efforts for instances when the variance will prevent students from moving forward. If there's a chasm between what different students will need before moving on, then (and only then) differentiate for readiness.

Finally, it may come as a surprise that teachers' biggest asset in using formative assessment results to create readiness-based tasks is a strong command of subject matter. When teachers grasp the underlying principles and intricate connections in what they are teaching, they are better able to discern a variety of ways for approaching and interacting with that content (Hattie, 2012). In other words, it's very difficult —if not impossible—to "see" what students are and aren't grasping, and to think about and plan for students' next steps, without deeply understanding the content. Studying math, science, reading, writing, and social studies at the targeted grade level and at least minimally at the grade levels immediately below and above one's own can go a long way toward equipping a teacher to differentiate for student readiness.

Figure 6.2 │ Protocol for Developing Tiered Tasks from Formative Assessment Results

1. ***Read all the assessment responses*** without focusing too long on any one question or student. Get a sense of where each student is relative to the content or skills, as well as the general patterns that begin to emerge.
2. Based on the learning goals and the assessment results, ***decide what all students could probably benefit from*** going forward, and devise an introductory activity centered around one or more of those ideas. This could be a demonstration, an illustrative video clip, a well-chosen problem, a discussion for the class, or a clarification from the teacher.
3. ***Look for distinguishing patterns*** in student responses and make piles of those that seem to "go together" in some way (there are usually between two and four piles). It's OK to focus on the one or two questions that yield the greatest variance among student answers. If students' responses to one particular question provide a great deal more insight into how to move forward than do their other answers, you'd want to focus on that question.
4. ***Make general notes*** about anything that stands out to you in each pile of responses. For example, you may find that certain students share the same misconceptions or that a small group of students made minor (albeit different) errors but seemed to understand the general process. Still others may demonstrate a sophisticated or fluid understanding of the content.
5. Look more closely at what each pattern reveals and ***determine what students will need to move forward***. For example, some students may benefit from a clarifying or annotated example. Others may require step-by-step directions to walk them through a process. Still others may be ready for a challenge that asks them to examine how the concept is used in other situations.
6. ***Generate ideas for tasks*** that students at each of these different readiness levels can complete and that will provide them with the feedback, scaffolding, or challenge they need to grow toward and beyond the goals.
7. ***Develop the most advanced task first***. This helps you avoid the trap of simply giving more work to students who already get it and instead ensures that those students will receive "more appropriate work" (Tomlinson, 2014a). In addition, establishing a high-quality advanced task first gives you something to emulate when developing the additional tasks (albeit with more scaffolding or support) so that you don't have to start from scratch with each task.
8. ***Develop a clear process, directions, and/or materials*** for each pattern: these are your differentiated tasks. Constructed properly, these tasks should provide all students with the feedback they need to grow.
9. Design a way to ***bring everyone together*** for whole-class closure.

Strategies for Readiness Differentiation

The following sections discuss several strategies for designing or delivering readiness-based tasks that double as feedback. A *strategy* is any vehicle that a teacher can use to deliver and differentiate *content* (what students learn), *process* (how they learn it), or *product* (how they show what they've learned). Regardless of which strategy a teacher uses, three principles govern the implementation of tasks that differentiate content, process, or product for student readiness:

- Varying levels of tasks should assess the same core learning goals.
- Decisions about instructional adjustments should be based on recent information from students' classroom performance—not on labels, assumptions, or even performance in previous classes.
- All tasks should provide students with the feedback they need to correct misconceptions; move forward in knowledge, understanding, or skill; and take the next step in their learning.

Keep in mind, differentiation is not synonymous with a set of strategies. There are no instructional strategies that are exclusive to differentiation or whose use automatically results in quality differentiation. However, teachers need strategies of all kinds to bring instruction—differentiated or otherwise—to life. Some strategies are especially well suited to making adjustments for student readiness.

Tiering

Tomlinson (2014a) explains that Tiering is useful "when a teacher wants to ensure that students with different degrees of learning proficiency work with the same essential ideas and use the same key knowledge and skills" (p. 133). Tiering can be thought of as either a *process* or a *concept*:

- Tiering is a *process* when it involves designing tasks differentiated for readiness based on pre- or formative assessment data. The steps listed on page 228 describe the process of engineering Tiered Tasks to meet student readiness needs as revealed from the results of a specific formative assessment.
- Tiering is also a *concept* that can be superimposed on other strategies. "Tiering" a strategy means creating different *levels* or *versions* of the tasks within the strategy in response to students' varying readiness needs. By this definition, anything can be tiered, including prompts or questions, resources, perspectives, or more complex structures or strategies. Each of these is discussed below.

Prompts, questions, or tasks. Teachers can tier prompts or questions for small-group instruction, in-class processing, or take-home work or tasks, and they can present the prompts orally or in writing. The examples in Figure 6.3 are ordered from more sophisticated to more accessible.

Figure 6.3 | Sample Tiered Prompts

Theme
- A. What does the author of this story want you (the reader) to understand after reading this story? Why do you say so?
- B. What lesson does the main character in the story learn? How do you know?

Poetry Analysis
- A. The most powerful writing appeals to all five senses. With that in mind, what line(s) in the poem is/are the most "powerful"? What makes it/them powerful? Defend your choice as the best one.
- B. Which of the five senses is the strongest in the poem: touch, taste, smell, sound, or sight? In other words, does the author do the best job getting you to "feel" the story, "taste" it, "smell" it, "hear" it, or "see it"? Support your choice with words, phrases, and lines from the poem.
- C. Think about your five senses. What senses are in this poem? Find specific words and phrases that give you clues. Is there one sense that you see (or hear, taste, smell, or feel) more than the others? Which one? Why do you say so?

Math Homework (Wiliam, 2012)
Given after teacher has reviewed student work.
- A. You solved all of these problems correctly. Now make up three problems for others to solve: one that's harder than those you just solved, one that's at about the same level, and one that's easier.
- B. [This number] of the problems you solved are incorrect. Find the incorrect solutions and fix them.

Finding Mistakes
- A. Review this set/list of [problems/answers/ideas/statements/sentences/word sorts] and decide if there are any mistakes. Correct any mistakes you find. Then explain how you found those mistakes and what you did to make changes. If there are *no* mistakes, explain how you can be sure.
- B. [This number] of these [problems/answers/ideas/statements/sentences/word sorts] have mistakes. Figure out which ones have mistakes and correct them. Then explain how you identified the mistakes.
- C. These [problems/answers/ideas/statements/sentences/word sorts] have mistakes. Use the questions provided to fix the mistakes. Explain why you did what you did.

How-To (Tomlinson, 2003)
- A. Write a set of directions for someone who is going to solve a problem or address a challenge in his or her life by using what we've learned about how to [write a strong persuasive letter/read a map/use fractions] this week. Explain the problem or challenge first.
- B. Write a step-by-step set of directions, including visuals or diagrams, to show someone who has been absent from class this week how to [write a strong persuasive letter/read a map/use fractions].

Science (Strickland, 2009)

A. Select an important part of today's [experiment/demonstration] and change it in some way. What would happen in the [experiment/demonstration] with that change? Why? What would that show or prove? Be sure you identify a change that focuses on the "science" of what happened.

B. A classmate had to leave the room today just as the [experiment/demonstration] was beginning. Write that student a note explaining what happened, why it happened, and what practical use there is in the real world for what the [experiment/demonstration] shows us. You are this student's only hope for clarity! Be as helpful as possible.

Access to resources. When teachers have upfront information—be it from assessments, observations, or performance on previous tasks—that suggests students will need a range of support with literacy, they can differentiate content by pulling resources that vary in complexity. Students who are proficient readers may excel with a website that is written for the general adult population, whereas other students may need a web-based resource written in language that is more easily understood. Newsela (www.newsela.com), for example, provides nonfiction articles from news organizations both in their original forms and in "cloned" variations written at different reading levels. CommonLit (www.commonlit.org) features fiction and nonfiction texts around themes such as *freedom, friendship,* and *education.* For younger students, numerous web-based platforms and dedicated apps feature hundreds of read-along children's e-books with features like built-in dictionaries, checks for comprehension, and interactive words and images.

To manage student access, teachers can bookmark or create QR codes for various sites and assign them strategically to give students access to the sources that work best for them. With research tasks around informational texts, consider whether students need to read all of the text in order to answer key questions. Use sticky notes to mark targeted pages and help students locate facts and ideas more efficiently.

Another approach is to highlight key material for students with reading difficulties. For example, some students may be ready to independently tackle a letter written in the "pioneer days," while others may need important passages indicated and unfamiliar words defined. These adjustments can benefit students with reading difficulties, language acquisition needs, or attention deficits.

Similarly, teachers can use Tiered Graphic Organizers (pp. 235–243) that ask students to exercise the same skills in different ways. For example, a T-Chart may support the majority of students as they compare and contrast different elements, while a few others may be more appropriately challenged by a three-way Venn diagram that asks them to add an additional layer to their comparisons.

Reading journals are another structure that is easily tiered. Teachers can provide some students with definitions, page numbers, and key points to guide them through the text in a supported manner. Other students may receive prompts that ask them to synthesize large chunks of material, consider conceptual connections, and refer to previously read chapters to make unusual connections.

Perspectives. In a story, a historical account, or even certain textbook chapters, there are often a variety of perspectives represented. Only examining the text through all of these different lenses will produce a full understanding of it. Usually, some of these perspectives are "right there" (e.g., the narrator, the main character, the population of focus in the article), while other perspectives require the reader to make significant inferences.

Such diversity in perspectives offers rich opportunities for tiered explorations of content. Students who need the most support in their learning can examine the story, account, or issue through the perspective with the most information available or the most obvious connections. This may be the main character in a story (e.g., Alice in *Alice's Adventures in Wonderland*); the voice of the author(s) in an important document (e.g., the signers of the Declaration of Independence); or the population being studied in a scientific journal article (e.g., bluefin tuna). Other students may be ready to examine all or part of the text from a perspective without as much access (e.g., the enigmatic Cheshire Cat) or information (e.g., British loyalists in the colonies, fishers living and working in regions with fishing restrictions).

Tiered perspectives can also bring students together around a key question related to a text—for example, "Who *really* saved Wilbur?" in *Charlotte's Web* (White, 1952). Students can be assigned (or choose) one of several possible answers (Wilbur, Charlotte, Templeton, or Fern) through which to reexamine and gather evidence from parts of the story. Although all students will have to search for evidence, support for Charlotte or Fern as Wilbur's "savior" is more obvious to and easier for students still struggling with analyzing the story. On the other hand, searching for evidence supporting the idea that Templeton, or Wilbur himself, saved Wilbur challenges students who are ready to dive more deeply into the nuances of the text. After studying the story through their specific lenses, students meet in both like-perspective groups and pooled-perspective groups to get a multidimensional picture of the events.

This same approach can apply to read-aloud picture books for younger students. For example, following a brief mini-lesson on overcoming obstacles, a teacher could assign each student one of two perspectives for listening to and processing *Martin's Big Words* by Doreen Rappaport, a biographical text on Martin Luther King Jr.:

- *More abstract*: "Listen for an obstacle that *America* was facing and how Martin helped America overcome that obstacle."
- *More concrete*: "Listen for an obstacle that *Martin* was facing and how he overcame that obstacle."

The difference is subtle, but for this text, the first prompt is more advanced and compels the listener to make a bigger "leap."

Sense-making strategies. Chapter 4 presented numerous strategies that teachers can use for sense making. Many of the descriptions of these strategies also include suggestions for Tiering (e.g., Looking/Listening Lenses, Debate Team Carousel, ThinkDots, and Jigsaw). In a Jigsaw, for example, the teacher can tailor expert group materials and tasks to meet the specific readiness needs of students (e.g., strategic choices of reading levels, number of facets addressed, complexity of material).

Contracts and Agendas

Contracts and Agendas can both serve as vehicles for differentiated tasks. Both structures outline a collection of learning activities and organizational measures to ensure student success and grasp of learning goals, but they vary in how they are prepared and implemented.

With *Contracts*, students do not choose what they will learn—the teacher determines the learning goals—but they do select how they'll demonstrate their mastery of those goals, usually from a list of discrete tasks or problems. Teachers generally use Contracts to assign varying levels of reinforcement or practice to students with varying learning needs. For example, the teacher may create two levels of a Word Study Contract if students in the class are operating at two different levels of sophistication with language. Each version has its requirements, but students receive several choices of how they can meet those requirements.

An *Agenda* is a teacher-created and -directed schedule of learning experiences and tasks that gives students choices only in terms of the order in which to complete the tasks. Teachers can fill in the appropriate homework, in-class tasks, teacher conference points, and peer partners for students at various readiness levels.

Teachers can pull from textbooks and other instructional resources when compiling a Contract or an Agenda. Because Contracts and Agendas are generally designed to reinforce skills and provide practice (rather than introduce students to content or summatively assess their mastery of learning goals), it is not hard to find varying levels of terms, problems, websites, and so on. Part 2 (pp. 244–249) includes descriptions and examples of both structures.

Small-Group Instruction

Small-group instruction is a widely used and potentially effective strategy for differentiating according to student readiness. Typically, small-group instruction involves convening groups of students in a smaller configuration (often between three and eight students per group) within the classroom for teaching, practice, or discussion. Teachers or specialists may meet with each group of students for 10–20 minutes to engage in an activity or a lesson that is focused on

- Reteaching.
- Reviewing.

- Scaffolding.
- Modeling.
- Providing focused or supervised practice.
- Clarifying misunderstandings.
- Extending student proficiency.
- Making interest-based connections.

The formation and composition of groups should be driven by evidence gathered through observation or recent formative assessment. The teacher might bring students together who have similar struggles or proficiencies with content, ideas, or skills; who lack or have attained prerequisite knowledge; or who have the same misconceptions or motivations.

Meeting in small groups for instruction can have several benefits, such as increasing student participation, engagement, and focus; providing manageable opportunities for formative assessment; and creating relationships among group participants. What teachers do—and what they have students do—both in and as a result of small-group instruction is more important than the "event" of meeting with the group. Small-group instruction is a better use of time when it doesn't simply repeat what was done (or what could have been done) with the whole class. Lessons and tasks within and across small groups should be closely connected to common and important learning goals.

Although small-group instruction is student-centered by design, it can become a mini version of a teacher-centered lesson, with give-and-take between the teacher and each student but little or no interaction among students. At its best, small-group instruction leverages the teacher-student ratio by intentionally engaging students with one another. Convening groups at places in the classroom other than a table, as purpose and task permit, can go a long way toward making the group feel more collaborative.

The overall goal of small-group instruction is to enhance *all* students' growth. It's not the case that some students (e.g., students with lower readiness, struggling readers, or English language learners) are more in need of small-group instruction than other students. When only certain students meet with the teacher—or when some students meet with the teacher far more often than do others—both their status in the classroom family and their sense that they can learn and work independent of teacher support are negatively affected. Instead, teachers should plan small-group instruction around the idea that every student has a next step; no one is "finished" learning or beyond the targeted teaching that small groups can afford.

With this in mind, teachers can also offer "opt-in" small-group instruction opportunities. These can begin with an "advertisement" like this one: "Friends, I noticed that there is still some confusion about how to say where the information in your opinion writing pieces came from. If you'd like to walk through some examples that you can transfer to your own writing, come over to this table in 10 minutes." Students can sign up in advance or decide to join in the moment. The teacher can also prompt or urge individual students to opt in to the group. This strategy can help remove the stigma from small-group instruction as well as serve as a readiness assessment.

Respectfully Differentiated Tasks

When travelers in a road caravan take different routes for a stretch of time, it's important for them to make sure that their vehicles are in good shape—that each one can carry its passengers safely and comfortably to the rendezvous point. In the classroom, when students are diverging from a shared route to take slightly different paths for a time, the tasks they work on—individually or with others—should all but guarantee progress and engagement and be closely connected to one another.

Whether teachers are designing tasks in direct response to recent and specific formative assessment patterns or using strategies that anticipate typical or predictable patterns, all students should be working with tasks that honor the content, the goals, and the learner. Carol Ann Tomlinson calls such tasks "respectful" (2014a). Tasks are respectfully differentiated when they meet the criteria outlined in Figure 6.4 (p. 214).

Respectful tasks are the insurance policy of differentiation. They support the development of a growth mindset and increase student buy-in to the idea of differentiation in general. Using the list in Figure 6.4 as a "respect check" in a self- or collegial review of differentiated tasks can help ensure that all students are working with motivating activities that are a good fit for their readiness needs.

Mindset, Student Status, and Readiness Differentiation

It's no secret that even very young students are acutely aware of any implied or actual differences between tasks that they and their peers choose or are assigned. Teachers understandably worry that students will label readiness-based tasks or groupings as "dumb" and "smart" and that student confidence and classroom community will be negatively affected by any suggestion that some students are working at a more or less advanced level, even if it is toward common goals. Children's general desire to belong and tendency to compare themselves with others further fuel teacher concerns about using readiness-based differentiation in the classroom. Indeed, such apprehension prevents some teachers from putting students into groups or using differentiated tasks of any kind.

It's true that without careful attention to key principles of differentiation, attempts to differentiate for readiness can easily create a status hierarchy or discernible "pecking order" in the classroom as well as reinforce a fixed mindset (Dweck, 2006). If some students or groups appear to be working on tasks that are meaningful while other students or groups have tasks that are menial—or if some students are always receiving help from the teacher while others are always expected to work independently—then students may begin (or continue) to develop a fixed mindset.

Figure 6.4 | Criteria for Respectfully Differentiated Tasks

1. ***The tasks are aligned with the same learning goals (understanding, knowledge, skills), and with one another.*** Tasks that are not connected by common goals are not differentiated; they are just different. The same "glue" must hold the tasks together, with understanding as the focus. Likewise, the tasks should be designed so that all student work can be evaluated according to the same criteria.

2. ***The tasks are equally interesting, appealing, and engaging from the students' perspective.*** If some tasks are the instructional equivalent of limp broccoli while others are delicious ice cream sundaes—that is, if some students are working with tasks that are boring, passive, or a waste of time while others work with tasks that draw them in and keep them hooked—there is little chance that respectful differentiation is occurring.

3. ***The tasks ask all students to work at high levels of thought.*** When differentiating for readiness, it's tempting to think in terms of "high-level" and "low-level" questions and prompts, but all students should work with cognitively demanding tasks. Designing the top task first, as we suggested in Figure 6.2, is one way to circumvent this potential pothole. Another strategy is to think about how to differentiate within a targeted skill. For example, if a skill goal is to analyze and compare primary sources, adjustments for readiness might include differentiating the sources being analyzed and compared or the process used to do so, but each task should engage every student in the targeted skill.

4. ***The tasks mimic what people or professionals in the real world do, or how they think.*** All tasks, including differentiated tasks, should approximate or represent in some way authentic ideas, knowledge, processes, or products. It's not respectful to have some students complete a low-level worksheet on measurement while other students use what they have learned to design a living space for a new animal at the local zoo. This is a stark example, but it vividly illustrates what differentiated tasks must avoid at all costs. All students should work with the authentic task, albeit with different levels of scaffolding and support.

5. ***The tasks represent a wise use of students' time.*** Tasks created in the name of differentiation should be substantive tasks that make learning more efficient than it might have otherwise been and move students toward or beyond the learning goals. A task that is a fun or interesting diversion but has little to do with curricular outcomes may actually get in the way of progress.

6. ***The tasks are comparable in terms of workload or time required for completion.*** When compared side by side, the time and workload implied or required by differentiated tasks should be equal. Do the tasks sound simply like "more work" versus "less work"? Avoid assigning different products that—by their nature—demand different amounts of sweat (e.g., a half-page diary entry versus a video documentary).

7. ***The tasks are constructed in such a way that they lead naturally to whole-class closure.*** In addition to being aligned with the same learning goals, differentiated tasks should be constructed in such a way that all students—no matter which task they are completing—can engage in the same closing discussion, summarizing prompt, or final problem. This helps the teacher make sure the tasks are not diverging from one another too drastically and solidify the class's sense of community.

Principles for Building Student Status and Developing a Growth Mindset

In addition to making sure that all readiness-based tasks are respectfully differentiated, as described above, teachers can ensure that differentiation builds student status and develops a growth mindset by adhering to these three principles:

1. **Practice flexible grouping.** Flexible grouping facilitates the belief that intelligence is dynamic and malleable. If students remain too long in any one grouping type or configuration, they may begin or continue to view their intelligence, strengths, and weaknesses as static or immutable. Tomlinson (2003) defines flexible grouping as students consistently working in a variety of grouping configurations over a relatively short time. Groups can vary by

   » Configuration (whole-group, half-class, small-group, individual).
   » Size of small group (partners, trios, quads).
   » Element of student learning (readiness, experience, interest, learning preference).
   » Composition in terms of elements of student learning (homogeneous or heterogeneous).

   At times, depending on learning goals and the purpose of a task, it makes sense for students to work with peers who share similar readiness in background or prerequisite knowledge or skills, to support academic growth. Other times, students should work with peers who share their interests or learning preferences to increase motivation and persistence in the task (see Chapter 7). Teachers can also use student-selected groups and groups configured at random (for more on this, see Chapter 8).

2. **Honor all tasks.** The way in which teachers make transparent and honor readiness-based tasks can also build student status. When possible and sensible, base task design and grouping decisions directly and explicitly on the latest evidence of what students know, understand, and can do—not on a blanket sense of their ability. Assuming the tasks are respectful, there's no need to keep it a secret that students are working on different things. Often the best way to honor what all students have done and to show that everyone "got the good stuff" is to conduct a discussion or synthesis activity that requires students to share, make sense of, or draw from one another's work. The Jigsaw strategy employs this component by design, as do several examples of tiered lessons featured in Part 2 of this chapter (pp. 230–234).

3. **Mix up the "flavors" of differentiation.** Teachers can differentiate content, process, and product for at least three aspects of the learner:

readiness (the focus of this chapter) as well as interest and learning profile (the focus of Chapter 7). Cindy Strickland (personal communication, August 16, 2016) calls these the "flavors" of differentiation. They serve different purposes and build on different aspects of a student's strengths. For example, differentiating *only* for readiness, even driven by evidence from recent formative assessment, sends the wrong message to students about what matters in learning—and robs at least some learners of opportunities to show what they can really do.

There is no special magic that happens purely because students are grouped in a certain way or with certain peers, and grouping alone does not make a learning experience differentiated. Differentiation is what teachers *do* to a task or process that students engage in, not a reference to the kind of group students are in.

Frequently Asked Questions

The following are common concerns among teachers and administrators about readiness differentiation, with responses stemming from research and practice.

What about labels or designations (e.g., students with IEPs, English language learners, gifted students)? Do those mean anything in the context of readiness?

Labels can be helpful insofar as they convey information that teachers need to consider as they plan instruction and accommodations to fit their students' learning needs. Labels do not, however, serve as boxes into which teachers can conveniently group students for every instructional experience. Here are just a few examples illustrating why:

- English language learners do not all speak the same native language, and they are not all at the same stage of language acquisition. They come to the classroom with varying school and life experiences that affect the way they will learn best. Too often, teachers conflate students' English language proficiency with their readiness in other subjects.
- Students who have been identified as gifted are most likely not advanced in every academic respect or with regard to specific concepts, topics, or skills in a given unit.
- The autism spectrum is indeed a spectrum: no two students with the diagnosis will require the exact same supports or excel in the exact same areas.
- A student can simultaneously struggle with attention issues and excel in problem solving, or be a talented storyteller who also happens to have dysgraphia or to be learning the English language.

Because students have such a wide array of learning needs that may or may not be communicated by a label, formative assessment is still the best way to determine what a student requires for successful learning. This is true even when that formative assessment is administered with accommodations. It's important to discover where students are with respect to learning goals—not just where they are in terms of their label—and plan accordingly.

Should I let students choose from differentiated tasks? What if they choose the wrong one?

When it comes to tasks differentiated for interest and learning profile (see Chapter 7), the idea is for students to do what seems most motivating and efficient from their perspective. So go ahead and let them choose, unless there's another reason you want certain students to work with certain tasks.

With tasks differentiated for readiness, the goal is to propel students' academic growth. The teacher has designed the tasks with students' particular readiness needs in mind, having interpreted where they are based on evidence. Most of the time, letting students choose from readiness-based tasks not only leaves their growth to chance but also places the onus for differentiation on the students. In general, students understand and accept the idea that sometimes they can choose from tasks and sometimes tasks are assigned to them. Maintaining a balance between the different "flavors" of differentiation can help ensure that differentiated instruction reflects a cooperative and collaborative relationship between teacher and student.

Strategies like Contracts and Agendas (see Part 2 of this chapter) can be used to present students with different readiness-based options while ensuring that students are choosing from tasks that you can live with them doing.

At my school, we regroup at some grade levels for math (or reading), with students going to different teachers based on their levels. That's readiness differentiation, right?

As presented in this book and others (e.g., Tomlinson, 2003, 2014a), differentiation is a model for individual classrooms. It is not dependent on sending students to another teacher's classroom for all or part of the instructional day. Often, when schools practice "between-class regrouping," the rationale is twofold: (1) teachers at any given grade level have different levels of skill and comfort with a particular subject (e.g., math), and (2) regrouping students for a specific subject reduces the readiness span that each teacher has to plan for.

Unfortunately, regrouping students in this way and for these reasons is problematic. The work of many researchers (Dweck, 2006; Perry, Steele, & Hilliard, 2003; Rosenthal & Jacobson, 1968) strongly suggests that teachers tend to adjust their expectations "up" or "down" in response to what they believe (or have been told) a group of students is or isn't capable of. Because students tend to perform in response to either elevated or lowered expectations, this model usually benefits students in high-readiness groups and is detrimental for students in lower-readiness groups. Whereas more advanced groups generally receive cognitively demanding instruction that requires students to engage in complex and meaningful tasks, students in the less advanced groups receive far less demanding instruction and tasks that may do more to keep them behind than to catch them up.

In theory, the readiness span in regrouped classes is more manageable. In reality, such "leveling" prevents teachers from seeking opportunities to study and respond to student differences. The class labels, in effect, tempt the teacher to view and treat the students in the regrouped classes as one student in terms of readiness, and to differentiate less, not more.

Regrouping students by readiness on account of *teacher* content knowledge or skill misses the boat on two counts: (1) Sending *any* student to a classroom where the teacher lacks strong content knowledge does a disservice to that student, and (2) There is no opportunity or incentive for the teacher to improve his or her command of the subject. In short, the "divide and conquer" strategy of regrouping students for instruction ignores the underlying issue. The more promising solutions are high-quality, sustained professional learning opportunities that help all teachers to build understanding and skill in content and pedagogy *and* support from specialists who can work alongside teachers to better meet a range of readiness needs.

What's the difference between differentiation for readiness and Universal Design for Learning? They seem similar.

Universal Design for Learning (UDL) is a set of principles or lenses that teachers can apply to unit or lesson design. It emphasizes maximizing the "fit" of the learning environment and instruction for students with certain needs by doing things that will likely benefit many students. UDL is driven less by classroom-level formative assessment than by general research about how the brain works, how people learn, and what groups of students with shared needs (e.g., students with learning disabilities) seem to benefit from. Broadly speaking, UDL suggests providing the entire class with multiple ways to represent, interact with, and show understanding of content. With differentiation, specific avenues are provided to specific students—or groups of students—based on needs emerging from ongoing assessment. In best-case scenarios, classrooms include both UDL and differentiation.

How does differentiation for readiness relate to RTI?

Both differentiated instruction (DI) and Response to Intervention (RTI) aim to optimize each student's academic growth. Whereas DI addresses a broad range of dynamic attributes—students' readiness, interests, and preferred ways of learning—RTI focuses mainly on identifying and addressing the needs of students when they demonstrate low readiness in fundamental skills (e.g., reading comprehension).

In practice, the success of the first level of intervention in the RTI model (Tier 1) depends largely on the classroom teacher's ability to differentiate for all learners. RTI assumes that differentiation is happening in the regular classroom and that fewer students are likely to need more intensive and out-of-classroom interventions (i.e., Tier 2 and Tier 3) when classroom and special services teachers alike continue to grow and apply their skills in differentiation. (Note that the way we use the term *Tiering* in this chapter—to describe designing tasks that are differentiated for student readiness and aligned with the same goals—is *not* the same as the way *Tier* is used in RTI.)

What about curriculum compacting?
Is that readiness differentiation?

Curriculum compacting is a multistep strategy that involves teachers pre-assessing student readiness against lesson or unit learning goals, documenting evidence of student mastery, and replacing the goals that each student has mastered with more challenging alternatives or interest-based activities (Reis, Burns, & Renzulli, 1992). The idea is to modify or streamline curriculum to allow students who demonstrate higher readiness to move at a quicker pace and have time to pursue an alternative topic or go into greater depth in an area of study.

Compacting can be used to differentiate for readiness whenever students (or teachers) need to save or buy time in the curriculum, but as designed it works best with skill- and memory-driven areas of study. Examples include filling out maps, recalling math facts, or spelling words correctly.

Compacting is most defensible when teachers use pre-assessments that gauge student understanding, not just knowledge and skills, and when any "replacement" activities are aligned with curricular goals (as opposed to being disconnected from the curriculum or just "fun" things to do). Also, if more than one student "exits" significant portions of a unit—or the whole thing—it probably means that the unit is pitched too low for all students and doesn't focus on important concepts and understandings.

Finally, the rationale behind compacting is that students should spend less time on what they already know and can do and more time on what they *want* to learn. This makes sense for all students in some form and at some point. As we discussed in Chapter 3, pre-assessment should guide and inform instructional planning in any differentiated classroom. All students—not just those who would be "compacted"—covet and deserve chances to explore and pursue topics of interest. For these reasons, strategies like Contracts and Agendas (see Part 2 of this chapter) and Learning Menus and Choice Boards (see Chapter 7) can be used in conjunction with compacting to optimize time and opportunity for everyone in the class.

How do I grade work that has been differentiated for readiness?

In both this chapter and Chapter 5, we have discussed formative assessment as a way of *gathering evidence of* student learning, and instructional tasks (differentiated and otherwise) as forms of *feedback* to students. Because formative assessment results are collected during the learning cycle, assessment experts advise de-emphasizing them when calculating students' grades. Students should still receive feedback on their work, but it need not include points or grades.

Generally speaking, readiness-based tasks are not summative assessments: they are instructional interventions. When teachers structure readiness tasks in the manner discussed in this chapter, it is with the goal of growth in mind. A mile runner's split times are interesting and can be noted, but they matter less in judging overall performance than the time when he or she crossed the finish line. Likewise, teachers don't need to record or calculate grades for students as they grapple with readiness-based differentiation. Rather, teachers should calculate grades summatively at designated, whole-class points in the units.

I learned "content-process-product" as a way of thinking about readiness differentiation. How does that fit in?

In the Tomlinson (2014a) model of differentiation, teachers can differentiate three elements of curriculum to meet student needs: content, process, and product.

Content is what students will learn, or how students will gain access to the information, skills, and ideas that are critical to understanding the content. *Process* refers to the activities through which students make sense of key ideas in the content using essential knowledge and skills. *Product* is how students demonstrate and extend what they know, understand, and can do as a result of a unit or series of lessons.

If students require different levels of *resources*, that's differentiating *content*. Providing *tiered prompts* usually involves differentiating the *process*. *Contracts* can be used to differentiate *product* when students are demonstrating their knowledge for different audiences with varying levels of "sophistication" (e.g., fellow students versus the school board).

Although these terms and the distinctions among them can be useful in describing how a task or learning experience can be or has been differentiated, avoid getting caught up in the vocabulary of differentiation. Talking about content-process-product is less important than studying and responding to needs in sensible ways, as directed by assessment results.

A Readiness Differentiation Upgrade

Second grade teacher Monica Helfand taught a series of lessons aligned to the following geometry standard:

CCSS.MATH.CONTENT.2.G.A.3: Partition circles and rectangles into two, three, or four equal shares, describe the shares using the words halves, thirds, half of, a third of, etc., and describe the whole as two halves, three thirds, four fourths. Recognize that equal shares of identical wholes need not have the same shape. (National Governors Association Center for Best Practices [NGA Center] & Council of Chief State School Officers [CCSSO], 2010)

Before Upgrade

Monica's first lesson focused on partitioning circles and rectangles into two and four equal shares. Most students did well with this, although a few students struggled to find more than one way to represent four equal shares of a rectangle. The second lesson focused on partitioning circles and rectangles into three equal shares. Using an interactive feature on the SMART Board, Monica modeled partitioning both a circle and a rectangle into three shares each. Student volunteers helped her find multiple ways to divide the rectangle. She then let students practice by drawing circles and rectangles partitioned into three equal shares and cutting them up to "check their work."

During this practice time, Monica realized that students were "all over the place" with their understanding of the lesson. Although the concept appeared to connect for some students, others struggled, especially with the circles (for example, many students cut the circles into three strips rather than three equal shares). Monica felt like she was running around trying to put out fires during the entire practice session. Although she had planned to pull a small group to reinforce the previous lesson's skill of finding different ways to divide rectangles into four equal shares, she ran out of time to do so. The class felt so chaotic that Monica decided she should just review everything the following day with the whole class. She conducted a SMART Board review on partitioning circles and rectangles into both three and four equal shares. Unfortunately, the lesson still didn't "click" for the students with questions and seemed to bore the students who had already grasped the content.

After Upgrade

The following year, Monica proactively planned two different Agendas to address the standard, which she articulated as specific learning goals to ensure alignment and emphasize understanding of mathematical concepts. She also made sure that all students engaged in mathematical thinking by highlighting several relevant mathematical practices from the Common Core standards (NGA Center & CCSSO, 2010) (see Figure 6.5, p. 222).

Monica began the lesson the same way she had the previous year. This time, she used the second lesson's drawing and cutting exercise to determine which Agenda each student would receive (see Figures 6.6 [p. 223] and 6.7 [p. 224]).

During Agenda time, she used the *Teacher Meet* portion to pull small groups for support or extension with partitioning different shapes into three and four equal shares in the context of authentic tasks. She incorporated content from the previous lesson on dividing circles and rectangles into four equal shares into the *Partner Practice* and *On My Own* sections of the Agendas. For easy reference, Monica named the Agendas "Cut the Cake" and "Break the Cookie" based on the Teacher Meet tasks.

Figure 6.5 | Learning Goals and Practices After Upgrade

Essential Question
- **EQ1:** Do equal shares have to be the same shape?

Understanding Goals
- **U1:** Shapes can be combined to make larger shapes [*composition*] and divided to make smaller shapes [*decomposition*].
- **U2:** Equal shares of identical wholes need not have the same shape.

Knowledge Goal
- **K1:** Terminology such as *equal, whole, halves, thirds, half of, a third of*

Skill Goals
- **S1:** Partition circles and rectangles into two, three, or four equal shares.
- **S2:** Describe the shares using proper terminology (see knowledge goal).
- **S3:** Reason with shapes and their attributes.

Common Core Mathematical Practices Emphasized
- Make sense of problems and persevere in solving them. (CCSS.MATH.PRACTICE.MP1)
- Construct viable arguments and critique the reasoning of others. (CCSS.MATH.PRACTICE.MP3)
- Look for and make use of structure. (CCSS.MATH.PRACTICE.MP7)

Figure 6.6 | Agenda 1: Cut the Cake

Assessment patterns: These students (a) had a firm grasp of decomposing circles and rectangles into two, three, and four equal shares but (b) needed a push to develop varied approaches to decomposing rectangles into three and four equal shares (U2).

> Focuses on the "building" portion of the standard overview while reinforcing area for growth.

> Focuses on area for growth as suggested by assessment for growth.

> Provides challenge by requiring students to make mathematical links; tasks are situated in a real context and explanation addresses a real audience. Also gives practice using mathematical terms.

Teacher Meet	Partner Practice	On My Own
(Student view) You will meet with the teacher to complete a mathematical task focused on cutting a cake. *(Teacher notes)* Work with students in a scenario involving cutting a rectangular birthday cake into three and four equal shares. 1. Using manipulatives (square tiles) or pencil and paper, students individually plan two different ways to cut the cake into three equal shares and four equal shares. 2. Students then share their mathematical processes and compare answers to see if anyone devised the same methods. 3. Each student explains the method that seemed the most "tricky" to him or her and why.	1. Use the square tiles to create two rectangles composed of three equal shares. Use a different strategy for each rectangle. Then draw what you did and be ready to explain it. 2. Use the square tiles to create two rectangles composed of four equal shares. Use a different strategy for each rectangle. Then draw what you did and be ready to explain it. 3. Find another pair that completed the "Cut the Cake" practice exercises and compare and contrast your results.	1. Use words and pictures to tell someone how to solve a problem or address a challenge in his or her life by using what we've learned about how to divide circles into three equal shares. 2. Use words and pictures to tell someone how to solve a problem or address a challenge in his or her life by using what we've learned about how to compose rectangles using both three and four equal shares. 3. Make sure your solutions address the problems. Also, be sure to use the math vocabulary on the board in your directions.

Figure 6.7 | Agenda 2: Break the Cookie

Assessment patterns: These students (a) had a firm grasp of decomposing circles into two and four equal shares and of decomposing rectangles into two equal shares but (b) struggled to grasp decomposing circles into three equal shares and (c) needed to develop more than one approach to decomposing rectangles into three and four equal shares (U2).

Focuses on the "building" portion of the standard overview while reinforcing area for growth.	Moves students beyond a region model to an area model.	Provides challenge by requiring students to make mathematical links; tasks are situated in a real context and explanation addresses a real audience. Also gives practice using mathematical terms.

Teacher Meet	Partner Practice	On My Own
(Student view) You will meet with the teacher to complete a mathematical task focused on breaking a big cookie. *(Teacher notes)* Work with students in scenarios involving breaking a big round cookie into three equal shares. 1. Using manipulatives (fraction circles) or pencil and paper, students work individually to generate solutions. 2. Students then share their mathematical processes and compare answers. 3. Students repeat the process to break the cookie into four equal shares. 4. Students discuss which method seems to result in the biggest "share" for each person.	1. Use the fraction circles to create a circle composed of three equal shares. Then draw what you did and be ready to explain it. 2. Use the square tiles to create two rectangles composed of three equal shares. Use a different strategy for each rectangle. Then draw what you did and be ready to explain it. 3. Use the square tiles to create two rectangles composed of four equal shares. Use a different strategy for each rectangle. Then draw what you did and be ready to explain it.	One of your classmates was absent! Use words and pictures to create two sets of step-by-step directions: • One set for how to divide a circle into three equal shares • Another set for how to divide a rectangle into four equal shares Use a different approach than this: Be sure to use the math vocabulary on the board in your directions.

First, Monica distributed the square tiles to all students and gave them some time to construct the shapes displayed on her Geometry bulletin board. During this experimentation time, she called students to the manipulatives table in two groups (one for each Agenda) to explain their respective Partner Practice directions. She had also made instructional videos of herself explaining the two different tasks so that students could play back the instructions if they got stuck or needed spoken-language support.

Once everyone was working on the Partner Practice tasks, Monica began to call groups of four to six students of like readiness to the small table for the Teacher Meet part of the Agenda. This setting allowed Monica to focus on students' specific readiness needs and to provide the necessary accommodations for her IEP students, also extending those supports to other students who needed them even if they hadn't been formally identified.

When students were finished with their teacher-led and collaborative activities, they moved to their On My Own tasks. They had answered journal prompts with a similar structure (albeit with different content) at other points in the year, so they were able to work independently. Students knew that they could use words and pictures in any combination as long as they got their point across.

By the time Monica finished her small-group meetings, most students either were moving to or had begun their independent work. She was able to circulate and check in with students who needed more challenge or support—information she had been able to gather both from her meetings and from student illustrations generated during partner work.

To close the lesson, Monica partnered a "Cake" student with a "Cookie" student to share their drawings and discuss what they had learned. Before convening as a class, Monica had posed the lesson's essential question: "Do equal shares have to be the same shape? Discuss with your partner and be ready to show what you mean." After partners had a chance to share with each other, the class members came together on the rug to discuss their thinking.

For Monica, this proactive approach felt much less exhausting and more productive than had her reactive approach the year before. It took some upfront planning, but it was worth it both in terms of student learning and in building students' capacity to work independently. She was also able to reuse the Agenda structure in other lessons and content areas.

Part 2:

Tools and Strategies

Tiering

What It Is:

Tiering, developed by Tomlinson (2014a), is best thought of as a *process* for designing tasks differentiated for readiness based on pre- or formative assessment data. Essentially, teachers use the patterns of student learning revealed in *recent* and *relevant* assessment results to create tasks that will move different groups of students toward the same learning goals. Tiering can also be considered a *concept* to be superimposed on other strategies in response to varying student needs. Examples include tiered prompts (p. 220), tiered perspectives (p. 210), and tiered graphic organizers (pp. 235–243).

How It Works:

After articulating learning goals, administering a pre-assessment or formative assessment of students' progress toward those goals, and reviewing the assessment results with the desired response(s) in mind, answer the following questions to guide the process of devising tiered tasks (see the template in Figure 6.10, p. 234).

1. *Does there seem to be something that* all *students need to do to move forward?* Devise introductory or review elements around those ideas.

2. *Do you see any distinguishing patterns in assessment responses? Are there responses that seem to "go together" in some way?* Make piles that reflect those patterns.

3. *What stands out to you about student responses in each pile?* Make general notes about anything that distinguishes one pile from the others (e.g., some students made minor errors but followed the process, whereas others missed steps of the process).

4. *For the students in each pile, what kind of feedback will fill in their learning gaps and advance their thinking?* Make notes about what each group of students will need specifically (e.g., a clarifying example, step-by-step directions, a chance to examine the concept in a new context).

5. *For each pile or pattern, what tasks could you design that will provide this specific feedback?* Generate ideas for tasks that will provide students at each readiness level with the scaffolding or challenge they need to grow toward and beyond the goals. Develop the top task first to avoid the trap of simply giving more work to students who "get it" and to create a model to emulate when developing the additional tasks.

6. *What specific directions will students need to successfully complete the tasks you've designed?* Develop clear directions and materials for each group. Consider structures for fostering independence (e.g., recorded directions, models). Build in time for *every group* to check in with you to demonstrate progress.

7. *How can all students come together after they have completed their tasks and synthesize or share their learning?* Develop a closure step that will reunite the class and prepare students to move forward.

What It's Good For:

- Tiered tasks are useful when assessment results reveal *significant* differences in student readiness for a particular concept or skill and students need different things to grow toward and beyond the learning goals or grade-level standards. (Minor gaps in student understanding, knowledge, or skill can be addressed through individual feedback, small-group "huddles," or other low-prep strategies.)
- Done well, tiered tasks allow teachers to maintain fidelity to learning goals and grant all students access to important content and ideas. It helps us teach *up* rather than dumb down.

Tips:

- The number of tiers (or whether Tiering is necessary at all) should be determined by the *patterns* that emerge from the formative assessment information. The patterns may reveal the need for one, two, or three tasks.
- If the assessment results lead you to see the need for five or more tasks, then it's likely that the learning goals are too narrow (or too low or too high), the pre- or formative assessment prompts need revision, or your "patterns" need to be broader and more encompassing.
- Often, Tiering involves making minor adjustments to one top-tier task rather than creating multiple parallel tasks.
- Use Tomlinson's (2014a) Equalizer as a visual thinking tool for Tiering or adjusting a task for student readiness.

Tiering Examples:

Figures 6.8 and 6.9 offer examples of Tiering at the primary and upper-elementary grade levels.

Figure 6.8 | Tiering Example: Measurement and Data (CCSS.K.MD.3), PreK–Kindergarten

Learning Goals

Understanding Goals
- Objects can have similar and different *attributes*/characteristics.
- Objects can be sorted into *categories* that represent the *attributes*/characteristics they share.
- The *number* of objects in a category can be counted and put in an *order*.

Knowledge Goals
- Terms/concepts: *attribute, category, order* (least to greatest)
- Counting numbers 1–10

Skill Goals
- Classify objects into given categories.
- Count the number of objects in a category.
- Sort categories of objects by count (i.e., the number of objects in the category).

Pre-Assessment

The teacher sorts some paper cookies using a think-aloud ("Let's see, here's a big chocolate cookie. I'll put it on this plate. Here's another chocolate cookie, but it's small, so I'll put it on another plate. Here's another small cookie, but it's vanilla. I'll put it on a third plate and see if I find any other small vanilla cookies. . . ."). Students then receive envelopes of cookies to sort and paper plates (or circles) on which to sort them. The teacher observes students as they sort and prompts students who are ready to count the number of cookies in each category.

Patterns from Assessment

Pattern 1	Pattern 2	Pattern 3	Pattern 4
Students are unsure how to sort.	Students sort by color but not by size (or vice versa).	Students sort by size and color.	Students sort by size and color and attempt to or successfully create additional categories.

Tiered Tasks			
• Students work on identifying the most obvious attribute (color) as well as an additional attribute (size). • The teacher uses modeling and guided practice with sorting objects first into one category, then into another.	• Students work on identifying multiple attributes and assigning categories to attributes. • Independent or partnered practice sorting objects into given categories. Students are encouraged to come up with an additional category.	• Students work on identifying multiple categories (cookie flavor, size, color, and "extras" [e.g., nuts, raisins]). • Independent or partnered practice coming up with and sorting according to obvious and nonobvious categories.	• Students work on identifying categories that could be used to sort multiple objects. (What else could be sorted by size? What would the sizes be?) • Independent or partnered practice showing how and why objects can fit into multiple categories and that the same categories can be used for different objects.
Whole-Class Closure			
Regroup students into mixed-task pairs (Pattern 1 with Pattern 2; Pattern 3 with Pattern 4). In their mixed pairs, they talk about how they sorted their cookies and what was easy about sorting them and what was hard. As a whole class, students discuss what else they could sort and how they would sort those things.			

Source: C. A. Tomlinson (2005). Used with permission.

Figure 6.9 | Tiering Example: Figurative Language in Poetry (CCSS.RL5.4&W.5.3.D), Grades 4–5

Learning Goals		
Understanding Goal	**Knowledge Goal**	**Skill Goals**
Words have the *power* to create pictures in readers' minds.	Terms/concepts: *Imagery, simile, metaphor,* and *rhythm.*	• Use imagery to communicate sensory information. • Use similes to communicate description. • Use line division to influence rhythm.

Pre-Assessment
The teacher gives students the following prompts: • Describe a family member by explaining what he or she is like. • You can compare your family member to anything in nature, in our classroom, in your lunch, on the playground, in your toy box, and so on. The only thing you should *not* compare your family member to is another person. • At the end of each comparison, tell *why* you made that comparison.

Patterns from Assessment	
Pattern 1	**Pattern 2**
Comparisons are specific and students display clear reasoning for choosing each comparison (e.g., "My little brother is like the fire alarm because he is so loud when he cries!" or "My Nanna is like a blanket because she is cozy.").	Comparisons are either very literal or missing, and students cannot explain the reasoning behind the comparisons they do make (e.g., "My mom is like a nice person because she is nice," or "My baby sister is like an ice cream sundae because . . . .").

Whole-Class Introduction
1. Students are given a two-column organizer with a blank space for their favorite color at the top and the five senses listed along the left-hand column. After writing down their favorite color, they are to list items in the right-hand column that are their favorite color and correspond to the sense in the left-hand column. For example, a student who lists red as his favorite color might write "a cardinal" next to *sight,* "a strawberry" next to *taste,* "a police siren" next to *hearing,* and so on. Students learning English can draw their images. 2. The teacher creates "crayon box" groups of students who chose different colors. One by one, the group members share what they chose for each sense. Students can get ideas from their peers to help fill in their own graphic organizers. For example, a student who chose blue as her favorite color but who has an empty space next to *taste* may hear her classmate share "strawberry" and get the idea to list "blueberry" in that section. 3. The teacher reads aloud the poem "What is Gold?" from *Hailstones and Halibut Bones* by Mary O'Neill (1961). 4. On a graphic organizer like the one students already completed, projected on the interactive whiteboard, the teacher and students fill in the sensory images featured in the poem. 5. The teacher gives an example of a simile and a metaphor from the poem, and the class discusses the form and effect of each. The class locates other examples of similes and metaphors from the poem and records them on the board.

Tiered Tasks

Task 1
(Corresponds to Pattern 1)

- Students receive a copy of "What is Gold?" with the first few similes and metaphors highlighted in different colors. Students must continue to find and highlight the similes and metaphors and then check their work with the answer key and discuss in their "crayon box" groups.
- The teacher checks in to answer questions.
- Students use the images from their graphic organizers and the examples of the similes and metaphors from the mentor text ("What is Gold?") to begin to write their own poems about their favorite colors.
- Students must use images that appeal to at least four senses in their poems. They must also use at least three similes and one metaphor.
- The teacher checks in to answer questions.
- When they are finished, students trade poems with a partner and try to find the following in their partner's paper: (1) imagery for each of the four to five senses, (2) the similes, and (3) the metaphor(s).

Task 2
(Corresponds to Pattern 2)

- Students are given back their descriptions from the pre-assessment. The teacher leads them in editing their comparisons to be similes or metaphors, using the examples on the board for modeling.
- Once all students have successfully revamped at least two of their pre-assessment responses, they take out their graphic organizers and work on writing a simile appealing to one sense. The teacher models with a color no one in the group has chosen.
- Once all students have one simile started, they can begin writing their poems, adding similes for each of the senses.
- Students must use images that appeal to at least four senses in their poems. They must also use at least four similes. They can use a metaphor if they want to, but they are not required to do so.
- The teacher checks students' papers as they finish and strategically pairs students for peer editing.

Whole-Class Closure

- The teacher reads "What is Gold?" again but asks students to listen for when she pauses in her reading. Through modeling and class discussion, students discover that pauses occur when the lines break.
- Students pair up with a classmate who was in the other task group earlier. Each reads his or her poem aloud to his or her partner, and together the pair decides where each student should "break the lines" in his or her poem to create the desired rhythm.
- Students mark line breaks on their papers. This will remind them of their decisions when they type up their poems later in the week.

Figure 6.10 | Tiering Template

Content Area/Topic: _____ Grade Level: _____

Learning Goals
Understanding Goals
Knowledge Goals
Skill Goals

Pre- or Formative Assessment Items

Patterns from Assessment (as many as are observed)		
Pattern 1	**Pattern 2**	**Pattern 3**

Whole-Class Introduction (if needed)

Tiered Tasks (to correspond to patterns)		
Task 1	**Task 2**	**Task 3**

Whole-Class Closure

Tiered Graphic Organizers

What They Are:

Graphic organizers are visual displays that show relationships or connections between concepts, ideas, or facts. They provide a framework for students' thinking as they make sense of new or previously learned information. Widely used examples include concept maps and webs, T-Charts, Venn diagrams, K-W-L charts, and fishbone models. Tiering a graphic organizer can involve changing the facets of the organizer, making points of comparison more or less sophisticated, or altering the content on which students focus.

How They Work:

1. Select or create a graphic organizer to match instructional purpose.
2. Consider whether to adjust content or process for student readiness.
    » Content: (a) All students use the same graphic organizer but access different resources or information that varies by reading level or thinking level or (b) The prompts or focus of the organizer are differentiated for readiness.
    » Process: The thinking process represented in the organizer (e.g., compare/contrast, problem/solution, cause/effect, sequencing) is adjusted to be more or less complex.
3. If students are working with different organizers around the same general topic, bring them together in mixed-organizer pairs or groups—or as a whole class—around a common question (e.g., "What did we find out about how shapes are similar and different?").

What They're Good For:

- Helping students organize information
- Engaging all students in high-level thinking
- Appealing to various student preferences for taking in and making sense of content

Tips:

- Tiered or not, graphic organizers should be the means to a clear and important end—not the end in themselves. The information gathered and processed through graphic organizers should be transferred to another task. In other words, students complete graphic organizers "en route" to something else.
- Frame graphic organizers with a driving purpose, question, or prompt (e.g., "How are plants and animals similar and different?" or "How were the effects of the Civil War linked to the causes?").
- On their organizers or through oral instruction, ask students to draw conclusions, pose questions, or make predictions based on the information they have just processed.

Examples:

Three-Column Organizers: Historical Fact Versus Historical Fiction

These tiered organizers are ideal for distinguishing fact from fiction in read-aloud or independently read texts about historical figures and events, such as *If a Bus Could Talk: The Story of Rosa Parks* by Faith Ringgold (1999) or *John, Paul, George, and Ben* by Lane Smith (2006). They also work with fictionalized movies about history, such as Disney's *Pocahontas*. In the examples shown in Figure 6.11, Organizer 1 is more accessible, starting with a focus that is closer to the student (his or her favorite part) but still requiring the key skills. Organizer 2 begins with the key skills and works back to the student's preference. Organizer 3, designed to be the most advanced, assumes that identifying the "most real (factual)" part of the text or movie is more difficult than identifying the most fictional part and asks students about their preferences in wholes rather than parts.

Character Analysis Organizers

Teachers can use one or more of these organizers to differentiate close reading and analysis of characters in stories. Using only one organizer, the teacher can assign students different characters that are more or less difficult to analyze. Using two or three organizers invites varied levels of complexity in analysis (Tomlinson, 2005) (see Figure 6.12 for examples).

Two- and Three-Way Venn Diagrams

Using two- and three-way Venn diagrams is a simple way to differentiate for student readiness. Note that each example in Figure 6.13 includes a question or prompt to lend purpose to the processes of comparing and contrasting and asks students to reflect further or draw conclusions from the information they have displayed.

Cause-and-Effect Organizers

These organizers can help students determine cause-and-effect relationships in multiple content areas (e.g., events in history, science experiments and scientific phenomena). They are flexible enough to be used with different grade levels, and, as the examples in Figure 6.14 illustrate, Tiered Graphic Organizers do not need to look the same. Organizer 2 (Cause-and-Effect Chain) is more advanced because it requires students to sequence, draw multiple conclusions, and make predictions. Organizer 1 (Cause-and-Effect T-Chart) is more open and allows for fewer direct connections between causes and effects but still asks students to draw a conclusion and then pose a question. Students could examine the causes and effects of weather events, character actions, or following or breaking laws.

Figure 6.11 | Three-Column Organizer Examples

Organizer 1

Favorite Part	Is This Part Fact or Fiction?	How Do You Know?

Organizer 2

Most Pretend (Fictional) Part	How Do You Know?	Did You Like This Part? Why or Why Not?

Organizer 3

Most Real (Factual) Part	How Do You Know?	Did You Like the Fact or Fiction Parts Best? Why?

Figure 6.12 | Character Analysis Organizer Examples

Organizer 1

Character:	
Physical Traits What the character looks like	
Personality Traits How the character thinks or acts	
Important Thing The most important thing to know about the character	

Organizer 2

Character:	
Actions What the character says or does	
Motives What the character *really means* to say or do	
Important Thing What the character most likely wants the reader to know about him or her	

Organizer 3

Character:	
Clues Clues the author gives about what the character is like	
Motives What the character's *true* motives are	
Bottom Line The author's "bottom line" about this character	

Figure 6.13 | Two- and Three-Way Venn Diagram Examples

Organizer 1 (More Accessible): Economies of Ancient Civilizations
Question: Were the economies of these ancient civilizations more alike than different, or more different than alike?

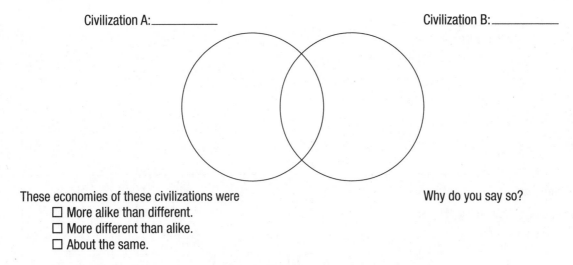

Civilization A:_____   Civilization B:_____

These economies of these civilizations were   Why do you say so?
    ☐ More alike than different.
    ☐ More different than alike.
    ☐ About the same.

Organizer 2 (More Advanced): Economies of Ancient Civilizations
Prompt: Compare the economies of these three ancient civilizations to decide which one had the strongest economy.

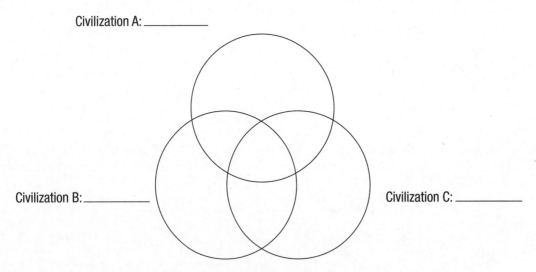

Civilization A: _____

Civilization B: _____   Civilization C: _____

Which civilization had the strongest economy? Why do you say so?

Organizer 1 (More Accessible): Comparing and Contrasting Decimals and Fractions

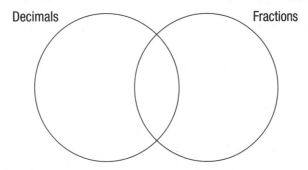

Answer on another piece of paper: What can decimals do or show that fractions can't? What can fractions do or show that decimals can't? How can someone decide whether to use a decimal or a fraction to solve a problem in his or her own life?

Organizer 2 (More Advanced): Comparing and Contrasting Decimals, Fractions, and Percentages

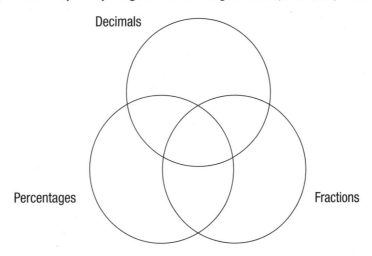

After comparing and contrasting decimals, fractions, and percentages, come up with three different real-world math situations: one that is *best* expressed with decimals, one that is *best* expressed with percentages, and one that is *best* expressed with fractions.

Figure 6.14 | Cause-and-Effect Organizer Examples

Organizer 1: Cause-and-Effect T-Chart

Causes	Effects

Overall Conclusion:

Burning Questions:

Organizer 2: Cause-and-Effect Chain

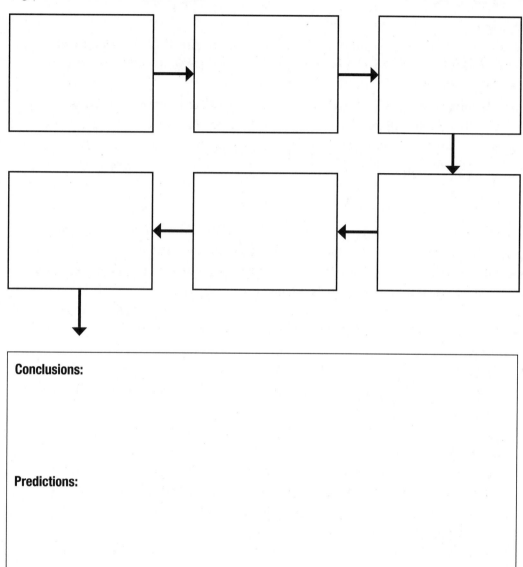

Contracts and Agendas

What They Are:

Contracts and Agendas are both mechanisms for delivering differentiated tasks.

- A Contract is a teacher-initiated framework that has students select tasks to complete to fulfill the expectations of the Contract.
- An Agenda is a schedule of learning experiences and tasks created and directed by the teacher that is differentiated for or tailored to student needs. Students have some choices about the order in which they complete the tasks, but not which tasks they will complete.

How They Work:

1. Determine the learning goals and standards that the Contract or Agenda will address. Include grade-level standards, prerequisite knowledge and skills for students who need review and practice, and next-step or deeper exploration possibilities for students who need to be stretched.
2. Make a list of learning experiences that the whole class will engage in. Ideally, these activities would be at grade-level proficiency. Some or all of these activities can appear on all versions of the Contract or Agenda.
3. Decide what students who need extra support should do to close gaps in their learning. Add the appropriate task(s) to the lower-readiness version of the Contract or Agenda.
4. Figure out how students who are already proficient could grow in their knowledge, understanding, or skill. This does not necessarily mean moving to the next skill set (although it can). It could involve asking high-readiness students to tunnel more deeply into standards by working with complex levels of the content or skills or by working with the content or skills in ways that mirror what professionals in the working world might do.
5. Devise a task (Agenda) or collection of tasks (Contract) for each version that includes
   » Tasks all groups will complete.
   » Tasks tailored for specific learning needs.
   » Tasks that weave content with literacy or research.
   » A combination of teacher-led, individual, and partner or group tasks.
6. Evaluate each version of the Contract or Agenda to make sure the tasks
   » Appear equally respectful.
   » Will require comparable time for the target groups to complete.
   » Stress the same core learning goals.
   » Use materials that are available or obtainable for classroom use.

What They're Good For:

- Promoting and supporting individual student growth and independence
- Freeing the teacher to work with small groups or individual students
- Modeling structure for completion of tasks in the "real world"
- Both Contracts and Agendas outline a collection of learning activities, along with teacher meeting times and other organizational measures, to ensure student success and grasp of learning goals. They allow for differentiation by providing the teacher with a structure for communicating different levels of resources, tasks, structure, and practice.
- Agendas may require less preparation to create but more preparation to implement.
- Contracts require more time to prepare but may free up the teacher during implementation.
- Contracts require students to make some kind of choice about what they are or aren't going to do for the Contract to be established and fulfilled; this choice can be motivating to students who seem to be reluctant learners.

Tips:

- Create or modify a template that students can get used to seeing.
- Offer "sets" of Contracts and Agendas according to patterns of need (versus a different one for each student).
- Design Contracts and Agendas for use over the course of several days or a week (versus one day).

Examples:

Show Me the Money!

One example of a Contract is Show Me the Money!, a structure that lends itself well to use with preexisting sets of problems, questions, or tasks. For example, mathematics texts and resources organize practice problems by level of complexity, with simpler problems sequenced before multistep problems. With the Show Me the Money! strategy, the teacher reviews the problem sets and selects groups of potential problems, making sure they represent a range of difficulty as well as the necessary concepts and skills. Each group or range is assigned a "money" value (e.g., problems 1–5 are each worth $100, and problems 6–10 are each worth $200). Students can choose which problems to do within parameters that the teacher sets—for example, "Complete $1,500 worth of problems—no more than one $100 problem, at least two $200 problems, and at least one $300 problem." See Figure 6.15 (p. 246) for blank and filled-in versions of these Contracts.

Figure 6.15 | Show Me the Money! Contract

Show Me the Money! Homework

Assignment: _____

Completion Amount Required: $_____

Problem/Task Values:

- _____ = $_____ each
- _____ = $_____ each
- _____ = $_____ each
- _____ = $_____ each

Guidelines:

You must complete _____

Show Me the Money! Homework

Assignment: Problems on pp. 135–136

Completion Amount Required: $1500

Problem/Task Values:

- Problems 1–5 = $100 each
- Problems 6–10 = $200 each
- Problems 11–15 = $300 each
- N/A = $N/A each

Guidelines:

You must complete: no more than one $100 problem, at least two $200 problems, and at least one $300 problem.

Show Me the Money! Student Receipt

Assignment: _____

Completion Amount Required: $_____

Problems I've completed:

- _____ @ $_____ each = $_____
- _____ @ $_____ each = $_____
- _____ @ $_____ each = $_____
- _____ @ $_____ each = $_____

Total: $_____

1 Realization and 1 Remaining Question:

Show Me the Money! Student Receipt

Assignment: Problems on pp. 135–136

Completion Amount Required: $1500

Problems I've completed:

- Problem 3 @ $100 each = $100
- Problems 7–10 @ $200 each = $800
- Problems 11–12 @ $300 each = $600
- N/A @ $--- each = $---

Total: $1500

1 Realization and 1 Remaining Question:

R = If I don't show my work, I make dumb mistakes.

? = What happens if there's a remainder?

Shape Up! Contract

The Shape Up! Contract (see Figure 6.16, p. 248) is designed to give younger students choice as well as practice with motor skills (i.e., with cutting and pasting shapes).

In this example, the teacher offers nine tasks related to stories about friendships that students are reading. Note that each set of tasks is aligned with a common purpose: the Circle tasks are focused on how characters solve problems in a story; the Triangle tasks ask students to come up with their own problem and solution, inspired by the stories they've read; and the Square tasks call on students to think about what traits they have that make them a good friend.

Figure 6.16 | Shape Up! Contract Example: Stories About Friends

Directions: Choose an activity for each shape group. Cut your three choices and glue or tape them below. You are responsible for finishing these activities by [day]. Have fun!

This contract belongs to _____

Draw a picture of the problem in the story. Then use words to tell about the problem and how the characters solved it.

Meet with a friend and make a puppet show about a problem and solution in your book.

Make a poster advertising yourself as a good friend. Use words and pictures to help people want to be your friend. Make sure your name is an important part of the ad.

Write a letter to one of the characters in your book. Tell him or her about a problem you have. Then have the character write back with a possible solution to your problem.

Meet with a friend and act out a problem and its solution.

Make a two-sided circle. Use it to show and tell people what makes you a good friend. Use words and pictures and make sure your name is an important part of the display.

Think about another problem that one of the characters in your book might have. Write a new story for the book about the problem and tell how it was solved.

Meet with me and tell me about a problem and solution from the story. Then tell me about a problem you had and how you solved it.

Make a collage that shows what makes you a good friend. Write your name on the collage in beautiful letters.

Source: Brenda Spurgeon. Used with permission.

General Agenda

Second grade teacher Monica Helfand (see pp. 220–225) is using differentiated Agendas. See Figure 6.17 for a general Agenda template.

Figure 6.17 | General Agenda Template

Student: _____

Teacher Meet	Partner Practice	On My Own
You will meet with the teacher on [day] to [learn about/practice/discuss] the following:	Complete these steps/tasks with your partner, _____:	Complete these steps/tasks on your own:
Teacher and student initials upon completion_____	Teacher and student initials upon completion_____	Teacher and student initials upon completion_____

7 | Differentiating According to Student Interest and Learning Preference

Part 1:

How Do I Increase Motivation and Investment?

"I learn best when the teacher does exciting things and not boring ones" (Wiggins, 2014). This claim—a 5th grader's response to a survey question asking students what would help them learn better—presents a challenge. On a cross-country journey, this might feel like a passenger's request to go off road to get ice cream when the driver is concerned with staying the course.

In terms of the way the brain works, however, it is *very* important to make learning a pleasurable experience for students. Neurologist Judy Willis (2007) explains that "when students are engaged and motivated . . . information flows freely through the affective filter in the amygdala [the brain's emotional center] and they achieve higher levels of cognition, make connections, and experience 'aha' moments" (para. 3). In other words, students make more progress when they are "revved up" about what they are doing.

How, then, do teachers put more fuel in students' tanks so that students persist in learning? *Do more fun activities* comes to mind—and students certainly would agree. In the same survey referenced above (Wiggins, 2014), students gave the following advice to their teachers:

- "Maybe make the work more fun so I understand it and it's fun."
- "[Have us do] more hand[s]-on work."
- "Have a more fun variety of activities in class."

Of course, just because students are having fun doesn't mean they are learning. Fun is merely "fluff" if it doesn't cause students to grow in their understanding, knowledge, and skills. A "hands-on" approach to learning doesn't necessarily lead to a "minds-on" approach (Wiggins & McTighe, 2005, 2011).

Consequently, a more complete driving question for this chapter might be "How do I increase motivation and investment *while making sure students are engaged in important tasks that address common learning goals*?" How can teachers plan lessons that address required content and standards while fostering student investment?

In this chapter, we explore how to strategically use student interests and learning preferences to plan instruction. This goes beyond simply asking, "What do kids like? What will be 'fun' for them to do?" Rather, it requires deep consideration of what will compel students to invest in the content and persevere in their learning even when the going gets tough.

Appealing to Students' Interests

There are inevitably spots in the curriculum—or even periods of the day or times in the year—that bring out the "reluctance" in many students. Repeated failed efforts to engage students at these points might lead a teacher to conclude, "Some kids just aren't motivated." But *all* human beings have passions, kinships, and areas of intrigue that motivate them to learn. Kids are no exception. If a student seems chronically unmotivated, it is most likely because what motivates him or her hasn't come to light.

Few things motivate learners of all ages more than choice. Choice not only satisfies the innate human desire for autonomy and ownership but also can increase student engagement in a task. Teachers can offer choice by appealing to two kinds of interests: personal interests and situational interests (Schraw, Flowerday, & Lehman, 2001).

Personal Interests

Personal interests are those that students bring to the classroom. Students "own" personal interests and develop them over time. Examples include taking care of pets, shooting hoops, writing or recording music, and cartooning. Teachers can proactively uncover personal interests by asking students to a make a pie chart or graph of their interests, as discussed in Chapter 1 (p. 28).

Interest surveys can be another rich source of information about what potentially motivates students. In any beginning-of-the-year survey, it's a good idea to ask at least a few questions that will uncover what students are interested in outside school. The following are the kinds of survey questions that tap into student interests and provide a starting point for forging connections:

- What is your favorite animal? Food?
- What do you enjoy spending time on?
- What are you really good at?
- What is hard for you to do? Explain.
- If you could invite a famous person to your house for a party, whom would you invite and why?

- What's the best story you've ever read, seen, or heard (e.g., from a book, an article, a movie, a TV show, a friend, or a family member)?
- Fill in the blank: "To me, numbers are like _____." Explain.

These questions need not be asked all at once, or even in writing. Teachers can pose them through various methods (e.g., Attendance Questions, journal prompts, interviews) to give all students an opportunity to respond.

Interest cards, a tool designed by Carol Ann Tomlinson (2005), offer a streamlined method for more directly gathering information about student interests and for building connections between the subject and what students care about. The four-square format (see Figure 7.1) provides an at-a-glance view of each student's interests. The cards can also be cut into fours and easily sorted to create groups based on shared or varying areas of student interest.

Figure 7.1 | Interest Cards

Directions: I'll be a better teacher for you if I understand some of your interests. In each box below, record an interest of yours. Write briefly about how you are involved with that interest, and note ways in which the interest might connect with this subject.

Name:_____ Interest #1:_____ Experience with it? Connection with this subject?	Name:_____ Interest #2:_____ Experience with it? Connection with this subject?
Name:_____ Interest #3:_____ Experience with it? Connection with this subject?	Name:_____ Interest #4:_____ Experience with it? Connection with this subject?

Many teachers gather this kind of information as the basis for building relationships with students. But teachers can also study that information to discover patterns among students' interests, which can help them strategically plan and direct instruction. Whether through formal surveys or via pre-assessment prompts (see Chapter 3), taking this active step in discovering what matters to each student can provide teachers with the ingredients to make school palatable—even delicious—for their students.

Harnessing students' personal interests may be as simple as allowing students to access informational texts on a topic of their choice while they practice analyzing how the author uses details. Or a teacher could provide students with ads for products corresponding to their personal interests to serve as "practice fields" for calculating discounts and sales tax. Although not all personal interests relate directly to curricular topics and skills, teachers can find and use "patterns" among students' personal interests—like technology, sports, music, and animals—to form interest-based groupings, design tasks, and build connections among school, learning, and real life.

Situational Interests

Situational interests are those that arise from or in a situation, such as a teacher-designed lesson or task. They are more spontaneous or "in the moment" than are personal interests. Teachers can uncover students' situational interests before or during a unit by providing straightforward prompts such as these:

- Here are some things we will be learning about: _____. Which sound most interesting to you? Rank your top three, and explain why you chose each one.
- On a scale of 0–5 (0 = not interesting at all, 5 = super-duper interesting), how interesting do you find what we're working on right now? Explain your rating.
- What was the most interesting thing you learned [today/this week]?
- What might make you *more* interested in [topic]? "This might be more interesting to me if . . . ."

Research (Schraw et al., 2001) suggests that situational interest in a text or task actually *increases* with choice, even when personal interest is low. Teachers can activate situational interest even in the most mundane tasks simply by providing students with different contexts for exploring content and exercising skills. Figure 7.2 illustrates how a writing prompt can be tweaked to reflect students' activities and curiosities. These adjustments have the potential to increase students' investment in the writing task without compromising important learning goals. Increased investment may in turn improve their performance. In fact, recent studies (e.g., Walkington, 2013) have discovered that students who were given math word problems reflecting typical out-of-school interests (e.g., sports, movies, music, food) solved those problems faster and more accurately than did students who received traditional story problems (see Figure 7.3). These effects were most pronounced for students who tended to struggle with math.

Figure 7.2 | Interest-Based Writing Prompts

Choice Topic	Task Description
Animals	The zoo has decided to move your favorite animal, the _____, out to make room for another animal! Write a letter to the zookeeper explaining why he should keep your favorite animal in the zoo. Be sure to give at least three reasons to support your opinion.
Cartoons	The new television schedule just came out and your favorite cartoon, _____, has been canceled. Write a letter to the network president explaining why she should put your cartoon back on TV. Be sure to give at least three reasons to support your opinion.
Toys	You brought the money you've been saving from birthdays and chores to the store to buy _____, a toy you've been wanting. When you got there, you found out that the store had run out. Write a letter to the store manager explaining why he should order more of the toy you want. Be sure to give at least three reasons to support your opinion.
Playground	The park has decided to take down your favorite piece of playground equipment, the _____, to make room for a new piece of equipment. Write a letter to the park director to convince her to keep your favorite part of the playground. Be sure to give at least three reasons to support your opinion.

Figure 7.3 | Math Story Problems with Adapted Contexts

Original problem	The doctor's office needs new carpet. The estimated cost of the carpet is $5.50 per square foot. How much will the carpet cost if the doctor's office is 12 square feet?
Sports	You and your 11 friends want to go to the local basketball championship! Tickets are $5.50 each. How much will it cost for all 12 of you to go to the game?
Friends	You want to have a birthday party and invite all of your friends. The cost for the food, decorations, and party favors will be $5.50 per guest. How much money will you have to save in order to invite 12 guests to your party?
Art	You have been painting pictures all year and are ready to sell them at the art show for $5.50 each. How much money will you make if you sell all 12 of your paintings?
Drama	You are performing in your community's play! Tickets to the play are $5.50 each. How much money will your family need to bring if 12 family members want to watch you act?

In these problems, the numbers, operations, and setup remain the same; only the context changes. Still, this small change has the potential to reap big rewards in student performance.

Higher-Prep Strategies for Designing Tasks Differentiated for Interest

There are many points in everyday instruction where making small changes for student interest can make a big difference. There are also points in the curriculum that call for assignment options that require more planning on the teacher's part. Often such tasks are used when teachers want students to transfer what they have learned to a new context or situation (e.g., tasks used for assessment, ongoing station work, or independent study). In each of these situations, motivation is key.

RAFT, Learning Menus, and Choice Boards are three higher-prep strategies that are great for leveraging students' interests. Each one provides students with a context, asks them to engage in higher-order thinking, and requires them to exercise their learning in a meaningful way. These strategies are engaging to students both because of their novelty and because they offer choices.

A RAFT (Buehl, 2009; Santa, 1988) asks students to take on a *role* to address a specific *audience* in an appropriate *format* about a particular *topic*. This novel approach in itself piques student interest, but the teacher can appeal to more students' preferences by designing several different options for role, audience, format, and topic—all aligned to the same learning goals—and inviting students to select the combinations that most intrigue them (see examples on pp. 287–288).

Learning Menus (Cummings, 2000) also motivate through offering choices. They function much like specially priced tasting menus that present customers with just a few dishes to select from for each course. Similarly, a Learning Menu presents students with several options in different categories (main courses, side dishes, desserts) and encourages them to design the "meal" that is most appealing to them and that will best help them "digest" the unit's learning goals (see examples on pp. 294–297).

Choice Boards are similar to Learning Menus in that they ask students to make choices in several categories. Choice Boards generally contain three sets of three assignment options in a 3x3 grid. Each row addresses different learning goals, with the three options in each row addressing the same set of learning objectives. Students choose one option from each row to demonstrate a grasp of all learning goals. This strategy, also known as "Think-Tac-Toe" (Tomlinson, 2003), offers teachers a means for presenting students with a variety of assignment options while ensuring that all students walk away having grappled with the same learning goals (see examples, pp. 300–305).

Part 2 of this chapter presents further instructions as well as examples of these strategies to help teachers craft their own interest-based assignments.

Appealing to Students' Learning Preferences

Learning profile is an umbrella term that refers to anything that might influence how students prefer to learn and how they seem to learn best (Tomlinson, 2009, 2014a). This can include learning-style theories about how people take in and process information, various intelligence-style theories, and ideas about how culture and gender might influence learning preferences.

The goal of differentiating for learning profile is to make learning more efficient, appealing, and effective. There is no scientific basis, however, for saying that a student is one kind of learner or another, or that a child's brain is hardwired to learn in one way all of the time (Hattie & Yates, 2014). Even intelligence-style theorists (e.g., Gardner, 1995; Sternberg & Grigorenko, 2007) caution against surveying students, "diagnosing" a profile, and assigning tasks accordingly.

Still, certain ways of taking in, processing, and demonstrating learning seem to work better for some students than for others. Accordingly, *learning preference* is a phrase that may better capture the essence of how students seem to learn best. It serves as a reminder that giving students *choices* about how they learn is what provides instructional power. In other words, learning preferences provide teachers with yet another way to activate situational interest. In the following sections, we explore two categories of learning preferences: *modalities* and *intelligence preferences*.

Modalities

Most teachers are familiar with modality preferences that their students express. For example, students may prefer to take in, "crunch on," or demonstrate their learning through visual, auditory, or kinesthetic means. Again, although research (e.g., Hattie & Yates, 2014) does not support the practice of *labeling* and *assigning* students these modalities, it does support teachers (1) using a variety of methods to represent content and (2) allowing students choice in how they engage with and produce evidence of learning (Sousa & Tomlinson, 2011).

Teachers can harness these different modalities simply by offering options for how students will take in, process, or express their learning. These options can be small in scope or more developed. Asking a class, "Tomorrow, would you rather learn about this topic by watching a video, reading about it, or listening to a podcast?" is a small adjustment that can pique student interest and heighten engagement during the following day's lesson. Alternatively, teachers can create task options that require a little more time for students to complete. This is particularly useful for allowing students to practice with content and skills in a way that enables the teacher to check for group understanding.

For example, Ms. Ball presented her kindergartners with the following task options, telling them it was time to "show what you know!" (Brighton, Moon, Jarvis, & Hockett, 2007):

- *Option 1 [visual task]*: Draw a mural or a series of pictures showing facts about how Pocahontas helped the new American settlers. Try to trick your classmates by including one "pretend" picture in the mural, and see if they spot it. Begin by planning a list or storyboard.
- *Option 2 [auditory task]*: Make an audio recording that tells facts about how Pocahontas helped the new American settlers. Try to trick your classmates by including one "pretend" part in your story, and see if they find it. Begin by planning a list or storyboard. Once the story is together, try to work in sound effects.
- *Option 3 [kinesthetic task]*: In a play, pantomime, or puppet show, act out the facts about how Pocahontas helped the new American settlers. Try to trick your classmates by including one "pretend" part in your performance, and see if they spot it. Begin by planning a list or storyboard. Once the story is together, work in props and cues.

Ms. Ball placed students in groups based on the task they liked best; she did not label the tasks as visual, auditory, and kinesthetic because she wanted children to base their choices on their own task preferences rather than on how fun (or scary) the *label* seemed. Students worked together, and each group presented its product to the class. This activity gave students the chance to practice distinguishing between fiction and nonfiction while giving Ms. Ball the opportunity to gauge the understanding of the class. She stopped after each presentation to ask clarifying questions and clear up anything that seemed "fuzzy."

Intelligence Preferences

Whereas modalities represent ways of taking in or demonstrating learning, intelligence preference models are rooted in theories of human cognitive capacity. Intelligence preferences are best viewed on a continuum; that is, all people possess these intelligence preferences to some degree, and they can be developed through experience. Howard Gardner and Robert Sternberg offer two conceptions of intelligence preference that are particularly useful for creating task options for students: multiple intelligences and triarchic intelligence.

Multiple intelligences. Howard Gardner's theory of multiple intelligences is perhaps the best-known theory about what human intelligence is and how it develops. According to Gardner (2006), human cognitive ability comprises multiple sets of capacities, or "intelligences," that all normally developing people have to some extent. The most recent iteration of multiple intelligences theory describes eight intelligences, with a possible ninth: verbal-linguistic, logical-mathematical, musical-rhythmic, visual-spatial, bodily-kinesthetic, interpersonal, intrapersonal, naturalistic, and (potentially) existential.

Although Gardner did not have teachers and education in mind when he developed his theory, educators have been some of the biggest fans of his work, probably in part because the theory aligns so well with what they observe in children day to day.

One practical application of Gardner's work can be seen in a strategy he developed himself called Entry Points. Gardner "collapsed" his intelligences into six ways of thinking:

- Narrational (i.e., storytelling)
- Logical (i.e., giving reasons)
- Existential (i.e., thinking big)
- Aesthetic (i.e., activating senses)
- Quantitative (i.e., working with numbers)
- Experiential (i.e., using experience)

Gardner advises users of the strategy to think of a topic as a room with multiple doorways or "entry points" into it, and to create tasks that serve as those doorways, allowing students to choose the Entry Points that most appeal to them (see examples, pp. 272–273).

Triarchic intelligence. According to cognitive psychologist Robert Sternberg, the human intellect comprises three sets of capacities (Sternberg & Grigorenko, 2007):

- *Analytical intelligence*: The ability to analyze, compare and contrast, see the parts and the whole, examine cause and effect, and think in linear and logical-sequential ways
- *Practical intelligence*: The ability to put ideas into action, apply knowledge and skills to the real world, execute tasks efficiently, and solve problems or resolve conflicts on the spot
- *Creative intelligence*: The ability to imagine possibilities, think outside the box, innovate, invent, ask insightful questions, propose novel solutions, and intuit

School tasks typically emphasize analytical intelligence at the expense of developing or valuing practical and creative intelligence. Sternberg (2006) believes that if teachers used a balance of tasks that require analytical, practical, and creative thinking, more students would be successful in school. Using a technique called TriMind, teachers can differentiate for learning preference by providing students with options for processing material that are aligned to analytical, practical, and creative ways of thinking (see examples, pp. 277–281).

Both Howard Gardner and Robert Sternberg caution against relegating each student to one particular intelligence preference "box." Instead, they recommend expanding the instructional options offered in the classroom with the goal of harnessing every student's strengths (Gardner, 1995; Sternberg & Grigorenko, 2007). Part 2 of this chapter presents further instructions, templates, and examples of these strategies to help teachers craft their own interest-based assignments.

Defensible Use of Strategies Differentiated for Interest and Learning Preference

Entry Points, TriMind, RAFT, Learning Menus, and Choice Boards can be used at various points during the instructional process to gauge student understanding of principles, content, and skills. For all five strategies, the teacher must take care to craft assignment options with the following criteria for success in mind:

- All assignment options should address the same understanding, knowledge, and skill goals.
- All assignment options should involve the same degree of rigor (unless strategic readiness adjustments are made; such adjustments are discussed within the context of each strategy).
- All assignment options should appear equally respectful to students.
- All assignment options should be accompanied by clear task descriptions as well as transparent expectations and criteria for success.
- Students may be allowed to propose alternative options that the teacher can approve *if* those options adhere to each of the criteria listed above.
- Assignment options should offer a true variety of approaches rather than multiple versions of the same kind of thinking.
- All assignment options should be able to be assessed using the same criteria or rubric in order to ensure alignment of learning outcomes and streamline the evaluation process.

This last criterion is vital. As stressed in Chapter 1, if the task options for any assignment don't cause students to arrive at the same learning destination, then the tasks are not differentiated; they are just "different."

Frequently Asked Questions

The following are common concerns among teachers and administrators about differentiating for interest and learning preference, with responses stemming from research and practice.

How does the "content-process-product" model fit with interest and learning preference differentiation?

As discussed in the Chapter 6 FAQs, *content* is what students will learn, or how students will gain access to the information, skills, and ideas that are critical to understanding the content; *process* refers to the activities through which students make sense of key ideas in the content using essential knowledge and skills; and *product* is how students demonstrate and extend what they know, understand, and can do as a result of a unit or series of lessons. Teachers can adjust content, process, or product as separate elements or in combination (Tomlinson, 2014a).

Adjusting the context of story problems and writing prompts, such as those represented in Figures 7.2 and 7.3, is a way to differentiate *content* according to *interest*. Similarly, giving students the choice of reading, listening to, or viewing material is a way of differentiating *content* according to *learning preference*.

Allowing students to select their Looking/Listening Lens (see Chapter 4, p. 129) is one way to differentiate *process* according to *interest*. Likewise, letting students choose from among TriMind or Entry Point options is a means of differentiating *process* according to *learning preference*.

Ms. Ball's use of multimodal choices (see p. 260) allowed her to differentiate *product* according to *learning preference*. Part 2 of this chapter describes more complex strategies (Learning Menus, Choice Boards, and RAFT) for differentiating *product* to appeal to situational *interest*.

Again, although these terms and the distinctions among them can be useful in describing how a task or learning experience can be or has been differentiated, avoid getting caught up in the vocabulary. Talking about content-process-product is less important than studying and responding to students' interests and learning preferences in sensible ways.

What's the difference between differentiation for interest and learning preference and Universal Design for Learning? They seem similar.

Broadly speaking, Universal Design for Learning (UDL) suggests providing the entire class with multiple ways to represent, interact with, and show understanding of content. It emphasizes the need to provide varied learning avenues and touts the power of choice. As such, UDL has quite a bit of overlap with differentiation for learning preference, especially in terms of modalities. With differentiation, however, specific avenues are provided to specific students—or groups of students—based on personal interests emerging from purposeful inquiry on the part of the teacher. In addition, differentiation suggests and describes specific strategies for constructing varied learning paths (see Part 2 of this chapter) rather than simply recommending their existence. In other words, differentiation embraces UDL but takes it a few steps further.

You've recommended interest surveys. Should I also give students a survey to determine their preferred multiple intelligence or triarchic intelligence?

Neither Gardner nor Sternberg recommends—nor does research support—the idea of "diagnosing" and labeling student learning profiles through surveys or inventories. That is not to say, however, that there isn't a place for learning preference surveys. These types of inventories are useful simply for developing both teachers' and students' awareness of the many different approaches to learning and for reinforcing the reality that students are both alike and different in many ways.

Should I label tasks that have been differentiated for learning preference?

In general, it's a good idea to use names or labels that students will understand and that increase the appeal of the task options. For example, a "verbal-linguistic" task might be a "Word Wizard" task. Tasks can also be numbered (e.g., option 1, option 2, and option 3) so that students make their choice based on the nature of the *task* rather than on its label.

Should students always work with their first-choice task?

If all tasks offered are high-quality, respectful, and aligned with common learning goals, then task choice can be left up to students, especially since their choices won't necessarily stay consistent across lessons and subjects. If a student does tend to gravitate toward one particular kind of task, the teacher can encourage him or her to try a new approach periodically, especially when content is familiar. For new material or higher-stakes assessment tasks, however, students should work with their first choice to foster both investment and success.

If a teacher wants to expose students to other task options, "Jigsawing" tasks or asking students to share their task results in mixed groups (e.g., analytical, practical, and creative) can accomplish the same goal. This gives students access to multiple perspectives and may even encourage them to try a new type of task in a future assignment.

One practical tip: when forming groups or partnerships according to interest or learning preference, it's a good idea to have students rank their choices and then to try to give students their first or second choice. This provides the teacher with more flexibility in forming groups.

What happens if no student chooses a task?

With all choice-based tasks, it's a good idea to conduct an "autopsy": Who chose which task? Which tasks were most popular? Least popular? Why? If the problem with a less popular task seems to lie with the task itself (e.g., it doesn't appear as engaging as the others or it seems denser than the others), tinker with it a bit to bring it up to par. However, if the task is respectful, important, engaging, and clear, try it again the following year. It may just be that the task hasn't met its "student match" yet.

So are differentiating tasks and giving students choices the same thing?

Not necessarily. There are many ways to give students choices in their learning that aren't differentiated; conversely, teachers can differentiate without giving students a choice. As noted elsewhere in this chapter and in Chapter 6, there are some general guidelines around letting students choose from differentiated tasks:

- When tasks are differentiated for readiness, it's because assessment evidence suggests significant differences in students' understanding, knowledge, or skill. In order for each student to grow, he or she has to get the "right" task. So, most of the time, letting students choose would put growth at risk.
- When tasks are differentiated for interest or learning preference, teachers are trying to increase motivation and make learning more efficient. So, most of the time, it makes sense to let students choose what's most appealing to them, or at least "have a say" by ranking their preferences.

Where do other learning-style theories fit in?

Teachers have long observed that children don't seem to learn in the same ways or have the same preferences in how (or even where) they learn. Learning-style frameworks such as those by David Kolb, Anthony Gregorc, and Rita Dunn and Kenneth Dunn are educationally appealing because they try to explain differences in how people take in, perceive, and process information. But experts across neuroscience, cognitive and learning sciences, and educational psychology rightfully point out the lack of research that supports these theories. In light of the criticism, what should teachers "do" with learning styles?

If a learning style or modality theory sparks ideas for rich and respectful tasks that are aligned with important knowledge, understanding, and skill goals, then it can probably be as useful as any instructional strategy. Likewise, such frameworks can potentially extend teachers' understanding of possible ways to present content and skills and upgrade learning experiences for all students. But relying on learning style as the best or only approach to differentiation, labeling students as *X* types of learners, or using a learning-style theory to justify tasks that fall short of quality standards is not a defensible practice.

The bottom line is this: learning-style theories can provide useful inspiration for the crafting of *task options*, as long as those tasks are authentic, aligned to the same important learning goals, and chosen by students rather than assigned by the teacher.

A Preference-Based Differentiation Upgrade

Julian Dankel's kindergartners had been learning about the basic needs of goldfish. To heighten motivation, he decided to give them several task choices to apply and demonstrate what they had learned.

Before Upgrade

Julian initially offered his students the following task options:

- *Option 1*: Write a letter to your teacher about why you think a goldfish would make a good pet.
- *Option 2*: Draw a series of pictures that show other kindergartners a day in the life of our class goldfish.
- *Option 3*: Make a list of the steps in taking care of a goldfish.
- *Option 4*: Create a model of the ideal goldfish tank.

He was excited about the activity and asked his principal, Dr. Layman, to observe the lesson to get some informal feedback.

As Julian and Dr. Layman studied students' responses after the lesson, they realized that although the students had seemed motivated to complete their tasks and enjoyed working on them, very few had demonstrated an understanding of the basic needs of goldfish. Although he thought it was implied, in reviewing his task descriptions Julian realized that he had not necessarily emphasized this learning goal in his instructions. Further, students who chose option 4 hadn't come close to finishing their models, while students who chose option 1 were finished in only a few minutes. Julian realized he'd have to go back to the drawing board to make sure that each task option (1) addressed the same learning goals, (2) was truly different from the others in terms of learning preference, and (3) involved the same amount of work as the others.

After Upgrade

Based on a recommendation from Dr. Layman, Julian attended a summer professional development workshop that stressed the importance of aligning tasks to learning goals. He realized that it wasn't just the task *options* that required this attention; it was also the task *setup*. Somehow, he needed to unite his task options in both clarity and purpose. He started by articulating his learning goals and essential question (see Figure 7.4).

Figure 7.4 | Learning Goals for Goldfish Task

Understanding Goals
EQ: How do living things stay alive?
- **U1:** All living things have basic needs.
- **U2:** In order to survive, animals (including goldfish) need air, food, water, and a clean place to live.

Knowledge Goal
- **K1:** Vocabulary associated with the structure, behavior, and basic needs of fish

Skill Goals
- **S1:** Organize information.
- **S2:** Apply knowledge of the characteristics and basic needs of living things.

Next, Julian set the tone so that students would launch into their tasks with purpose, increasing the likelihood that all students would arrive at the same learning destination together. He enlisted his principal's assistance to make this happen, surmising that a real audience would help the tasks feel as important as they were fun. To provide such a setup, Dr. Layman wrote the following note to Julian's students:

> Dear Kindergartners,
>
> I have heard from Mr. Dankel that you want a new tank for your class goldfish. That sounds like a big responsibility! Keeping goldfish healthy in a fancy tank takes a lot of work. I know you've been learning in science about goldfish's basic needs. I'll come visit you at the end of the week. Maybe you can convince me that you're ready for that tank!
>
> Love, Dr. Layman

Finally, Julian designed task options using Sternberg's triarchic intelligence theory. This focus helped him narrow his options from four to three, guided his construction of the tasks so that their differences were purposeful, and helped him craft more deliberate instructions for students (see Figure 7.5, p. 268).

Figure 7.5 | Instructions for Goldfish Task

We need to convince Dr. Layman that we understand the basic needs of goldfish, their environment, and how to take care of them well. Choose one of the following tasks to show her you know what it takes! (Complete your planning guide before you start working.)

1. *Dear Dr. Layman [analytical]:* Write a letter to Dr. Layman that persuades her to let you take the class goldfish home for the summer. Make sure you show her that you understand the basic needs of a goldfish and explain what you will do to do the best job of taking care of the goldfish.

2. *How to Take Care of a Goldfish [practical]:* Create a "How to Take Care of a Goldfish" booklet that you can show Dr. Layman. Start by taking photos with a partner that show all the important things to do to keep a goldfish healthy. Then write a detailed how-to that anyone could follow. Remember to include all the things fish need to live and have fun.

3. *Amazing Tank! [creative]:* Plan and sketch an amazing tank for goldfish to live in. Remember to include all the things that goldfish need to have their basic needs met. Label the parts of your tank and be ready to explain how the parts help meet the fish's needs. Then take your plan to the block area, build your tank, and be ready to explain how it helps meet the basic needs of a goldfish.

When students completed their work, they presented it to the principal in mixed groups (with each task represented). The students were even more engaged and invested than were the previous year's students, and they emerged from the experience with a firm grasp of the learning goals and a shared sense of accomplishment and purpose.

Source: Tasks developed by Lara Galicia and Frances Collins, Willard Elementary School, Evanston, IL. Used with permission.

Part 2:

Tools and Strategies

Entry Points

What It Is:

This strategy developed by Howard Gardner can be used to pique students' interest in a new unit of study or topic. Gardner (2006) tells us to "think of the topic as a room with [multiple] doorways into it" (p. 139) and design tasks accordingly.

How It Works:

1. The teacher uses the points of entry (as few as two or as many as six) to create differentiated learning tasks according to interest (Gardner, 2006) (see planning template in Figure 7.6):

   » *Storytelling:* Use story or narrative structure to communicate ideas or principles.
   » *Giving reasons:* Use reasoning, argument, or cause-and-effect relationships.
   » *Thinking big:* Pose or think about big questions about life and the world; emphasize big ideas and meaning making.
   » *Activating senses:* Emphasize sensory or surface features; activate sensitivities.
   » *Working with numbers:* Provide or look at data; examine numerical relationships.
   » *Using experience:* Use a hands-on approach, dealing directly with materials (physically or virtually), simulations, and personal explanations.

2. Students choose a task to complete alone or with a partner and share their work in small groups or with the whole class.

What It's Good For:

- Hooking students into content or topics that typically lack intrinsic appeal for young students
- Offering "tastes" or "previews" of lesson activities that all students will do throughout the unit
- Designing "Jigsawed" tasks or brief small-group discussion prompts

Tips:

- Because the primary goal is to motivate students, Entry Point tasks need not all be aligned with the same learning goals. Having students share their work exposes them to a variety of Entry Points and gives them a broad initial perspective of the unit topic(s).
- You can assign Entry Points, but it's better to let students choose from limited options (e.g., four) or have students come up with their own Entry Point tasks after they have experienced a few.
- Entry Points is also a useful framework for planning learning activities or assessments that will be used throughout the unit, either as differentiated tasks or as tasks that all students will complete.

Figure 7.6 | Entry Points Planning Template

Concept/Topic/Text: _____

Storytelling _Use story or narrative structure to communicate ideas or principles._	**Giving Reasons** _Use reasoning, argument, or cause-and-effect relationships._
Thinking Big _Pose or think about big questions about life and the world; emphasize big ideas and meaning making._	**Activating Senses** _Emphasize sensory or surface features; activate sensitivities._
Working with Numbers _Provide or look at data; examine numerical relationships._ **1, 2, 3, 4, 5**	**Using Experience** _Use a hands-on approach, dealing directly with materials, simulations, and personal explanations._

Classroom Examples:

Figure 7.7 offers examples of Entry Points across the content areas.

Figure 7.7 | Entry Points Examples

Math Entry Points: Patterns		
Storytelling Tell a story using this number pattern: 3, 2, 1, 3, 2, 1 . . . . (e.g., *Three friends went to the store and bought two apples . . . .*). Or use your own number pattern. Continue the pattern until you reach the end of the story.	**Giving Reasons** Look at the three number patterns on the sentence strips. These patterns involve adding or taking away from each number to get the next number in the pattern. Can you guess the rule for each pattern?	**Thinking Big** Draw or tell your answers to these questions about patterns: • Is this a pattern? Why or why not? • Who uses patterns? • What can patterns help us do?
Activating Senses Use markers or paints to create three different color patterns. Show your patterns to a friend and see if he or she can tell you what the patterns are. Let your friend know if he or she is right and explain why or why not.	**Working with Numbers** Count how many different patterns you see around our classroom. Use the camera/tablet to take pictures of each one, and be ready to tell why you think each one is a pattern. **1, 2, 3, 4, 5**	**Using Experiences** Choose a certain number of items from each of the small tubs (e.g., buttons, paper clips, Unifix cubes, pom-pom balls) to make three different patterns. Don't add or take away objects once you've made the first pattern.

Geography Entry Points: Directions	
Storytelling Tell the story of how you get to your room, the playground, or school. Use words like *near/far*, *above/below*, *left/right*, and *behind/in front*.	**Giving Reasons** Make a chart that shows how these words help us every day: *near/far*, *above/below*, *left/right*, and *behind/in front*. Put the words in one column and write or draw their uses in the other column.
Activating Senses Think about a monster, ice cream, and a puppy. Share where you would rather be for each of them: Near or far? Above or below? On the left side or the right side? Behind or in front? Why?	**Using Experiences** Draw and label a map of how you get to your room, the playground, or school. Label your map with words like *near/far*, *above/below*, *left/right*, and *behind/in front*.

Science Entry Points: Earth's Movements

Giving Reasons

Look at the pictures depicting where the Big Dipper constellation appears in each of the four seasons. What differences do you note about its changing position? What reasons can you give for this?

Activating Senses

Look at the pictures of how the shadow of a tree changes during the day. Re-create that pattern in four drawings of yourself at the same times of day. Now choose two additional times of the day. Draw what you think your shadow might look like at those times. Explain your guesses.

Working with Numbers

Look at the table of sunrise and sunset times for one week in each season. What patterns do you notice within each week? How do the times differ from season to season?

1, 2, 3, 4, 5

Using Experiences

Think about how dark or light it is when you wake up in the morning in the summer and in the winter. How about at dinner time and bedtime? Explain what is different about how dark or light it is in each season.

ELA Entry Points: Heroes

Storytelling

Make up a new story starring your favorite cartoon or book hero. You can sketch or write the main points of your new story.

Giving Reasons

Why do kids like your favorite cartoon or book hero? Explain, list, or draw the traits this hero has and why you think they make him or her so popular.

Activating Senses

When you think of your favorite cartoon or book hero, what do you see in your head? What do you smell? What tastes does the hero make you think of? What kinds of textures do you feel? Write or draw your answers.

Using Experiences

What have you seen your favorite cartoon or book hero say and do? How does what he or she says or does make you feel? Use words or pictures to share some of this hero's actions and words and explain how they make you feel.

TriMind

What It Is:

A strategy for designing instructional and assessment task choices that appeal to analytical, practical, and creative thinking

How It Works:

According to cognitive psychologist Robert Sternberg (Sternberg & Grigorenko, 2007), the human intellect comprises three sets of abilities—thus, the triarchic theory of intelligence:

- *Analytical:* The ability to analyze, compare/contrast, see the parts and the whole, examine cause and effect, and think in linear and logical-sequential ways. The kinds of abilities measured on most standardized tests. Think: *Hermione Granger*
- *Practical:* The ability to put ideas into action, apply knowledge and skills to the real world, execute tasks efficiently, and engage in on-the-spot problem solving. Think: *Ron Weasley*
- *Creative:* The ability to imagine possibilities, think outside the box, innovate, invent, dream, ask insightful questions, propose novel solutions, or intuit. Think: *Harry Potter*

Generate three tasks—all aligned with the same learning goals—that appeal to creative, practical, and analytical thinkers. Then present those tasks as options to students.

What It's Good For:

- Helping more students be successful in school
- Differentiating the thinking process according to student learning preference
- Designing unit or lesson "hooks," creating individual or group-oriented sense-making tasks, or generating summative assessment choices

Tips:

- In practice, analytical, practical, and creative are types of *thinking* and do not themselves dictate a particular kind of product. For example, creative tasks should emphasize innovative and fresh thinking but do not require artistic responses. Therefore, begin to design tasks by looking at the *thinking* represented in each Sternberg intelligence preference (see Figure 7.8) rather than by selecting a "product."
- After using the prompts from the TriMind Template (see Figure 7.9, p. 276) to generate three tasks (one for each intelligence preference), present those tasks as *options* to students; don't diagnose students' thinking styles and assign the tasks accordingly.

- Instead of labeling the tasks with their associated intelligences, present them as numbered options. That way, students will select the task (rather than the label) that appeals to them most.
- If the analytical task is critical for all students to complete, have them do so, and then use practical and creative tasks as follow-up or transfer task choices.
- Letting students choose their task most of the time heighten their investment. If you want students to step outside their typical preference, it's generally better to do so once they're more familiar with the content in the unit of study.
- It is wise to strive for a balance of analytical, practical, and creative teaching methods and examples in a given unit of study, even if you're not using TriMind to provide differentiated task choices.

Figure 7.8 | Designing Tasks According to Sternberg Intelligences

Sternberg Intelligence	Consider first, "What kinds of thinking can the task emphasize?" . . .	. . . Not "What kind of product?"
Analytical	Comparing, analyzing, critiquing, evaluating, seeing the parts and the whole, using criteria, judging, thinking logically, sequencing, ranking, defending	~~Make a Venn diagram.~~
Practical	Putting to use, adapting, making practical, applying to real-world situations, translating ideas for an audience, demonstrating, teaching, convincing	~~Design a how-to booklet.~~
Creative	Making new or unusual connections, inventing, innovating, synthesizing, predicting, transforming, making metaphors or analogies	~~Draw a picture.~~

Source: From *Differentiation in Middle and High School: Strategies to Engage All Learners* (p. 217), by K. J. Doubet and J. A. Hockett, 2015, Alexandria, VA: ASCD. Copyright 2015 by ASCD.

Evaluation Criteria:

When using TriMind as an assessment, create a rubric that will assess students' performance. When developing criteria for success, think back to the learning goals for the task. No matter which of the three options students complete, what must they demonstrate that they understand, know, and are able to do? Think about evaluating students' grasp of these learning goals (LGs) rather than the products they create, as well as what "expert," "developing," and "novice" levels of demonstration would entail. See Figures 7.19 and 7.20 at the end of this chapter for two possible evaluation tools.

Figure 7.9 | TriMind Template

Subject/Grade: _____   Lesson/Unit Topic: _____

Learning Goals		
Understanding Goals: **Knowledge Goals:** **Skill Goals:**		
Analytical Task Prompts	**Practical Task Prompts**	**Creative Task Prompts**
• Show the parts of _____ and how they work together to achieve _____. • Explain why _____ works the way it does. • Diagram how _____ affects _____. • Identify the key parts of _____ and tell why each part is important. • Present a step-by-step approach to _____. • Analyze/evaluate/assess _____. • Compare and contrast _____ for an audience of _____ to show that _____ is better suited for _____. • Justify/defend the position that _____.	• Demonstrate how someone uses _____ in his or her life or work. • Show how we could apply _____ to solve this real-life problem: _____. • Based on your own experience, explain how _____ can be used for _____. • Here's a problem at school: _____. Using your knowledge of _____, develop a plan to address the problem. • Apply this lesson in _____ to your life [or this situation/context]. • [Teacher decides what career might use this skill and devises a situation asking the student to assume that role and use the skill in context.]	• Find a new way to show _____. • Use unusual materials to explain _____. • Use humor to show _____. • Invent a new and better way to _____. • Make connections between _____ and _____ to help _____ understand _____. • Become a _____ and use your "new" perspectives to help _____ think about _____. • Create a new _____. • Design an approach to or interpretation of _____. • Imagine what it would feel like to _____.
Analytical Task Idea	**Practical Task Idea**	**Creative Task Idea**

Classroom Examples:

Figure 7.10 offers several TriMind examples across the content areas.

Figure 7.10 | TriMind Classroom Examples

Math: Number Sense
Understanding: Numbers help us understand our world better.   **Knowledge:** Numbers from 1 to 10   **Skill:** Explain how numbers are used in the real world.

Analytical	Practical	Creative
Decide which number you think is most important. Make a list (words or pictures) of your reasons for why that number is the most important.	On your way home from school today, notice all the different places you see your favorite number. How does it help you when you see it?	Imagine that your favorite number is running for "Number President." What might that number say to prove to people that he or she is the best?

Continued

Figure 7.10 | TriMind Classroom Examples *(continued)*

Squares and Rectangles

Understanding: Students will understand that a square is a rectangle, but a rectangle is not a square.

Knowledge:
- Students will know the properties of a rectangle and of a square.
- Students will know that rectangles and squares share certain properties.

Skills:
- Students will be able to differentiate between a rectangle and a square.
- Students will be able to compare and contrast the properties of a rectangle and a square.

Analytical	Practical	Creative
Compare and contrast the properties of a square and the properties of a rectangle. • Examine the given square and rectangle and list the properties you notice for each. • Create a trifold poster where each outside section lists the properties that belong only to a square or only to a rectangle. • In the middle section of the poster, list the properties that the two quadrilaterals share and include the mathematical thinking involved in distinguishing one from the other. • Provide a corresponding visual representation to go with each property listed.	Show how we could apply the properties of squares and the properties of rectangles to solve this real-world problem: You are an architect asked to design a rectangular building. Your blueprint of the building ends up looking more square-shaped. • Using your knowledge of the properties of squares and rectangles, develop an argument to defend how your square-shaped building is, in fact, a rectangle. • In your argument, include details on possible alterations that could be done to make the building rectangular without also being square.	Create a new way of explaining the similarities and differences between a rectangle and a square through a skit where Quadrilateral Quincy is confused about his identity. • Your two-act skit should incorporate the properties of a rectangle and a square. • The first act should tell the story of Quadrilateral Quincy meeting Rectangle Rachel and seeing the ways they are the same (share the same properties). • The second act should tell the story of Quadrilateral Quincy meeting Square Sammy and seeing the ways they are the same (share the same properties). • In the end, Quadrilateral Quincy must decide if he is a rectangle or a square based on the shared properties he saw.

Source: Jenny Tashjian, Chesapeake City School District, Chesapeake, VA, and Katie O'Brien, Loudoun County School District, South Riding, VA. Used with permission.

ELA: Opinions and Reasons
(To be used with Mo Willems's *Don't Let the Pigeon Drive the Bus*)

Understanding: To get someone to agree with your opinion, you have to give good reasons.

Knowledge: Terms: *opinion*, *reason*

Skills:
- Distinguish between convincing reasons and unconvincing reasons.
- State and support an opinion.

Analytical	Practical	Creative
Evaluate the Pigeon's reasons. What was his most convincing reason and why? What was his least convincing reason and why? Give him some specific pointers to help him give better reasons.	Which of the reasons in the Pigeon's opinion have people used with you? How well did those reasons work? Explain. What kinds of reasons usually work best on you and why?	Roughly storyboard a new book in which the Pigeon uses more effective reasons than he did in the previous book. Include an "author's note" that explains your choices.

ELA: Setting

Understanding: Story elements are interdependent.
Knowledge:
- Definition of *setting*
- Elements of a given story

Skills:
- Analyze setting for its effects on other story elements.
- Compare the effects of time and place on other elements of a story.

Analytical	Practical	Creative
Make two charts: one showing all the changes that would result from a change to the story's place and one showing all the changes that would result from a change to the story's time. Make a case for which is more important—place or time.	What if this story happened today in our town? List all the changes that would occur in the other story elements. Include an explanation of which changes would result from the different time and which would result from the different place, and which of the two would have a bigger effect.	Imagine that this story was set in another time or place (your choice). Outline or rewrite the new story incorporating these setting changes. Explain why you made the choice you did.

Continued

Figure 7.10 | TriMind Classroom Examples (continued)

Social Studies: Communities		
Understanding: Compromise is a way we can cooperate. **Knowledge:** Definitions of *compromise* and *cooperation* **Skills:** • Explain how to cooperate. • Give examples of compromise.		
Analytical	**Practical**	**Creative**
Pretend a new student joined our class. Write a role-play dialogue of you explaining to the new student what the rules are for how students in the class cooperate with one another. Be sure to talk about compromise. Give examples.	Choose your favorite piece of school playground equipment. Create a poster that will show through words and pictures how students can cooperate to share this piece of equipment. Be sure to show examples of compromise.	Pretend you are our classroom clock. Write a letter to our class that describes what you notice when you watch students cooperate. Be sure to give examples of ways you see students compromise.

Source: Lindsay Kookoothe, Hammerschmidt Elementary School, Lombard, IL. Adapted with permission.

Social Studies: Rules and Laws		
Understanding: People need rules and laws in order to solve problems in a community. **Knowledge:** Types of rules and laws **Skills:** • Identify the relationship between problems and solutions. • Explain and defend a law.		
Analytical	**Practical**	**Creative**
Make a list of school problems that need solutions through rules. Include at least five ideas on the list. Then rank the problems from most important to least important. Write an argument that gives good reasons for why you ranked the problems the way you did. Then create a list of similar problems in our community. Do all of these have laws? How could you find out?	Pick a rule or a law in a community that you think is particularly important for our community to have. Write the law at the top of your paper. Draw a picture of what might happen if people didn't obey it. Write an advice letter to other kids telling them what might happen to the community if the law or rule isn't followed or is broken.	Create a story or comic strip about a community situation that needs a new or better rule or law. Start by deciding what the problem situation is and who or what is causing it. (Tip: the problem should be related to a rule or law not being followed.) Either in your story or in a separate paragraph, explain what new or revised rule or law would prevent or solve the problem in the situation, and why.

Source: Patti Satz, Evanston/Skokie School District 65, Evanston, IL. Adapted with permission.

Plant Parts

Understanding: The parts of a plant are interdependent; when something happens to one part of the plant, the whole plant is affected.

Knowledge: The parts of a plant and their functions (jobs)

Skill: Explain the parts and functions of plant parts.

Analytical	Practical	Creative
Identify the key parts of a plant, the parts' functions, and the effect that each part has on the life of the plant and its survival.	Show how knowing the parts of a plant and their functions could help people understand how best to care for them in different kinds of weather.	Make connections between the parts of a plant and the parts' functions, and the parts of the human body and their functions.

Animal Migration

Understanding: Animals migrate in order to meet their needs.

Knowledge: Animals' traits and needs

Skill: Trace an animal's migratory path and explain why it follows that pattern.

Analytical	Practical	Creative
Find two animals that share a similar migration pattern. Chart their similarities and differences. Be sure to include information on each animal's characteristics, habitat(s), adaptations, needs, migratory path, and movement time frames, as well as the reasoning behind these facts. Include an explanation as to why you think these two animals share the same migratory pattern.	*National Geographic* magazine has asked you to research the migratory habits of [animal of your choice]. They would like you to share your findings with other scientists *and* to offer them recommendations about the best manner of observing in the future. Be sure to include information on the animal's characteristics, habitat(s), adaptations, needs, migratory path, and movement time frames, as well as the reasoning behind these facts. Include a "how to" checklist for future scientists to use in their research pursuits of this animal.	You have just discovered a new species of [animal of your choice]. You have been given the honor of naming this creature and sharing your discovery with the scientific world in a presentation. Be sure to include information on this newly discovered animal's characteristics, habitat(s), adaptations, needs, migratory path, and movement time frames, as well as the reasoning behind these facts. Include a picture of the animal detailed enough that other scientists will be able to recognize it.

RAFT

What It Is:

A strategy for creating differentiated performance tasks, originally developed to help teachers think about and plan for teaching different kinds of writing (Buehl, 2009; Santa, 1988). RAFT encourages students to assume a *role* and consider their *audience* while working in a *format* and examining a *topic* from their chosen perspective. RAFT is motivating because it gives students choice, appeals to their interests and learning profiles, and can be adapted to student readiness levels.

How It Works:

The teacher designs several horizontal "strips" or role-audience-format-topic combinations that serve as assignment options from which students can select.

1. Decide on the purpose for using the RAFT (e.g., for sense making, as a Jigsaw task, as a summative assessment).
2. Craft learning goals for the assignment in terms of what students should understand, know, and be able to do.
3. Generate several RAFT assignment choices for students to choose from that will get them to the same learning goals (for an assessment) or that, in combination, will address all the content you want to address (for a strategy like a Jigsaw).
4. When using a RAFT as an individual assessment, design all RAFT combinations so that no matter which option students select, they can be evaluated with the same criteria or rubric (see pp. 306–307).

What It's Good For:

- Designing introductory unit hooks, sense-making activities, Jigsaws, homework tasks, applications and extensions, or summative assessments
- Helping students consider multiple perspectives and develop empathy
- Introducing novelty and encouraging creativity in student work

Tips:

- Present RAFT options in an at-a-glance grid format so that students can quickly identify the essence of the task; for substantial RAFTs, provide more specific guidelines for each option, if needed.
- To guide students to success as they complete their RAFTs, provide a list of required vocabulary or add a fifth column outlining points of discussion for each RAFT grid.
- Students can "mix and match" roles, audiences, formats, and topics as long as the mixing and matching generates a task or situation that makes sense and is aligned with the learning goals. Students can also create their own RAFT tasks. Use a blank row to invite this option.
- The best RAFTs have clear knowledge, understanding, and skill goals, with all activities leading to those same goals. However, sometimes learning goals are not met in

full until students have shared their RAFT tasks in the large group or in mixed small groups. This is most often true if students are not completing the RAFT as an individual assessment.

- Figure 7.11 offers ideas for crafting RAFT prompts. Although these lists are not exhaustive and do not necessarily include content-specific examples, they may get the creative juices flowing during the design process. Potential "topics" are not included, as those are usually content-dependent.

Figure 7.11 | Ideas for Crafting RAFT Prompts

Possible Roles	Possible Audiences	Possible Formats	
• Advertiser	• Ad agency	• Advertisement	• Newspaper
• Architect	• Art lovers	• Argument	• Painting
• Art critic	• Attendees	• Article	• Petition
• Artist or illustrator	• Author	• Award	• Photographs
• Author (biographer, poet)	• Board members	• Banner	• Play
• Botanist	• Boss	• Biography	• Poem
• Campaign manager	• Business	• Blog	• Poster
• Candidate	• Celebrities	• Blueprint	• PowerPoint presentation
• Cartographer	• Committee	• Brochure	• Program
• Cartoon character	• Community members	• Calendar	• Public service announcement
• Coach	• Concert-goers	• Campaign	• Puppet show
• Designer	• Consumers	• Cartoon/comic strip	• Puzzle
• Detective	• Editor	• Catalog	• Questionnaire
• Engineer	• Experts	• Chart	• Quiz show
• Film critic	• Family members	• Dance	• Recipe
• Filmmaker	• Friends	• Debate	• Research project
• Geographer	• Government or elected leader	• Demonstration	• Review
• Historian	• Historical figures	• Diagram	• Scrapbook
• Interviewer	• Judge	• Dialogue	• Skit
• Inventor	• Jury	• Diary	• Song
• Journalist	• Library visitors	• Dictionary entries	• Speech
• Lawyer	• Museum visitors	• DVD	• Story
• Manager	• Neighbors	• Editorial	• Survey/data
• Museum director/ curator	• Packaging company	• E-mail exchange	• Television script/show
• Musician (composer/ lyricist)	• Pen pals	• Film	• Terrarium
• Nutritionist	• Publisher	• Flowchart	• Test
• Photographer	• Radio listeners	• Game	• Testimony
• Researcher	• Readers (newspaper, magazine)	• Graph	• Text message conversation
• Scientist (all fields)	• Relatives	• Interview	• Time line
• Statistician	• School staff	• Invention	• Tour
• Travel agent	• Students	• Machine	• Trial
• Zookeeper	• Travel agents	• Magazine	• Video
	• Viewers	• Map	• Website
	• Visitors	• Model	
		• Mural	
		• Museum exhibit	

Source: Adapted from *Differentiation in Middle and High School: Strategies to Engage All Learners* (p. 234), by K. J. Doubet and J. A. Hockett, 2015, Alexandria, VA: ASCD. Copyright 2015 by ASCD.

Important Design Notes:

- Although there is no "right" number of options, all tasks must be meaningful and aligned with the learning goals. It's better to have 3 high-quality options than 10 low-quality ones.
- High-quality RAFTs don't need to sound cute or funny. Strive first for alignment with clear learning goals. Often, writing out each task as a short paragraph can help ensure that the task is challenging and achievable and makes sense.
- Students can include a reflection to accompany their products, as in Figure 7.12.
- Use the template in Figure 7.13 to design the RAFT.

Figure 7.12 | "Inside My Mind" RAFT Reflection Sheet

Directions: Complete and turn in this form with your RAFT assignment.

- Task choice:

- Why did you choose this task rather than the other options?

- Explain what your work reveals about the big idea or essential question.

- The portion of this assignment I am most proud of is _____ because:

- I _____ did or _____ did not do my best work on this assignment. Explain:

Figure 7.13 | RAFT Planning Template

Learning Goals Understanding/uniting idea: Knowledge: Skills:	This RAFT is a(n) ☐ Introductory activity/hook. ☐ Sense-making activity. ☐ Anchor Activity. ☐ Jigsaw task. ☐ Assessment.	Evaluation criteria:
	This RAFT is differentiated for student ☐ Readiness. ☐ Interest. ☐ Learning profile. (Check all that apply.)	When and how this RAFT will be used:

Role	Audience	Format	Topic

Evaluation Criteria:

If using the RAFT as an assessment, create a rubric that will assess students' performance. When developing criteria for success, think back to the learning goals for the task. No matter which of the options students complete, what must they demonstrate that they understand, know, and are able to do? Think about evaluating students' grasp of these learning goals (LGs) rather than the products they create, as well as what "expert," "developing," and "novice" levels of demonstration would entail. See Figures 7.19 and 7.20 at the end of this chapter for two possible evaluation tools.

Classroom Examples:

Figure 7.14 offers examples of RAFTs across the content areas.

Figure 7.14 | RAFT Classroom Examples

Shapes
(CCSS.MATH.CONTENT.1.G.A.1)

Spoken directions: You will choose one RAFT task to show what you know about comparing shapes and one task focused on seeing and describing shapes in the world around you. Be sure to use the words related to shapes on the math word wall.

	ROLE Pretend you are . . .	AUDIENCE . . . talking to . . .	FORMAT . . . in a . . .	TOPIC . . . about . . .
Comparing shapes	A shape	Another shape	Series of cartoons	How you are alike and different
	A spokesperson for 2D shapes	A spokesperson for 3D shapes	Conversation (audio-recorded)	What you can do that they can't
Seeing and describing shapes in the world	A toy	Toy Museum visitors	Speech (written or audio-recorded)	The "shapes" you're in (detailed description of all of your shapes)
	A teacher	Kindergartners	Set of directions (words and map)	A shape scavenger hunt

Making Inferences
(CCSS.ELA-LITERACY.RL.4.1)

Directions: Choose one of the rows below and make inferences in order to complete the task. Make sure you support your inferences with evidence from the text.

Role	Audience	Format	Topic
Character	Reader	Secret note	Here are some things the author didn't tell you about me . . . .
Character	Another character	Apology	Excuse my actions. Here's why I did it . . . .
Character	Author	Dialogue	Why did you make me do this? Please explain.

Equivalent Fractions
(CCSS.MATH.CONTENT.3.NF.A.3)

Directions: Choose and complete one row from the three below. You should use a combination of words, pictures, and numbers in your response. Be sure to show all of your work so that we can see your mathematical thinking.

Role	Audience	Format	Topic
1/4	1/8	Comic strip	I don't care if you LOOK bigger, I AM bigger!
1/2	2/4	Role-play	Can you believe we're twins?
1 3/5	8/5	Conversation	I think we're the same. Let's see . . . .

Point of View
(CCSS.ELA-LITERACY.RL.5.6)

Directions: Choose the row that interests you most. You can begin by planning your writing, or you can begin writing right away if you have a good idea. Make sure you use specific images in your writing (just like Shel Silverstein did).

Role	Audience	Format	Topic
Narrator	Reader of Shel Silverstein's poem "Sarah Cynthia Sylvia Stout Would Not Take the Garbage Out"	Phone call	Did I get it right? Tell me what you pictured when you read the poem!
Sarah Cynthia Sylvia Stout		Note	Here are all the reasons why I did not take the garbage out.
Sarah's neighbor		Another poem	Here's how Sarah's garbage affected my house!

Continued

Figure 7.14 | RAFT Classroom Examples (continued)

Goods and Services in a Community

Spoken directions: We know that people in a community depend on goods and services to meet their needs and wants. Use your knowledge of these providers of goods and services in a RAFT task of your choice. No matter what you choose, be sure to show *how and why the good(s) and service(s)* are important to people. You will share your work in groups of three to four with peers who chose different tasks than you did.

Role	Audience	Format	Topic
Newspaper writer	Readers	List and explanation	The 10 most important providers of goods/services in our community
Provider of goods/services	Another provider of goods/services	Letter	Why I am more important than you
Provider of goods/services	Community	Speech	Why you can't do without me
Yourself	Newcomer to the community	How-to list or set of directions	How to get your needs met in our community

Historical Events and Figures

Directions: You have been assigned an event or a figure from the historical period we're studying. Choose one row and use a combination of words and pictures to complete the task. Be sure to use evidence from our informational texts and other resources in your answer.

Role	Audience	Format	Topic
News reporter	Today's television audience	News report script	New facts discovered about this historical event/figure: _____
This historical figure: _____	Future inhabitants of _____	Series of drawings	What my life was REALLY like
This historical figure: _____	Friend/family member	Letter of apology	They got it all wrong!
Inhabitants of _____ today	This historical figure: _____	Song	A tribute to you

Life Cycles

Spoken directions: We have been learning that all living things change in cycles. Now it's time for you to show what you understand about the life cycle of a butterfly. Choose one task that you think you can do best. I'll be here to help you with your work. Let's look at what the choices are . . . .

Pretend you are a . . .	. . . talking to . . .	. . . in . . .	. . . about . . .
Monarch butterfly	A caterpillar	A speech	How it will change
Tree	Children	A written story	What happened to the butterfly egg on my leaf
Teacher	A class	Picture cards	The life cycle of the butterfly in the book
Singer	An egg	A song	How it will grow and change

The Water Cycle

Directions: Choose one of the rows below and complete the task to show us all you know about the "journey" water takes in its cycle. Make sure you include all the details from our class diagram in your answer. You can use a combination of words and pictures to present your information.

Role	Audience	Format	Topic
Old water droplet	Young water droplet	"Grandfather story" of his experience with the water cycle	You ain't seen nothing yet!
Meteorologist	Science convention attendees	Speech and presentation	Tracking the water droplet—what we've discovered
The Water Police	Water public	Wanted posters	Have you seen this droplet? Don't be fooled by his various disguises!

Source: Developed by kindergarten teachers in Evanston/Skokie District 65, Evanston, IL. Used with permission.

Learning Menus

What They Are:

Learning Menus outline a variety of instructional options targeting important learning goals. Students select and complete the assignment options that most appeal to them.

How They Work:

1. The teacher articulates learning goals and creates a "menu" of tasks (appetizers, main dishes, side dishes, and desserts) that are designed to help students practice with and display their grasp of identified learning goals.
2. In most cases, students are assigned some or all of the main dishes, but they can typically choose the appetizers, side dishes, and desserts they want to focus on.
3. The menu's design works best when all options in each "course" address the same learning goals. The template in Figure 7.15 (p. 292) helps the menu designer ensure that all learning objectives are addressed through the task options.

What They're Good For:

- Organizing what students will be doing over the course of a week or unit rather than in a single lesson
- Supplementing whole-class instruction with sense-making activities (e.g., students move to menu work after a lecture or discussion)
- Acting as Anchor Activities (e.g., students move to menu work after completing other assigned tasks; see pp. 330–333 for more information)
- Serving as assessments, if designed as such (e.g., with an evaluation tool that contains assessment criteria for each key learning goal; see pp. 306–307)

Tips:

- Decide on the purpose for using the Learning Menu (sense making, Anchor Activity, assessment).
- Craft learning goals for the menu in terms of what students should understand, know, and be able to do. Decide which learning goals will be addressed in each "course." There is no need to address all learning goals in all courses; rather, you can spread them among the appetizers, main courses, side dishes, and desserts.
- Begin by designing one or more appetizers, which are opening activities that can serve as hooks for the menu. These could be introductory videos, readings, or tasks (e.g., interviews) that will get students thinking about the ideas they'll "chew on" for the rest of the unit.

Important Design Notes:

- **Main Dishes**—Create main dishes by identifying core tasks that all students should complete:
    - » The main-dish section can look the same for every student in the class, *or* there can be more than one version of the menu, each with different main-dish tasks. For example, two menus for different readiness levels could feature four main dishes: two that are common to both menus and two designed for different levels of readiness that look different in each version.
    - » Regardless of how many menu versions there are, each student will complete all of the main-dish items on the Learning Menu he or she is assigned. Each "dish" should be clearly tied to the learning objectives.

- **Side Dishes**—Design several side dishes to tackle learning goals other than those addressed in the main dishes *or* to deepen or expand the investigation of the learning goals introduced by the main dishes. Students should select a certain number of side dishes (e.g., two from a list of four), generally designed to address different interests or learning preferences.
    - » Determine the learning goal(s) that the side dishes will address or emphasize. All side dishes should address a common concept.
    - » Incorporate options based on *interest* (e.g., contextualized tasks for math); *learning profile* (e.g., Sternberg's triarchic model); or *varied products or modes of expression* (e.g., poems, flowcharts, or recordings).
    - » Allow students to select and complete the side dishes that most appeal to them.

- **Desserts**—Design several dessert tasks that students will be very motivated to complete (in other words, students shouldn't need to be convinced to "eat their dessert"!).
    - » Desserts should be appealing, engaging tasks that tap into students' interests as related to the topic.
    - » It may be useful to think of desserts as enrichment activities, in that they allow students to explore (or become exposed to) an area of interest not usually covered in the core curriculum.
    - » Desserts can range from short learning tasks to more extensive independent projects.
    - » Desserts can be included as optional activities that only some students choose to complete, *or* all students may be expected to complete at least one.
    - » In some cases, it might be appropriate for students to design their own dessert tasks.

- It may be helpful to pull appropriate tasks from textbooks or other associated resources (e.g., see math menu, p. 297).

- For all four "courses," choices can be tailored to different readiness levels. Consider—and gather, if necessary—resources (including technology) that might help students to succeed in each step.

Evaluation Criteria:

If using the Learning Menu as an assessment, create a rubric that will assess students' performance. When developing criteria for success, think back to the learning goals for the task. No matter which of the options students complete, what must they demonstrate that they understand, know, and are able to do? Think about evaluating students' grasp of these learning goals (LGs) rather than the products they create, as well as what "expert," "developing," and "novice" levels of demonstration would entail. See Figures 7.19 and 7.20 at the end of this chapter for two possible evaluation tools.

Source: Tips adapted from guidelines developed by Jane Jarvis, 2010. Used with permission.

Figure 7.15 | Learning Menu Template

Content/Topic:	
As a result of completing the assignments on this menu, students will reach the following goals:	"Course" in which each objective is assessed:
Understanding Goals:	
Knowledge Goals:	
Skill Goals:	

Courses

Focus/uniting idea	Appetizers
Learning goals and notes about readiness variations, resources, etc.	**Main Dishes**
Learning goals and notes about readiness, learning preferences, resources, etc.	**Side Dishes**
Learning goals and notes about readiness, connections, resources, etc.	**Desserts**

Classroom Examples:

Figure 7.16 offers several examples of Learning Menus across the content areas.

Figure 7.16 | Learning Menu Classroom Examples

ELA: Word Study

Learning Goals

Understanding Goals:
- **U1:** Words have family relationships with other words. (Main dishes)
- **U2:** Words enrich our ability to communicate. (Side dishes)
- **U3:** Words have "personalities." (Desserts)

Knowledge Goals:
- **K1:** Definitions and word origins of all assigned words (Main dishes)

Skill Goals:
- **S1:** Group words according to similar roots, derivations, and meanings.
- **S2:** Use personification and/or sense imagery to describe words.
- **S3:** Use words to describe daily activities.

U1 **K1** **S1**	**Main Dishes** *You must complete both of the following:* 1. *Word origins:* What language did each of your assigned words come from? Look for this information in the dictionary or online, and then record the word, its original form, and the language of its origin. Be sure to explain how we've changed it to work in our language. 2. *Word relationships:* For each of your assigned words, make a "Word Tree" to show the base ("root") word and at least four derived words. Circle the **prefix** and **suffix** in each derived word. Don't spend too long on the art, but make each word a different kind of tree, if you like!
U2 **S2**	**Side Dishes (connections to your free-reading book)** *Complete one of the following:* 1. *Hero or Villain:* Choose three of your words and decide whether each is a **superhero** or a **villain**. Does the word do "good" or do "bad"? (Or does it depend?) Use the tablet to record your video or audio explanations. Use strong reasoning and good examples in your descriptions to prove your point. 2. *Personification poem:* Choose three words from your list that are not already living things. Write a "personification poem" that brings these words to life. If you would like help, get the poem template from your teacher. 3. *Character-word match:* What fictional character (from a book, a movie, or a show) would use your words? Use the **speech balloon** template to write captions for what these characters would say when using three of your words. You can have the same character use all the words or have different characters use different words.

U3 **S3**	**Desserts** ***Complete at least one; you may complete more if you want to or have time.*** 1. *Photo album:* Take pictures of each word in action or "at work" in the classroom. Then compile a photo book (paper or electronic) using your words in the captions. Ask permission before you take a picture of a classmate! 2. *News feature story:* Write a newspaper story (on paper or electronically) about some of our daily classroom routines. Make sure to use all the words, and underline each word when you use it. You can interview classmates for this story if you would like.

Source: Some portions adapted from work developed by Jessica Hockett for the Tennessee Department of Education. Copyright 2017 by Tennessee Department of Education. Used with permission.

	Science: Food Chains (NGSS 5-LS2-1)

Learning Goals

Understanding Goals:
- **U1:** In a system, all parts must work together.
- **U2:** Change to one part of the system results in change to the other parts.

Knowledge Goals:
- **K1:** Definitions and examples of simple food webs and ecosystems

Skill Goals:
- **S1:** Discuss how systems work.
- **S2:** Explain how one organism depends on another organism to survive.
- **S3:** Compare and contrast different systems to find similarities and differences.

U1, K1, **S2**	**Main Dishes** ***Mr. Winston will assign you an ecosystem from class to study more closely. You must complete all of the following based on the ecosystem that Mr. Winston has assigned you.*** (NOTE: Mr. Winston assigns ecosystems of different complexities based on readiness.) 1. Draw the food web for this ecosystem. 2. Make sure that you use arrows to show relationships in the food web. 3. Make sure that you have included and correctly labeled all the parts. 4. Pick two organisms from your ecosystem and explain how one needs the other one to survive. 5. Find someone who has studied the same ecosystem as you and complete a "Checking Our Work" reflection sheet.

Continued

Figure 7.16 | Learning Menu Classroom Examples (continued)

Science: Food Chains (NGSS 5-LS2-1)	
U1, S1, S3	**Side Dishes** ***Complete one of the following:*** 1. Compare your main-dish food web with another system we've discussed in class (e.g., our bodies, weather, the water cycle). How is the food web like this system? How is it different? Complete a Venn diagram showing how the parts of the two systems work together in similar and different ways. 2. Find someone who has studied a different food web than you did and compare your own main-dish work with your partner's. Then complete a Venn diagram showing how the parts in your two systems work together in similar and different ways.
U2, S2	**Desserts** ***Complete at least one of the following:*** 1. Think about what you eat on a typical day. What would happen if all those food sources disappeared? What kinds of food would you have to eat to survive? Where would you find it? How would this affect your environment? Use words or pictures to tell your story. 2. Pick any food web from those we studied in class. What would happen if part of that food web disappeared? What would happen to the rest of the organisms? Tell a story about what happens to all of the other parts of the food web when one part of that food web is missing. 3. Write a letter to the creators of *SpongeBob SquarePants* explaining what they would need to change about the cartoon for it to show a real food web with all of the ecosystem's parts working together. Explain why changing any of these real parts would make the ecosystem "break" in real life.

Mathematics: Fractions

Mr. Last's Delicious Fractions Restaurant Menu

Appetizer
Bread basket: Whole-class discussion about writing word problems for fraction division

Main Dishes	Side Dishes
Complete both:	*Choose two:*
1. *Sirloin steak:* Lesson 8.5 on writing word problems [*Note:* You may complete your side dishes between your first and second main dishes.] 2. *Herb-encrusted breaded fish:* Chapter 8 review/test	1. *Green beans:* Dividing fractions worksheet 2. *Grilled asparagus:* Enrichment 8.5 3. *Roasted rosemary potatoes:* Khan Academy video and questions on dividing fractions 4. *Whipped potatoes:* Pie picture worksheet (serves two; complete in pairs) 5. *Macaroni salad:* Standards practice 8.5

Desserts
Choose one:

1. *Chocolate mousse:* Use Scratch to code a model for a dividing-fractions problem.
2. *Ice cream sundae:* Create a worksheet of dividing-fractions problems based on sports, music, or another topic of your choice.
3. *Fruit salad:* Design a poster for use in explaining how to divide fractions to other 5th graders.

Source: Stephen Last, Charles E. Smith Jewish Day School, Rockville, MD. Used with permission.

Choice Board

What It Is:

A Choice Board (also known as Think-Tac-Toe; see Tomlinson [2003]) presents task options aligned with common goals for students to select and complete in a given timeframe.

How It Works:

1. Design a Choice Board by setting up a 3x3 grid offering three sets of task options (see Figure 7.17).
2. Each of the three rows addresses a different learning goal, with the three options in each row addressing the same set of learning objectives.
3. Students choose one option from each row to demonstrate a grasp of all learning goals.
4. At the teacher's discretion, students can either work independently on the assignments they have chosen or work with others who have chosen the same options.

What It's Good For:

- Differentiating for student interest by inviting students to select the learning options that seem most appealing to them
- Differentiating for readiness and learning profile, if the teacher creates different levels of each board (readiness) or strategically positions learning options that cater to differing intelligence preferences or modalities
- Structuring Anchor Activities (see pp. 330–331) either alone or in conjunction with calendars, contracts, and other "monitoring" devices

Tips:

- When designing a Choice Board, be clear about the learning goals each student should have reached, no matter what combination of options he or she completes.
- Make sure that all activities are aligned to specified learning goals. Remember that students will choose different tasks, but those choices should allow you to assess their work against the same goals.
- Use Sternberg's TriMind framework (analytical, practical, creative) to design each row of task options.
- Have students check in after they have selected their assignment preferences. Monitor students as they work to make sure they are progressing efficiently.

Evaluation Criteria:

If using the Choice Board as an assessment, create a rubric that will assess students' performance. When developing criteria for success, think back to the learning goals for the task. No matter which of the options students complete, what must they demonstrate that they understand, know, and are able to do? Think about evaluating students' grasp of these learning goals (LGs) rather than the products they create, as well as what "expert," "developing," and "novice" levels of demonstration would entail. See Figures 7.19 and 7.20 at the end of this chapter for two possible evaluation tools.

Figure 7.17 | Choice Board Template

Content/Topic:			
Learning Goals			
Understanding Goals: **Knowledge Goals:** **Skill Goals:**			
Learning Goal	**Choice 1**	**Choice 2**	**Choice 3**

Classroom Examples:

Figure 7.18 offers examples of Choice Boards across the content areas.

Figure 7.18 | Choice Board Classroom Examples

ELA: Kindergarten Anchor Activity

Learning Goals

Understanding Goals:
- Characters in stories have traits and experiences that are much like our own.
- The words and pictures in a story can help us understood who a character is and what he or she is like.

Knowledge Goals:
- Characters are people, things, or animals that play a part in the story.
- Characters often face trouble or have problems to solve.
- Characters can be described in terms of how they look, think, feel, and act.

Skill Goals:
- Distinguish characters from other story elements.
- Make connections between characters in a story and real-life experiences.

Background: Students complete three activities from the Choice Board (one from each column) over one month to demonstrate their understanding of characters. These tasks can be completed during Daily Five rotations or other flexible timeframes, with or without teacher assistance. Students choose a sticker to place over a square on their Choice Board after completing a task. (In this example, students have read and completed mini-lessons around the book *No, David!* by David Shannon.)

What a Character!	Characters Come to Life	A Character and Me
Look at the group of pictures from this story. Sort each of the pictures on our T-Chart into Character and Not a Character. Explain why you placed the pictures where you did.	Compile a list of changes that would need to take place in our room if David from *No, David!* visited for the day: "If David came in our room, we would need to . . . because . . . ."	Draw a picture of you and your favorite character sitting at your table group working on a project. Label yourself and your character. Tell why the character would be helpful to you in your project.
Select a book from the Book Nook. Find the characters. Then find things in the book that are *not* characters, but that someone might confuse for characters. Explain your choices to an adult in our classroom.	Think about our "Read to Self" time. Based on his actions in the book, what might David do during that time? How is that different from what you do? Use those ideas to come up with some "Do's" and "Don'ts" for David.	If you could have one book character help celebrate your birthday, whom would you choose and why? Design an invitation asking that character to attend your party. Be ready to explain what the character would like about your design.
Choose a character from a book you like. Then make up one noncharacter. Draw a picture of the character and the noncharacter in the empty boxes at the bottom of your graph. Ask five friends to choose which one is the noncharacter and explain why.	Think of a character from another book who you would want to be in our class for a day. Finish the following sentence frame and draw a picture: "I would want _____ to be in our class because . . . ."	Choose a character from a book who you think is a lot like you. List or tell about that character's traits and your traits. Draw side-by-side pictures of you and the character that show how you are alike.

Source: Lisa Roeschley, Mountain View Elementary School, Harrisonburg, VA. Adapted with permission.

Math: Playing with Numbers (Kindergarten)
(Related Common Core standards: MATH.CONTENT.K.CC.C.6-7, MATH.CONTENT.K.OA.A.1)

Learning Goals

Understanding Goals
- Objects can be counted to tell how many there are (the number of objects).
- Numbers can be compared with one another.
- Addition is "putting together" or "adding to"; subtraction is "taking apart" or "taking from."

Knowledge Goals
- Terms: *greater than, less than, equal to*
- Numerals 1–10
- Addition (+), subtraction (−), and equal sign symbols (=)

Skill Goals
- Identify whether the number of objects in one group is greater than, less than, or equal to the number of objects in another group.
- Compare two given numbers up to 10, when written as numerals, using comparative terms.
- Represent addition and subtraction in multiple ways (e.g., with objects, fingers, or drawings, or by acting them out).

Background: This Choice Board can be used to structure interest-based (and/or readiness-based) practice with key mathematical concepts and skills over the course of a week or as part of an ongoing routine. The student view is featured first, followed by the teacher view. Activities are organized according to whether students complete the activity alone, with friends (after teacher demonstration), or with the teacher, but they can be rearranged according to level of student independence. If the Choice Board is displayed on a screen, students can put initialed sticky notes on their choices.

Student View (on paper or projected on screen with icons)

By Myself	*With Friends*	*With the Teacher*
Whose Is "Greater"?	**Snap It!**	**Snack Stories**
Decide who has more items in his or her collection of something.	Play this game with one to two friends who also want to play.	Add and subtract piles of healthy snacks to tell number stories.
Quick Pick	**How Many Are Hiding?**	**Storyteller**
Pick two numbers from a hat to compare.	Play this game with one to two friends who also want to play.	Invent, tell, and show your own number stories.
Roll the Dice	**What's Missing?**	**Storyteller**
Roll dice to compare two numbers.	Play this game with one to two friends who also want to play.	Use other number stories to come up with your own.

Continued

Figure 7.18 | Choice Board Classroom Examples (continued)

Math: Playing with Numbers (Kindergarten)		
Teacher View (for planning and implementation)		
Comparing Numbers	**Number Compositions**	**Number Stories**
Whose Is "Greater"? Present students with a scenario about friends who have similar collections, and provide actual collections, with items in small bags. Students' task is to count each collection and decide who has more of each thing. For example: *Zoey and Anthony each have collections of the same things: pennies, rocks, and buttons. Who has more of each one? Count and write the number of the things in each bag on the sticky notes. Use the words on the vocabulary cards* (greater than, less than, equal to) *to tell who has more and how you know.*	**Snap It!** Students work together to make different combinations for a given number (visit https://www.youcubed.org/tasks/snap-it for directions). Model the activity for students before having them play with friends.	**Snack Number Stories** • Put a pile of snacks (e.g., raisins or cereal) on the table. *Option:* Model a number story before or while the student works. • The student counts the number of items. • The student places a cut-out addition symbol next to the pile. • The student puts another pile of snacks next to the symbol and counts them. • The student takes away the symbol, puts all the snacks together, and says how many there are in one pile. Make sure to prompt the student (or another classmate) to count again to check. • The student tells a number story that fits the model while he or she is working or after he or she is done. • Repeat with other numbers, snacks, and the subtraction symbol.
Quick Pick Put *two* sets of cards containing numbers 1–10 in a hat or box. Students pull out two numbers at a time and place them on the table. *Option 1:* Students write each number on a line and circle *greater than, less than,* or *equal to* to compare the numbers. *Option 2:* Students write each number and circle the bigger number of the two or draw an equal sign between them if the numbers are the same.	**How Many Are Hiding?** Students find the missing number to complete a number sentence while seeing different representations made by other students (visit https://www.youcubed.org/ task/how-many-are-hiding for directions). Model the activity for students before having them play with friends.	**Number Storyteller** Students use cut-out addition and subtraction symbols and manipulatives to tell, act out or model, and solve number stories that use addition or subtraction. For example: *Two kindergartners were sitting at a lunch table, and three more children sat down with them. How many children were there altogether?* Use pennies or other small objects and the addition symbol to act out or model the stories. Students then draw or write out one or more of their stories.
Roll the Dice Provide each student with a set of dice that are two different colors (e.g., one black die and one white die). Students roll the dice and decide which color die has the greater or lesser number, using a sentence like "Six is greater than 4" or "Five is equal to 5."	**What's Missing?** • Each partner begins with a set of 10 paper clips, a 10-piece puzzle, or 10 markers. • Partners work individually to make a "chain" (with the clips or markers) or a puzzle that has 10 or fewer items. • Partner 1 shows his or her work to partner 2, and partner 2 writes how many are missing on a card before showing it to partner 1, who says whether the answer is correct. • Students switch roles and repeat the process.	**Number Stories from Number Stories** With guidance and support, students review number stories and pictures similar to those featured here: http://everydaymath.uchicago.edu/community/student-gallery/number-stories. Students use these examples as inspiration or models for their own number stories.

Source: Developed by Jessica Hockett for the Tennessee Department of Education. Copyright 2017 by Tennessee Department of Education. Used with permission.

Social Studies: Historical Fact vs. Fiction (George Washington)
(Related Common Core standards: ELA-Literacy.RL.1.5, W.1.1 and 1.8, and SL.1.5)

Learning Goals

Understanding Goals:
- One person's contributions can change the world.
- Authors use facts and fiction for different purposes.
- We can distinguish between fact and fiction both by using our minds (reasoning) and by consulting informational sources.

Knowledge Goals:
- A *fact* is something that is true.
- *Fiction* or *fantasy* is something that is not true ("pretend").
- Stories often combine facts and fiction.
- Biographical details of George Washington
- How George Washington contributed to the foundation of the United States

Skill Goals:
- "Explain major differences between books that tell stories and books that give information, drawing on a wide reading of a range of text types" (ELA-Literacy.RL.1.5).
- "[S]tate an opinion, supply a reason for the opinion, and provide some sense of closure" (ELA-Literacy.W.1.1).
- "With guidance and support from adults, recall information from experiences or gather information from provided resources to answer a question" (ELA-Literacy.W.1.8).
- "Add drawings or other visual displays when appropriate to clarify ideas, thoughts, and feelings" (ELA-Literacy.SL.1.5).

Background: Students complete three activities from the Choice Board (one from each column) to demonstrate their understanding of fact versus fiction. Students will have already studied biographical information about George Washington from various sources. They will also have read the book *George Washington's Birthday: A Mostly True Tale* by Margaret McNamara. Tasks are designed according to Sternberg's triarchic intelligence preferences: row 1 is analytical, row 2 is practical, and row 3 is creative.

Book Versus History	Fact and Fiction	Purpose
You are getting ready to meet with the author of *George Washington's Birthday* to explain your opinion of how she portrayed George Washington in her book. Do you think the fact portions or the fiction portions were better? Why? Give specific reasons in your explanation. You may use words and pictures or audio-record your argument. Make sure you end your discussion with courtesy.	Lane Smith wrote the book *John, Paul, George, and Ben* about important American leaders. Read or listen to (on You-Tube) either the part about Paul Revere or the part about Benjamin Franklin. On a T-Chart, make a list (using words or pictures) of things you think are facts and things you think are fiction. Then check your work by listening to a short biography of your historical figure (get the recording from your teacher).	In the United States, George Washington's birthday is celebrated as a national holiday. In some places, students get the day off from school. Do you think George Washington's contributions were important enough for *everyone* to have a day off from school? Express your opinion, supporting it with specific facts about George Washington's life. You may write, draw, or record your explanation.
Your friend is getting ready to read *George Washington's Birthday*. You know that this book has both facts and fiction in it. Write a note to your friend about the three most important facts and the three most "pretend" things in the book. You may make a list or write in letter format and use words or pictures. Make sure you end your note with a friendly sign-off.	Make a slideshow to teach your classmates about a person you think is an important leader in our country, community, or school. Use pictures and captions on each slide. On half of the slides, include captions that are facts. On the other half of the slides, include captions that are fiction. Present your slideshow to two classmates to see if they can find your fiction.	Think about everything we have learned about the ways George Washington helped form the United States. List the five that you think are the most important. Now think of five things *you can do* to make a difference in your family, neighborhood, classroom, or school. Make a book of words and pictures showing how you are like George Washington in the ways that you help.

Continued

Figure 7.18 | Choice Board Classroom Examples (continued)

Social Studies: Historical Fact vs. Fiction (George Washington)		
Book Versus History	**Fact and Fiction**	**Purpose**
Imagine you are George Washington reading *George Washington's Birthday*. What do you think about the way you are being portrayed? Is it true or not? What parts do you like best? What parts do you like least? Write or record a note to our class from George's point of view. Be sure to end with a convincing last statement.	Think of a real person who is very important in your life and make up a story about that person. Your story—like *George Washington's Birthday*—should contain both facts and fiction. Plan your story as a storyboard, and then make an "answer key" that tells whether each frame in your storyboard is fact or fiction.	Pretend you are George Washington's horse. You've been through everything together, and you know all the important things George has done. Now you're in a new barn with new horses who don't know anything about George. Explain how he helped form the United States. You may use words, pictures, or a recording to tell your tale.

Science: Animals and Their Surroundings
(Related NGSS Standards: 2.LS2.1, 2.LS2.2)
Learning Goals
Understanding Goals: • All living things interact in interdependent systems. • Living things depend on their environment. • Living things depend on other living things. **Knowledge Goals:** • Traits of where animals live • Specific ways that animals depend on their surroundings and other living things to survive • Changes in the environment that can affect animals (e.g., temperature, deforestation, wildfires, pollution, salinity, drought, land preservation) **Skill Goals:** • Compare how different animals depend on their surroundings and other living things to meet their needs in the places they live. • Predict what happens to animals when the environment changes.
Background: This Choice Board can be introduced following or in conjunction with lessons on animal structures and functions and animals' habitats. The teacher can show students the whole board so that they have a "big picture" sense of what they'll be doing and can preview tasks. During implementation, students work with the *Research* tasks first, followed by the *Game Time!* tasks and concluding with the *Roles, Please!* Tasks.

Science: Animals and Their Surroundings

1. Research *How do different animals depend on their surroundings and other living things to meet their needs?*	2. Game Time! *How does this animal depend on its surroundings and the living things in it?*	3. Roles, Please! *What happens to the animal when there are changes to its environment?*
☐ Choose a NEW animal to research using teacher-provided resources. Record your findings using the same model/organizer we used together (to compare how different animals depend on their surroundings and other living things). Be ready to share what's unique about how this animal depends on its environment.	☐ Create a matching game with (1) pictures of things in your chosen animal's surroundings and (2) words that tell what the animal depends on each thing for. After your teacher has checked your work, choose a partner to play your game.	☐ Put yourself in the shoes of a scientist who studies this animal. Use your expertise to come up with a way to teach kids (in this grade/class) about what could happen to the animal when there are certain changes to its environment.
☐ Choose a NEW animal to research using teacher-provided resources. Record what you find out about how the animal depends on its surroundings and other living things in your own way—*different* from the model/organizer we used together. Be ready to share what's unique about how this animal depends on its environment.	☐ Design a Guess Who? Game by coming up with 8–10 clues about your chosen animal, based on how your animal depends on its surroundings. Arrange your clues from "hardest" to "easiest." After your teacher has checked your work, choose a partner and read your clues to him or her in order. Let your partner guess the animal after each clue.	☐ Imagine that you are a member of a wildlife protection group. Focusing on human activities that can affect your animal's environment, record a brief video that explains what people should (or should not) do so that the animal's habitat is not harmed. Make sure you give information about how changes to the animal's environment could affect the animal.
☐ Choose a NEW animal to research using teacher-provided resources. Record your findings using the blank fishbone, T-Chart, or web model/organizer. Be ready to share what's unique about how this animal depends on its environment.	☐ Play a game with yourself: Come up with as many answers as you can for this prompt: The way that [this animal] depends on ___ for ___ is like how humans depend on ___ for ___. Share your ideas with your teacher, and then with a partner. Have the partner give you other ideas for the human comparison.	☐ Act (or write or record) a conversation between a parent animal and his or her child about changes to the environment that could affect their habitat. Have the child ask the questions and the parent answer the questions.

Source: Developed by Jessica Hockett for the Tennessee Department of Education. Copyright 2017 by the Tennessee Department of Education. Used with permission.

Evaluation Tools for TriMind, RAFT, Learning Menu, and Choice Board Assignments

The evaluation tool in Figure 7.19, designed for use in the primary grades, can be used by both the teacher and the student to guide feedback, conferencing, and improvements.

Figure 7.19 | Primary-Grades Performance Checklist

In this task . . .	YES!	For the most part	Needs work
You have included all of the parts of your task.			
Your ideas and information are correct.			
Your ideas and information are complete.			
You have stayed on topic the whole time.			
You have "talked to" the right audience.			
Your work looks and sounds "polished."			
Other:			

What are you most proud of?	How can you keep growing?

The template in Figure 7.20, designed for use in the upper-elementary grades, can be used by the teacher to develop learning goal–focused rubrics.

Figure 7.20 | Upper-Elementary Rubric Template

	Expert	Developing	Novice
Criterion 1: LG Assessed:			
Criterion 2: LG Assessed:			
Criterion 3: LG Assessed:			
Criterion 4: LG Assessed:			
Criterion 5: LG Assessed:			

8 | Considering the Nuts and Bolts of Implementing Differentiation

Part 1:

How Do I Manage It All?

This book has presented differentiation through the analogy of a road trip. Many teachers buy into the value of taking that trip and can picture themselves embarking on the journey and implementing the strategies associated with it. At the same time, they can also picture the roadblocks that may pop up along the way to make the journey a bumpy one. Those roadblocks—often related to management—may give teachers qualms about even attempting to take the trip. Accordingly, this chapter examines such potential roadblocks to differentiation and offers ways to work around them.

Roadblock #1: Launching Differentiated Tasks

In a differentiated classroom, there will be times when not everyone is doing the same thing. What's the best way to talk about that with students? Recall from Chapter 1 how crucial it is to help students redefine what *fair* means. Using activities like Doctor Visit (p. 37) can stimulate open discussion about the purpose and benefits of engaging with differentiated tasks and experiences. Keep in mind that dialogue about fairness will mean little if the tasks fall short of the criteria for being respectfully differentiated (see Chapter 6, pp. 213–214).

When launching differentiated tasks or experiences, decide whether all students need to see all the tasks. Consider giving a common set of directions for the process that all students or groups need to use in addition to task-specific directions (see, for example, Check, Please! in Part 2 of this chapter). Display and briefly review the common protocol before giving students or groups time to digest their own tasks, circling to check in and clarify as needed.

If possible, limit initial verbal explanations to a general overview of the task and process—for example, "Based on your Exit Slip responses yesterday, you'll be working at different stations to make and record measurements. Each of you has a set of items to measure and questions to answer. Tomorrow, you'll be sharing your findings and thinking with classmates from other stations." Then provide crystal-clear, detailed electronic or paper-based directions at each station.

When creating directions for differentiated tasks, anticipate potential questions and areas of confusion by using a checklist format, providing visuals, or offering recorded instructions for groups to listen to on tablets (this is particularly helpful for students who are learning to read or who are learning English). Consider instituting a "1-2-3, Then Me" format in which students get one minute to go over the directions silently, two minutes to discuss the directions with one another, and three minutes to plan their approach to the task before being allowed to ask you for assistance.

If students do need to know more specifically what everyone else is doing, be sure to describe the tasks in a respectful, even engaging, way. There's usually no need to label tasks in a way that draws attention to differences in student readiness (e.g., Level 1, Level 2, and Level 3), but there can be value in giving groups equally engaging titles (e.g., ninjas, rock stars, and superheroes) or in framing each task with the role that students will adopt. Both the Looking/Listening Lenses strategy featured in Chapter 4 (pp. 129–131) and the Entry Points strategy highlighted in Chapter 7 (pp. 270–273) provide examples of using real-world jobs and professions to design and name tasks.

When letting students choose from several options or introducing a preference-based task, it can be tempting to spend a large chunk of time reviewing and clarifying directions and expectations for every option. It is more efficient, however, to give students time to discuss their understanding of and questions about the tasks with one or two peers before pulling the group together to clarify and answer questions. A major advantage of this approach—even with tasks that aren't differentiated—is that students "work" to make sense of and own the task rather than tuning out or waiting for the teacher to spoon-feed them the tasks.

Roadblock #2: Getting Students into Groups

As discussed in Chapter 1, using varied and flexible groupings over the course of a lesson, week, and month can go a long way toward helping students see differentiated tasks as a way of life rather than as an anomaly or a special event.

To this end, consider abandoning a single seating chart and instead making a flexible chart that depicts whichever arrangement suits the purpose for the day (e.g., a small-group discussion seating chart or a "map" for circle time). Some teachers have students create "nameplates" on index cards at the beginning of the year and use these to show students where to sit each day or for a set of days. Other teachers put students' pictures or names on magnets and move those into different configurations on the board to display the groups for each activity. Still other teachers let students choose where to sit most days as a "home base" and change seating as needed for instructional purposes.

One community-building strategy that also helps students get accustomed to working with different peers is Fold the Line (see Chapter 1, p. 21). Students quickly line up according to a characteristic (e.g., birth month and day) or a preference (e.g., how much they like hot dogs, with hot-dog haters at one end and hot-dog lovers at the other). Students can form groups of the desired size with classmates standing near them in the line, or you can "fold" the line and group students from there. This approach removes the stigma of getting into a new group because the teacher is always mixing things up.

Keep in mind that just because students are sitting next to each other doesn't mean they know how to talk to one another. They need modeling and practice in how to make social transitions between stations or how to talk to their partners during Think-Pair-Share discussions. Volunteers can act out example and nonexample conversations with "elbow partners" to emphasize what respectful and productive discussions sound like. Posting or providing sentence frames as scaffolds for group dialogue improves the quality of conversation even more. This kind of upfront investment pays off when students are able to move and converse efficiently.

Finally, it's important to *show* (not just *tell*) students the nuts and bolts of how to move into and operate in groups. No matter their age, students need rehearsal and explanation (in words and through visuals) for where they should move and how quickly. Conducting dry runs can provide fun, low-stakes opportunities for students to practice adjusting desks or chairs quietly and efficiently. This might involve using a stopwatch to time students as they move into groups and challenging them to beat their own best times from previous practice runs.

Roadblock #3: Ensuring Task Completion and Quality

A common concern regarding differentiated group work—or any group work, for that matter—is how to ensure that students stay on task and actually complete what's been assigned to them in a timely manner and at a high level of quality. The first principle for ensuring task completion is to design the task so that it is *actually a task*. Simply putting students in groups and asking them to "discuss" something is a recipe for disaster. By contrast, when students are asked to work on producing something specific to turn in, present, or share with another group, they are less likely to linger in off-task conversations. Products should require *all* group members' participation or contributions.

Steps to increase accountability might involve placing a poster in the middle of the table on which everyone records or "graffitis" ideas or having each student complete a graphic organizer (see Figure 8.1, p. 314). If each group is doing a different version of the task, announce that you will collect one paper per group, to be revealed at the end of the activity. When time is up, use random criteria, such as "group member with the shortest hair" or "person with the birthday closest to the teacher's" to

Figure 8.1 | ThinkDots Response Organizer

Side #	Question Key Word	Teammate Name	Response
1			
2			
3			
4			
5			
6			

determine whose paper it will be. Regardless of the strategy used, every student should be responsible for what happens in groups during task completion.

Another key to success is to make students partners, if not primary agents, in keeping tabs on their progress, the room's noise level, and the time. Keeping track of progress should be straightforward: if groups are producing something tangible, they can see what they have left to do. For monitoring noise level, a tool like Bouncy Balls (www.bouncyballs.org—accessible in Google Chrome) provides a visually appealing way to gauge the volume of the room. An online digital stopwatch or another easy-to-see timer is useful for tracking time. It's also a good idea to give students a bit less time than might be necessary in order to build a sense of urgency; when time is running low, check in to see if groups require more (e.g., "Fist to five—how many more minutes do you need?"). If some groups finish before others, have a next-step question or task or an Anchor Activity (see Roadblock #6) ready for students to tackle.

Finally, it is important to establish and enforce a clear protocol for bringing together a variety of responses during group work. Often, a group task requires students to pool the answers they came up with during an independent task. Students need a clear procedure for how to reach consensus in cases like these. Simply asking students to "compare answers" will most likely lead students to follow the "majority rules" principle or to let one student fill in all the answers. Instead, set up a *system* for students that requires them to listen to every group mate, defend their responses, and honor outliers. The Check, Please! protocol on page 328 is one structure for encouraging this kind of collaborative work. This system works when the whole class has completed the same work (in class or at home) as well as when different groups of students have completed different tasks (in class or at home).

Roadblock #4: Facilitating Group Work

Describing tasks clearly and requiring some measure of accountability are important first steps in helping learners become self-sufficient thinkers and workers. Of course, if we want students to be successful, then we must scaffold this process.

The first step is to provide instructions both to the whole class (see Roadblock #1) and to small groups (see Roadblock #3) that help students *begin work without teacher help*. Design tasks in such a way that you can be "off-limits" for the first five minutes. This frees you up to attend to any unanticipated bumps in the road while students use their directions and their resources to begin. Admittedly, your first attempt at this may be difficult; students won't *really* believe that you won't be available. But once they see it's "for real" and figure out that they can succeed in your absence, their perseverance will improve.

It's also important to design tasks in such a way that the teacher will be available to work with every group at some point. This may mean structuring tasks to meet with some groups at the beginning of their task, some midway through completion, and others toward the end (see the math Agenda upgrade on pages 221–225 for an illustration of this principle). This practice not only improves the flow of group work from a management perspective but also removes the stigma of a teacher-led group. When a teacher works exclusively with any one type of group (e.g., struggling learners), he or she may send status messages that are difficult to undo. All students, regardless of readiness, need teacher guidance and support, especially when the tasks are appropriately differentiated. There will be times when the first meeting should be with students who have the most advanced task.

Sometimes group work falters simply because students don't know, like, or respect one another—yet. This is another reason why the full-class community-building activities described in Chapter 1 are crucial. Small group–level bonding moments also reap rich rewards in helping groups gel, release tension, and exercise courtesy. This might involve using an opening prompt like "Before you start, share your favorite ice cream flavors" or asking students to fist-bump one another as they complete each step of the task. Consider displaying fun anchor questions for students to discuss once they are finished. Anchor questions keep students from drifting into uncharted work or conversations while providing a structure that lets students build connections with one another. They can relate to the task (e.g., "Where have you seen this kind of math used in real life?") or appeal to general interests (e.g., "If you could have any animal for a pet, what would it be and why?").

Roadblock #5: Fostering Independence

In many ways, a differentiated classroom relies on letting students exercise a certain degree of age-appropriate independence. Unfortunately, even at this early stage in their schooling, students may have developed a certain degree of dependence on adult help. Thus, it is especially important to help students develop skills of independence rather than to eliminate situations that require autonomy. Even the youngest children can work on their own with appropriate supports, provided they have been taught and are expected to do so. This last part is key; even students who seem self-sufficient will sometimes need guidance and routines for knowing how and when to seek assistance. The following strategies work toward accomplishing these ends.

- *Recorded Directions and Responses* are simple but powerful tools for helping students work independently, especially those who do not yet read or write due to age, language development, or special need. Many classrooms have a few MP3 players, tablets, or computers assigned to them; if not, most school media centers provide such technology for checkout. Using the voice memo function or a similar app, teachers can record themselves giving directions to students (groups or individuals) and house the device at the station or center where students complete their tasks. Teachers of older children can also post the voice recordings to class websites for students to access themselves. Students can play back these directions when needed, rewinding to listen to trouble spots or simply to hear the teacher's voice explaining the entire procedure again. Similarly, students can record themselves reading aloud, delivering responses to prompts, pronouncing words, and so on. Teachers can listen to young children's responses played back directly from the devices; older children can upload their responses to a class website. Use of digital recordings allows teachers to both deliver directions and listen to students' responses in a flexible manner, freeing them up to work with other small groups or individuals. It also allows students to complete tasks in a more flexible fashion, as they do not have to wait for the teacher to be their audience in person. Although the prospect of asking young children to use technology may seem intimidating, teachers are often surprised by how savvy children are with technology, which seems to become more user-friendly with each passing day.
- *Resource Files* provide another good way to offer assistance to students when the teacher is not immediately available. Resource Files include information about routines and problem-solving techniques that are used on a regular basis. Resource Files can be placed in a prominent area of the room and can consist of either physical files (i.e., in file folders) or digital files (e.g.,

bookmarked websites or computer desktop folders). These files can outline steps for troubleshooting (e.g., what to do when your screen freezes, how to push through writer's block) or provide other problem-solving "helps" (e.g., graphic organizers, peer editing protocols, rubrics).

- *Hint Cards* operate in much the same way as Resource Files but are usually lesson-specific resources. A teacher who is teaching a lesson on creating graphs, for example, can most likely anticipate the trouble spots and questions that will arise. Accordingly, she can create several Hint Cards that contain the probing questions she would ask students when they get stuck. It usually works well to have different Hint Cards for different "sticking points" in the process. Students must first use these resources before consulting the teacher; when they do, the teacher can use the prompts on the Hint Cards to talk students through getting "unstuck." Over time, this strategy will reinforce students' own problem-solving skills.

- *Colored Cups*, a signaling strategy, helps students develop the habit of relying on their own resources before seeking outside help. In this system, each group receives a stack of three colored cups (ideally, green, yellow, and red to mimic traffic light colors). When the green cup is on top, the group is working fine. When the yellow cup is displayed, students need help, but they can continue working on another step while they wait for assistance. The red cup signals a group's need for immediate attention. As the teacher circulates, he or she monitors the cups and works with groups according to the urgency indicated by the color displayed. On first implementation, teachers may find that students regard every question as a "red" question; this provides yet another opportunity to foster group independence by telling a group that its question is "yellow," pointing to another step the students can work on in the teacher's absence, and waiting a few minutes before returning to assist them.

- *Question Chips* help students self-monitor to determine whether their questions about tasks are "must-ask" or "could-find-out-myself." Each group— or each student, if they are working independently—receives a limited number of Question Chips (e.g., pennies, paper squares, or game chips). These chips represent the number of times students can call on the teacher for help. If students have only three chips, they are less likely to automatically raise their hands and summon the teacher for easy-to-answer questions. This doesn't mean that the teacher should refuse to answer important content-based questions; rather, Question Chips help students determine whether their queries truly relate to understanding or are simply procedural in nature. If a question is procedural, the teacher can hint, "Do you really want to use a chip on that question?" and even indicate a general area of the directions where students can find the answer.

Each of these strategies must be taught and modeled in order to run smoothly; students don't develop independence overnight. With guidance and experience, however, they will develop it over time.

Roadblock #6: Using Time Wisely

Time is teachers' most valuable resource. Understandably, they may be hesitant to spend extra time up front to launch a new initiative or make changes to class structures. However, like any other worthwhile venture, developing a differentiated classroom requires teachers to *invest* time in order to *save* time. In other words, time spent on establishing routines and teaching students how to use resources and move into groups efficiently gains back time in a smoothly running classroom. In general, the following procedures require some rehearsal before teachers can expect them to run self-sufficiently:

- *Introducing new strategies.* Some of the strategies discussed throughout this book will be unfamiliar to both teachers and students. Just as it's a good idea to have students do dry runs of getting into groups, it also makes sense to practice these strategies in a low-stakes or content-free situation before using them to connect students with content. For example, a RAFT can be used to review classroom routines and procedures. Students can engage in a ThinkDots activity to get to know one another or build community (see Figure 8.2). Quartet Quiz (see pp. 142–143) is a useful tool to help students generate questions about an upcoming classroom event or project. Introducing strategies in a stress-free manner allows students to relax into the strategies when they are used with content.
- *Spacing things out.* Introducing multiple strategies simultaneously can produce overload and confusion, so it's a good idea to spread out introduction of the routines outlined in this chapter slowly, over the course of the first week or two of school. Implement strategies deliberately and purposefully. Start with a few and allow students time to get comfortable with those before adding more to the rotation. Remember, too, that a differentiated class does not spend the entire time working in small groups or on differentiated tasks. Responsive classrooms use a combination of whole-class, small-group, and independent configurations.

Finally, it's important to acknowledge—and plan ahead for—the reality that kids will most likely complete tasks at different rates. Because of the nature of the authentic tasks students tackle in a differentiated classroom (as well as the different ways students do so), teachers should expect some degree of ragged finish time. As a rule, it's advisable to have a bit too much planned for a task, with the understanding that the last step

Figure 8.2 | Community-Building ThinkDots

If you could have any job in the world, what would it be and why?	Pretend you've been given some magic seeds. When you plant these seeds, and say the magic words, you can grow *anything* (not just plants). What would you grow?	Imagine you could invite any three people or characters—real or pretend—to a party. Whom would you invite and why?
You have been sent to a deserted island and can bring only three things with you. What will you bring? Why?	You've been given a special power to trade places with a famous person or character for one day. Whom would you trade places with? Why?	You won a million dollars! What would you do with all that money? Give us details!

or two will be "forgiven" if students don't get there. Even with preemptive planning, however, students will inevitably finish at somewhat different rates, so it's a good idea to have and communicate a plan for "what's next."

- *Anchor Activities.* One way to steer students who finish early toward continued meaningful engagement with content is to use Anchor Activities (Tomlinson & Imbeau, 2010). Anchor Activities engage students in tasks that are important to the discipline but that may not be related to the primary content focus on a particular day. Anchor Activities may involve practice with important skills, extension of vocabulary, or investigation into areas of interest. Agendas (see Chapter 6, pp. 244–245) and Learning Menus (see Chapter 7, pp. 289–297) provide efficient structures for delivering such tasks. Other examples of Anchor Activities are included in Part 2 of this chapter (pp. 330–333).

- *Coming Soon!* Once in a while, students may become so engrossed in a task or experience such major setbacks that they fall behind in their work. An important principle in a differentiated classroom is that "getting there" is more important than the time of arrival. Teachers can send this message by asking students to complete a Coming Soon! note when they are unable to meet the original deadline (see Figure 8.3, p. 320). This structure ensures that the student who is asking for the extension recognizes the importance of the task and takes ownership for its completion. It also sends the message that the teacher is flexible (within reason) and is invested in students' success.

Figure 8.3 | Coming Soon!

> ### *Coming Soon!*
>
> Dear _____ [teacher's name],
>
> I know that _____ [name of task/project] is due on
>
> _____ [day/date]. May I please have some extra time
>
> to turn it in? Here's why:
>
>
>
> I will turn it in on _____ [proposed day/date].
>
> Thank you for taking the time to read and think about my request.
>
> Your student,
>
> _____

Roadblock #7: Figuring and Reporting Grades for Differentiated Tasks

When it comes to grading, teachers are generally interested in reporting several categories of information: where the student is relative to content goals or standards (*performance*); how far the student has come with respect to those goals or standards (*progress*); and how the student is doing with certain work habits and dispositions (*process* [Guskey, 2011; Guskey & Bailey, 2010]). Most teachers mix these factors into a single grade so that each category is indistinguishable from the others. Although performance, progress, and process are related and likely influence one another, they are not *synonymous,* and lumping them together into one grade adds neither value nor clarity. Figuring and reporting these "3 Ps" separately—each as a grade or as grades and other ways of reporting—goes a long way to communicate better and more accurate information to stakeholders. It also makes sense for differentiated classrooms, whose teachers are rightfully concerned about seeing success in terms of performance, growth, and behaviors exhibited in pursuit of goals (Tomlinson & Moon, 2013). Ideally, the report card should be structured to provide information in this way (Guskey & Bailey, 2010; O'Connor, 2009).

Even in the absence of a multidimensional reporting system, it's important to make sure that a grade is based on student performance against clear standards. When it comes to figuring this grade, experts advise drawing from and weighting evidence that students have produced *later* in the learning cycle rather than earlier (Brookhart, 2008; Guskey & Bailey, 2010; Marzano, 2000; O'Connor, 2009; Tomlinson & Moon, 2013). The reasoning is simple: work that a student does toward the end of an instructional sequence around given learning goals paints a more accurate picture of what the student has learned. Therefore, summative assessments should be the primary data source for determining and reporting grades. This is one reason why it's important to have more than one kind of summative assessment in and across units. Formative assessment should be weighted less, with students' responses on Entry or Exit Slips, in-class sense-making tasks, and some kinds of practice work excluded from a grade altogether.

Remember that any differentiated tasks that you *will* grade should be aligned with the same learning goals and evaluated using the same criteria or rubric. Most of these will be differentiated for interest or learning profile (see Chapter 7 for examples). The vast majority of tasks that are differentiated for readiness are formative activities that shouldn't be counted in the performance grade.

Roadblock #8: Differentiating in a Certain Grade Level or Subject

Many teachers wonder—to themselves or aloud—if differentiation is more difficult or necessary in a particular grade level or subject area. Comments like these might sound familiar:

- "I see how this could work in writer's workshop, but not in math."
- "This seems easy with kindergartners, but not 5th graders."
- "Differentiation is really more of a remedial/ELL/special education/gifted thing than something for the regular classroom."

As with many endeavors, change often seems easier for other people than it does for us. No research suggests that certain disciplines, ages, or programs are inherently optimal for or resistant to differentiation. There is, however, plenty of research (Brighton, Hertberg, Moon, Tomlinson, & Callahan, 2005; Elmore, 2004; Fullan, 2007; Kennedy, 2005; Tyack & Cuban, 1995) that speaks to how difficult it can be to change instructional and assessment practices—including those that are connected to or reflect differentiation.

In truth, even when teachers believe that different students should be doing different things, they may be unable to envision how it would play out in their classroom. Learning Stations (see pp. 326–327) offer a flexible structure for giving students access to materials, tasks, and teacher instruction that are targeted to their specific needs. Whether a teacher decides to tackle two stations—or five—with or without a co-teacher, stations offer a palatable entry point for teachers of all grade levels to confront the logistical considerations of the differentiated classroom.

Many teachers can better "see" how to implement and manage differentiation in a subject or with a given population when they have high-quality examples that they can envision transferring to their own classrooms. For that reason, this book includes such examples across a range of grade levels and subject areas that can inspire and encourage teachers to grow and upgrade their approaches.

The Bottom Line

Let's face it: classroom management is hard, good classroom management is harder, and classroom management that facilitates differentiation calls for an incredibly sophisticated range of skills. Building those skills takes practice, and no teacher will every truly "finish" developing them. But, over time, every inch of progress adds up to miles of growth, both in teachers' efficiency and in students' self-sufficiency. For all teachers, the growing pains of managing differentiation are a part the never-ending, evolutionary process of understanding whom, what, and how to teach.

A Management Upgrade

Joshua Lawrence has been teaching for eight years. He loves his job and his students, and with his school's recent focus on differentiated instruction, he has been more than willing to experiment with changing his practice. Still, sometimes it is challenging for him to anticipate what will work and what won't. In an upcoming lesson, he wants to experiment with grouping. Josh's students have worked in groups before, but he and his fellow PLC members have all decided to try using *differentiated* groups.

Before Upgrade

For Josh's lesson, he's decided to have the groups work on different tasks that correspond with their varying readiness levels. Josh's tentative plan follows:

1. On Monday, when the students come to class, he will tell them that they'll be working on several different activities. Right now, he's not quite sure who will be in which group. He's thinking it might be best to let the students choose their groups.
2. Next, he'll describe all the activities to the whole class so that all students will understand the directions and what's going on in other groups. He will announce that every student must participate in completing the group's assigned task, but that he wants the students to collaborate on the work.
   » If he decides to have students choose their own groups, he'll let them find friends with whom they want to work and settle in a spot of their choice.

> » If he decides *not* to let students choose their own groups, he'll let them know which group they will be working with. Then they can find their group mates and find a place in the room to work.

3. Next, he'll ask each group to send a member to pick up the written directions for its work. The directions advise students to be sure to get materials that will help them with their particular task.

4. If students need him, they can come ask him for help. As students finish their work, they will bring it to him. He will grade it overnight so they can see how they did. If a group doesn't finish the work, it will have to turn it in unfinished.

After Upgrade

Josh's PLC met to talk through each teacher's upcoming experiment with using differentiated groups. They were all trying different strategies, and as his colleagues shared in turn, Josh realized that his plan blurred the lines between readiness and interest differentiation. Because his tasks were going to be differentiated by *readiness*, he needed to *assign* students to their groups, not let them choose. He would use a work sample he had just collected as a formative assessment to determine those groupings and tasks. He based his four groups on four common errors emerging from student work and decided that he would concentrate on asking students to correct those errors.

When it was Josh's turn to share his lesson plan, he sought his colleagues' advice on how to move students efficiently into readiness groups. Not only did his team members provide insights on how to address that issue in Josh's lesson, but they also brought up other potential trouble spots across all of their plans, including how to give directions, ensure accountability, and manage questions. After consulting their school's professional development resources and collaboratively working through their roadblocks, all team members emerged with new and improved versions of their differentiated lesson plans.

Josh's upgraded implemented plan follows:

1. On Monday, when the students came to class, Josh announced that they would be working in groups to get more practice with the skills they had worked on last week.

2. He explained that when students moved into their groups, they would find directions (both written and recorded on tablets) at their stations.

3. Displaying a "1-2-3, Then Me" poster he had created, Josh explained that students were to listen to and read the directions silently for one minute, spend two minutes discussing the directions with one another, and take three minutes to plan their approach to the task before being allowed to ask Mr. Lawrence for help. All of the materials students would need

were located at their stations, including their own work samples from the previous week and the Check, Please! protocol that each group had to complete as it worked through its corrections in a collaborative fashion.

4. After a representative from each group repeated these directions back to Josh, he told them that he believed they were ready to move into their groups.

5. Based on the formative assessment results, Josh had designed four tasks that he named according to the four Teenage Mutant Ninja Turtles (a favorite cartoon of many of his students):
   » Michelangelo (Mikey)—orange mask
   » Leonardo (Leo)—blue mask
   » Raphael (Raph)—red mask
   » Donatello (Donnie)—purple mask

6. Using the mask colors as his "key," Josh drew colored squares on the board and grouped magnets with students' pictures affixed to them to display who was in each group. He had also marked each station in the room with its proper mask color. He gave students 30 seconds to find their picture on the board and determine which "turtle" they were, 15 seconds to find their corresponding area of the room, and another 30 seconds to get to their stations and begin the 1-2-3 process.

7. After students finished their 1-2-3 powwows, Josh distributed three Question Chips to each group and told them to begin work. He stopped by each group periodically for status checks and to provide further directions if he found that students were experiencing common areas of confusion.

8. When groups finished their work, they followed their tasks' final directions, which told them to paperclip their work together with the Check, Please! sheet on top, have the person with the shortest hair bring the pile to Mr. Lawrence, and move to their choice of center (math games, free reading, or journaling). The centers served as Josh's Anchor Activity that day.

9. Only one group didn't finish, but the students marked their progress and submitted their work as instructed. They had completed enough for Josh to see what "clicked" for them and what would need more work.

As he walked his class to lunch, Josh reflected on the success of the lesson but realized that students would need much more practice with the routines before things would run smoothly. He briefly chatted with a colleague in the cafeteria who was left with the same impression. They high-fived each other, congratulating themselves on a winning effort and vowing to continue practicing until their classes became well-oiled machines.

Source: Scenario adapted from *The Common Sense of Differentiation: Meeting Specific Learner Needs in the Regular Classroom* (Facilitator's Guide) (p. 77), by C. A. Tomlinson, J. Hockett, & L. J. Kiernan, 2005, Alexandria, VA: ASCD. Copyright 2005 by ASCD.

Part 2:

Tools and Strategies

Learning Stations

What They Are:

Learning Stations are a structure for managing simultaneous instruction, learning activities, or tasks. Stations can be used to introduce topics or concepts, provide experience with or review material, or practice or reinforce ideas and skills.

How They Work:

The teacher plans the desired number of Learning Stations around clear learning goals. The plan for using the stations should address the following questions:

- How are the stations related or connected? What is the overall goal or purpose of the stations?
- What will students do at each station (complete a task, use a technological tool, receive peer-to-peer instruction, engage with the teacher)?
- With whom will students do what they need to do (with the teacher, with a peer, by themselves)?
- How will students know what they need to do—what process will they need to use or follow (task card; an individual menu, guide, or agenda; directions on a screen; recorded directions; a chart)?
- Where will the materials for station tasks be located (at the station, with the students)?
- Will all students visit all stations?
- How will students transition between stations? Will students rotate at specific times, or will they "wander" among stations?
- How long will each rotation/visit take? How will students know?
- Are the stations temporary or ongoing?

What They're Good For:

- Giving students "tastes" or previews of a new topic
- Providing interest-based activities
- Addressing a large amount of content in a short amount of time
- Giving students practice with specific concepts and skills
- Providing targeted instruction following modeling
- Providing feedback following formative assessment
- Reviewing content or practicing skills (e.g., in preparation for a summative assessment)
- Structuring feedback on or facilitating the sharing of student work
- Providing a structure to give all students access to limited resources, technology, and so on
- Providing a system for working with small groups

- Serving as a strategy/model for co-taught classrooms; both teachers can facilitate instruction in stations, one teacher can "float" while the other instructs at a station, or both teachers can "float."

Tips:

- Make sure that the number and focus of stations are meaningful and manageable.
- Tools for guiding students through station tasks include colored folders with directions inside, bookmarked websites or instructions on electronic devices, station guides for students to carry, and the use of QR codes.
- Establish a signal and a system for moving from station to station.
- Practice rotating among stations in a content-free manner to introduce the strategy; review rotation procedures periodically.
- Introduce stations that will be part of an ongoing routine gradually so that students get used to the expectations and the kind of work they will be doing at the stations.
- Use a card similar to the one in Figure 8.4 for student self-monitoring and teacher auditing.

Figure 8.4 | Station Report Card

Check, Please!

What It Is:

A protocol for having students check differentiated homework assignments

How It Works:

1. The teacher checks to make sure each student has completed the assigned homework.
2. Students who have not completed the work go to a designated area of the room to finish the assignment. The teacher floats to provide guidance and feedback and informally assess.
3. Students who completed the homework convene in groups of four to check their responses for agreement/disagreement.
4. All students mark each answer for agreement/disagreement and, when necessary, provide explanations of why an answer is wrong and how to make it right.
5. Students sign the Check, Please! form indicating agreement, staple the four papers together, and turn them in.
6. The teacher spot-checks and "grades" one assignment per set.

What It's Good For:

- Checking any assignment that has been differentiated (works for any subject, but especially math) and that students can self-check (e.g., spelling, vocabulary)
- Structuring discussion around any task that students completed independently and are meeting to go over or analyze, even if the assignment has not been differentiated
- Teaching students how to interact with one another
- Discussing text-dependent questions

Tips:

- Start by using the protocol with homework or tasks that have *not* been differentiated.
- When using the protocol with differentiated homework or tasks, it's not necessary to have 10 different assignments or problem configurations. Having two or three assignments differentiated by readiness is sufficient in most cases. It's OK to have more than one group checking the same assignment.
- Keep the groups small (three to four students).

Classroom Example:

See Figure 8.5 for a protocol that student groups can use, especially when they are first learning the process.

Figure 8.5 | Check, Please! Protocol

Team Members: _____

Today's Leader: _____

Overview:

- You and your fellow team members will engage in a conversation around your responses on the task that you each completed independently.
- The goal is to compare your responses and work through any differences you have by talking about how you [*solved the problem/resolved the issue/made sense of the text*], and why.

1. Has everyone in your group completed the task?
   - ☐ YES. (Go on to step 2.)
   - ☐ NO. (Ask the person to let the teacher know.)

2. Begin with the first [*question/part/problem*]. Does everyone have the same response?
   - ☐ If YES, go on to the next [*question/part/problem*].
   - ☐ If NO . . .

   Do *NOT* assume that one person is wrong and everyone else is right! Challenge one another!
   - Talk through your response! Have each person share how he or she arrived at his or her conclusion or solution.
   - If you still don't agree, use your resources (e.g., whiteboards, texts, notes, blank paper) to have one person walk through the thinking behind his or her responses for everyone as the group talks it out.
   - It's everyone's responsibility to make sure that your group arrives at consensus—even if you agree that you don't know, aren't sure, or disagree!

3. Use the same process for each [*question/part/problem*].

4. *Complete this step only if directed to do so by your teacher!* Check your answers with the [*key/model/ exemplar*] provided. If your team's response differs from that on the [*key/model/exemplar*], determine why and how you differ. If you believe that your team's response is actually more on target than that in the [*key/model/exemplar*], include a defense/an explanation of your reasoning.

5. When you're finished, staple all the responses together. *Make sure that the version that represents your group's consensus is on top!*

Consensus Check:
- ☐ We reached consensus on all [*questions/parts/problems*].
- ☐ We did not reach consensus on the following:

   Here's why:

Source: Inspired by the classroom of Linda Armbruster in Rockwood (MO) School District, as featured in *The Common Sense of Differentiation: Meeting Specific Learner Needs in the Regular Classroom,* 2005, Alexandria, VA: ASCD. Copyright 2005 by ASCD.

Anchor Activities

What It Is:

A strategy developed by Carol Ann Tomlinson and colleagues (Tomlinson, 2014a; Tomlinson & Imbeau, 2010), Anchor Activities have students engage in meaningful work related to core curriculum that students engage in independently during class on an ongoing basis (e.g., throughout a unit, over a month, in a grading period, or longer). Anchor Activities "anchor" students in important and motivating tasks *and* anchor the teacher's efforts to manage differentiation.

How It Works:

- The teacher provides structured tasks for students to complete at various "ragged" or down times in the classroom (e.g., after tests or quizzes or while waiting for the teacher), as part of a routine or rotation, or on dedicated "catch-up" days.
- Although Anchor Activities can themselves be differentiated, they are principally a mechanism for supporting differentiation. Figure 8.6 shows a four-stage model for using Anchor Activities to launch differentiation.

Figure 8.6 | Using Anchor Activities to Launch Differentiation

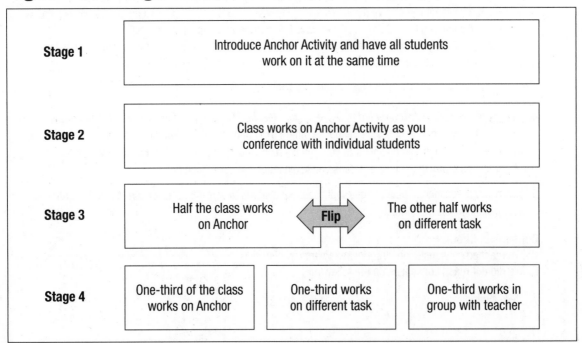

What It's Good For:

- Making sure that students are productive when they have completed other assigned tasks
- Giving students a chance to work on something that would be "nice" to do but is difficult to get to in the regular curriculum

Tips:

- Anchor Activities work best when
  - » Expectations are clear.
  - » Tasks are taught and practiced prior to use.
  - » Students are accountable for on-task habits and task completion.
  - » They have a choice component.
  - » Students look forward to them.
  - » Students have the prerequisite skills needed to complete them.
- Use the form on page 330 as a guide for planning Anchor Activities.

Examples:

- The following can make good Anchor Activities, provided that they are purposeful and interesting:
  - » Independent reading or writing
  - » Skill practice
  - » Math or vocabulary games
  - » Tasks on a Contract, an Agenda, or a Learning Menu
  - » Tasks at Learning or Interest Centers
  - » Computer-based or online programs or learning apps
  - » Ongoing projects
- Story Starter Ideas (see Figure 4.12, p. 150) can be posted and used as an Anchor Activity, either to generate story ideas or write stories from the ideas.
- Writing BINGO (see Figure 8.7, p. 332) can be tailored by the teacher or student to align with a certain content focus or meet readiness and interest needs. The number and kinds of options should be grade level–appropriate. A BINGO like this can also be delivered via an online platform like Padlet and linked to models.
- Figure 8.8 (p. 333) shows another example of an Anchor Activity.

Figure 8.7 | Writing BINGO

Directions: Try for one or more BINGOs this month. Use appropriate technology, and make sure you have a real reason and audience for your work. Use your writing goals and our class rubric to guide your work.

B	I	N	G	O
Recipe for _____	Thank-you note from _____ to _____	Letter to the editor of _____ about _____	Directions from _____ to _____	Rules for a game that _____
Invitation to _____ from _____	E-mail request to _____ from _____ for information about _____	Letter from _____ to a pen pal, friend, or relative	Skit or scene that shows _____	Interview between _____ and _____
Article in _____ about _____	Short story about _____	**FREE Your Choice**	_____'s grocery or shopping list	_____'s schedule for _____
Advertisement for _____	Cartoon strip about _____	_____ poem about _____	Instructions for _____	Greeting card from _____ to _____
Letter to your teacher about _____	Proposal to _____ about improving or changing _____	_____'s journal for a week	Design layout for a web page on _____	Book talk about _____

Source: Adapted from *Fulfilling the Promise of the Differentiated Classroom: Strategies and Tools for Responsive Teaching,* by C. A. Tomlinson, 2003, Alexandria, VA: ASCD. Copyright 2003 by ASCD.

Figure 8.8 | Innovate! Anchor Activity

Innovate!

We have been learning about inventions and innovation through books like *Toys! Amazing Stories Behind Some Great Inventions* [Wulffson, 2000] and *Mistakes That Worked: 40 Familiar Inventions and How They Came To Be* [Jones, 1991], as well as news articles and biographies. The truth is, we *all* have ideas that could change the way people think about and do things. But unless someone pushes us, or gives us time and resources, we might not have the chance.

Over the next few months, flex your innovation and invention muscles to generate and plan your own project. Work on your ideas whenever you have downtime in class. Here's a checklist to guide you in your efforts.

☐ Come up with an idea for an innovation or invention. It can be realistic or "sky's the limit" dreamy. Either way, include the following information:

— **A sketch or mock-up (hand-drawn or computer-generated).** What does your invention look like? Annotate your visual to fully explain the parts and features.

— **The invention's purpose.** What need or want does it address? What problem does it solve, or what challenge does it help overcome?

— **The target audience.** Who is your invention intended to help? Who would use it?

— **Effects.** How will it help or improve lives? What are the potential negative effects it would have on people, the environment, other businesses, and so on?

— **Feasibility.** How feasible or "possible" is your idea? Why do you say so?

☐ Receive and respond to peer feedback.

— Select two peers from whom you would like to get feedback on your idea. Your teacher can help you choose.

— Give your peers your mock-up and explanation as well as some questions for peer feedback.

— Meet with each peer separately to receive his or her feedback.

— Revise your invention in response to the peer feedback.

☐ Receive and respond to teacher feedback.

— Give your teacher your revised sketch and write-up, as well as blank copies of the feedback form.

— Meet with your teacher to receive his or her feedback.

— Talk with your teacher about potential candidates for professional/expert feedback.

— Revise your invention in response to the teacher feedback.

☐ Receive and respond to professional/expert feedback.

— This process will vary, depending on who the professional/expert is.

☐ Finalize your work and prepare it for our Innovation Expo. Details to follow!

Conclusion:
How Can I Continue to Upgrade?

Differentiation professionalizes teachers.

—Carol Ann Tomlinson

The goal of this book has been to show through principles, metaphors, and examples that differentiation is a practical—and desirable—approach to honoring and embracing classroom diversity. At its core, differentiation is about moving all students toward and beyond common, important learning goals. Sometimes (but not always) students share a route. Other times (but not always), ongoing assessment prompts the teacher to plan two or more routes that vary according to students' readiness, interests, or learning preferences (Tomlinson, 2014a).

To noneducators, the simplicity of such descriptions makes differentiation sound easy, like something anyone should be able to do if they take a class, go to a workshop, or read a book. Teachers know that the opposite is true: differentiation is a complex endeavor that "ups the ante" on what it means to be a professional teacher. It takes time and experience to do well, and it's a journey that continues throughout a teacher's professional life.

With that in mind, this conclusion addresses a few burning questions about differentiation: how much it matters in student outcomes, whether it really is something most teachers already do, and what all teachers, regardless of expertise, can do to "stay the course" of continuous improvement.

Does Differentiation Make a Difference?

A road trip isn't worth planning or going on unless the travelers come away better for having gone on it. Along those lines, if students aren't better off—if they don't know and understand more, aren't more engaged and motivated, or aren't better equipped to do challenging and important work—then is differentiation worth doing at all? Does differentiation make a difference in student learning?

In one sense, this is an easy question for any teacher to answer. Are students more likely to experience growth in a classroom where teachers plan with differences in mind or in a classroom where a teacher treats all students as one and the same? Both research and common sense say the former environment is better for more students than the latter. Put differently, a road trip that has been planned with someone's specific characteristics in mind is probably more effective than a uniform itinerary.

Here's another way to look at it: in essence, differentiation is an approach to teaching that pulls elements from many areas of education, including neuroscience, motivation, learning and cognition, curriculum, assessment, and instruction. The principles and practices highlighted in this book are informed by the theoretical and research bases in those fields. It is beyond the scope of this book to discuss the scores of studies that support, for example, taking a concept-oriented approach to curriculum, using ongoing assessment, appealing to student interest, or employing rich and respectful tasks. But each of those practices (and others associated with differentiation) draws from a deep well of compelling research. Together, they form a solid foundation for differentiation. Further, even though implementing differentiation as a schoolwide system is complex, studies of schools that have invested time and effort to do so report positive results in student achievement and other measures (Tomlinson, Brimijoin, & Narvaez, 2008).

Don't I Already Differentiate?

This question was posed in the Introduction: Don't all good teachers *already* differentiate? It's fair to say that, yes, most elementary teachers fall somewhere along a continuum from novice to expert in practicing and applying some of the principles and practices associated with differentiation.

The content, examples, and before-and-after scenarios in this book were designed to enable the teacher-reader to "see" himself or herself on that continuum and be both affirmed and challenged in his or her current practice. One teacher may have strong management systems and routines in place but struggle with seeing the patterns in formative assessment results. Another teacher may plan elegant and engaging tasks that respond to students' readiness but feel less confident designing tasks that attend to students' varying interests. Still another teacher may find that articulating learning goals comes naturally, but fostering healthy relationships among students is a challenge. Each of these teachers has strengths and weaknesses; saying, "I already differentiate" is like saying, "I'm already as good as I'll ever need to be."

The reality is, research on differentiation shows that although many teachers buy into the idea of differentiation and testify that they "do it," differentiation is *not* commonplace, well understood, or consistently applied in defensible ways, regardless of the characteristics of the students involved (see Tomlinson, 2014b, for a brief review). Why is that?

First, consider this: there are *numerous* research-based teaching practices that are neither easy to implement nor pervasive in schools. Formative assessment, timely feedback, and cooperative learning are just a few examples (Hattie & Yates, 2014). So although it's true that, in many places, differentiation is not the norm, that doesn't mean it's impossible or a waste of time.

Another reason why differentiation is not as widespread or well-applied as one might expect is that differentiation isn't a separate set of skills in a vacuum. A teacher's conceptions of and skills with differentiation are connected to his or her knowledge of the content area, pedagogy, management, how students learn, the nature of intelligence, and the role and purpose of assessment (Brighton et al., 2005; Hockett, 2010; Moon, Callahan, Tomlinson, & Miller, 2002). In other words, how "good" a teacher is with differentiation is strongly influenced by his or her skill with other aspects of teaching. Viewed positively, this means that there are multiple entry points and avenues for teachers to keep growing.

It's also worth noting that although many schools and districts spearhead initiatives aimed at increasing teacher skill in differentiation at one time or another, these efforts often lack the kind of sustained focus and feedback that teachers need to be able to understand and apply the principles and practices of differentiation (Tomlinson & Murphy, 2015). Professional learning opportunities that balance research, rationale, relevant examples, and transferrable strategies—supported by leadership that champions long-term growth over "quick fixes"—is more likely to build all teachers' capacity to build differentiated classrooms.

The Perpetual Beta Teacher

Some teachers might read a book like this one and respond by completely overhauling what they do in one fell swoop. For most teachers, however, small steps and incremental changes are the path to continuous improvement. Developers of computer apps and software who make constant minor changes to programs rather than releasing only full-blown "complete" iterations call this "perpetual beta." This approach invites a more nuanced testing process on the design end and a less jarring experience on the user side.

The teacher who is committed to differentiation is in a similar state. Whether strengthening classroom family bonds, planning learning goals, assessing student learning, designing rich learning tasks, or leading and managing the classroom, the teacher who is in perpetual "beta mode" pledges to maximize his or her own growth as well as students'. On a practical level, getting started or continuing with differentiation might involve some of the approaches modeled in the scenarios that close each chapter of this book, such as

- Engaging in peer observation to receive and give feedback on how well specific principles or practices related to differentiation are (or aren't) working (e.g., Mr. Dankel, Chapter 7).
- Collecting and studying student data (on interests, readiness, and learning preferences) and discovering what avenues the data reveal (e.g., Ms. Helfand, Chapter 6).
- Implementing specific strategies and applications on your own or (even better) with colleagues (e.g., Mr. Lawrence, Chapter 8).
- Focusing PLC conversations and tasks around understanding, transferring, and reflecting on aspects of differentiation (e.g., Ms. Collins, Chapter 2).
- Basing professional learning goals on different aspects of differentiation and building one's repertoire throughout the year or across years (e.g., Ms. King, Chapter 1).
- Using differentiation to make sense of and respond to state-, district-, and school-level initiatives (e.g., Ms. Areda, Chapter 4).
- Starting with a lesson that either goes really well (e.g., Mr. Knox, Chapter 5) or goes really poorly (e.g., Mr. McLaughlin, Chapter 3, and Ms. Helfand, Chapter 6) and infusing those plans with pertinent aspects of differentiation the following year.

Which of these approaches teachers take is less important than that they continue to do *something*—to keep upgrading in ways both obvious and subtle.

What's Next?

Apple founder Steve Jobs said in an interview,

> I think if you do something and it turns out pretty good, then you
> should go do something else wonderful, not dwell on it for too long.
> Just figure out what's next. (Williams, 2006)

That's what drives the teacher of a differentiated classroom. He or she is always figuring out what's next, asking what step or change will lead to the next differentiation upgrade. This never-ending search fuels the drive to engage and equip *all* learners.

So, what's next for *you*?

Appendix: Strategy Index

References

Anderson, L. W., & Krathwohl, D. R. (Eds.). (2001). *A taxonomy for learning, teaching, and assessing: A revision of Bloom's taxonomy of educational objectives*. New York: Longman.

Aronson, E., & Patnoe, S. (1997). *The jigsaw classroom: Building cooperation in the classroom* (2nd ed.). New York: Longman.

Beers, K. (2003). *When kids can't read: What teachers can do*. Portsmouth, NH: Heinemann.

Bergmann, J., & Sams, A. (2012). *Flip your classroom: Reach every student in every class every day*. Alexandria, VA: ASCD.

Berra, Y. (2001). *When you come to a fork in the road, take it! Inspiration and wisdom from one of baseball's greatest heroes*. New York: Hyperion.

Black, P., & Wiliam, D. (1998). Inside the black box: Raising standards through classroom assessment. *Phi Delta Kappan, 80*(2), 139–148.

Boushey, G., & Moser, J. (2006). *The Daily 5: Fostering literacy independence in the elementary grades*. Portland, ME: Stenhouse.

Brandt, R. (1993). On teaching for understanding: A conversation with Howard Gardner. *Educational Leadership, 50*(7), 4–7.

Bransford, J., Brown, A., & Cocking, R. (Eds.). (2000). *How people learn: Brain, mind, experience, and school* (Expanded ed.). Washington, DC: National Academy Press.

Brighton, C. M., Hertberg, H. L., Moon, T. R., Tomlinson, C. A., & Callahan, C. M. (2005). *The feasibility of high-end learning in a diverse middle school*. Storrs, CT: National Research Center on the Gifted and Talented.

Brighton, C. M., Moon, T. R., Jarvis, J. M., & Hockett, J. A. (2007). *Primary grades teachers' conceptions of giftedness and talent: A case-based investigation*. Storrs, CT: National Research Center on the Gifted and Talented.

Brookhart, S. M. (2008). *Grading* (2nd ed.). Upper Saddle River, NJ: Pearson.

Bruner, J. S., Goodnow, J. J., & Austin, G. A. (1956). *A study of thinking*. New York: Wiley.

Buehl, D. (2009). *Classroom strategies for interactive learning* (3rd ed.). Newark, DE: International Reading Association.

Carnegie, D. (1936). *How to win friends and influence people*. New York: Simon & Schuster.

Cummings, C. (2000). *Winning strategies for classroom management*. Alexandria, VA: ASCD.

de Bono, E. (1999). *Six thinking hats*. New York: Back Bay Books.

Dobbertin, C. (2005). *HOTTLINX study on differentiated instruction in middle school*. Charlottesville, VA: University of Virginia's National Research Center on the Gifted and Talented. Retrieved from http://curry.virginia.edu/academics/offerings/gifted-education/hottlinx

Doubet, K. J., & Hockett, J. A. (2015). *Differentiation in middle and high school: Strategies to engage all learners*. Alexandria, VA: ASCD.

Dweck, C. S. (2006). *Mindset: The new psychology of success*. New York: Ballantine Books.

Elmore, R. F. (2004). *School reform from the inside out: Policy, practice, and performance.* Cambridge, MA: Harvard Education Press.

Erickson, H. L. (2002). *Concept-based curriculum and instruction: Teaching beyond the facts.* Thousand Oaks, CA: Corwin.

Fisher, D. C. (1917). *Understood Betsy.* New York: Henry Holt and Company.

Frayer, D., Frederick, W. C., & Klausmeier, H. J. (1969). *A schema for testing the level of cognitive mastery.* Madison, WI: Wisconsin Center for Education Research.

Fullan, M. (2007). *The new meaning of educational change* (4th ed.). New York: Teachers College Press.

Fullan, M., Hill, P., & Crevola, C. (2006). *Breakthrough.* Thousand Oaks, CA: Corwin.

Gardner, H. (1995, November). Reflections on multiple intelligences: Myths and messages. *Phi Delta Kappan,* 200–209.

Gardner, H. (2006). *Multiple intelligences: New horizons.* New York: Basic Books.

Gordon, W. J. J. (1961). *Synectics: The development of creative capacity.* New York: Harper and Brothers.

Graff, L. (2014). *Absolutely almost.* New York: Philomel Books.

Guskey, T. (2003). How classroom assessments improve learning. *Educational Leadership, 60*(5), 6–11.

Guskey, T. R. (2007/2008). The rest of the story. *Educational Leadership, 65*(4), 28–34.

Guskey, T. R. (2011). Five obstacles to grading reform. *Educational Leadership, 69*(3), 16–21.

Guskey, T. R., & Bailey, J. M. (2010). *Developing standards-based report cards.* Thousand Oaks, CA: Corwin.

Hattie, J. (2009). *Visible learning: A synthesis of over 800 meta-analyses relating to achievement.* New York: Routledge.

Hattie, J. (2012). *Visible learning for teachers: Maximizing impact on learning.* New York: Routledge.

Hattie, J., & Yates, G. (2014). *Visible learning and the science of how we learn.* Thousand Oaks, CA: Corwin.

Himmele, P., & Himmele, W. (2011). *Total participation techniques: Making every student an active learner.* Alexandria: ASCD.

Hockett, J. A. (2010). *The influence of lesson study on how teachers plan for, implement, and understand differentiated instruction* (Unpublished doctoral dissertation). University of Virginia, Charlottesville.

Jarvis, J. (2010). *Learning menus* (Unpublished curriculum materials). The Flinders University of South Australia, Adelaide.

Jensen, E. (2005). *Teaching with the brain in mind* (2nd ed.). Alexandria, VA: ASCD.

Johnson, D. W., & Johnson, R. T. (n.d.). *Structured academic controversy (SAC).* Retrieved from http://teachinghistory.org/teaching-materials/teaching-guides/21731

Jones, C. F. (1991). *Mistakes that worked: 40 familiar inventions and how they came to be.* New York: Delacorte Press.

Kagan, S. (2008). *Kagan cooperative learning.* San Clemente, CA: Kagan Publishing.

Kennedy, M. M. (2005). *Inside teaching: How classroom life undermines reform.* Cambridge, MA: Harvard University Press.

Lemov, D. (2012). *Teach like a champion field guide: A practical resource to make the 49 techniques your own.* San Francisco: Jossey-Bass.

Levy, S. (1996). *Starting from scratch: One classroom builds its own curriculum.* Portsmouth, NH: Heinemann.

Marzano, R. J. (2000). *Transforming classroom grading.* Alexandria, VA: ASCD.

Marzano, R. J., Pickering, D. J., & Pollock, J. E. (2001). *Classroom instruction that works: Research-based strategies for increasing student achievement.* Alexandria, VA: ASCD.

McTighe, J., & Wiggins, G. (2004). *Understanding by Design professional development workbook.* Alexandria, VA: ASCD.

McTighe, J., & Wiggins, G. (2013). *Essential questions: Opening doors to understanding.* Alexandria, VA: ASCD.

Moon, T. R., Callahan, C. M., Tomlinson, C. A., & Miller, E. M. (2002). *Middle school classrooms: Teachers' reported practices and student perceptions.* Storrs, CT: National Research Center on the Gifted and Talented.

Moore, M. (2008, November 26). Stress of modern life cuts attention spans to five minutes. *The Telegraph.* Retrieved from http://www.telegraph.co.uk/health/healthnews/3522781/Stress-of-modern-life-cuts-attention-spans-to-five-minutes.html

National Council for the Social Studies (NCSS). (2010). *The National Curriculum Standards for social studies: A framework for teaching, learning, and assessment.* Atlanta: Author.

National Governors Association Center for Best Practices (NGA Center) & Council of Chief State School Officers (CCSSO). (2010a). Common Core State Standards for English language arts & literacy in history/social studies, science, and technical subjects. Washington, DC: Author.

National Governors Association Center for Best Practices (NGA Center) & Council of Chief State School Officers (CCSSO). (2010b). Common Core State Standards for mathematics. Washington, DC: Author.

National Research Council. (2012). *A framework for K–12 science education: Practices, crosscutting concepts, and core ideas.* Washington, DC: National Academies Press. Available: www.nextgenscience.org

O'Connor, K. (2009). *How to grade for learning* (3rd ed.). Thousand Oaks, CA: Corwin.

O'Connor, K. (2010). *A repair kit for grades* (2nd ed.). Boston: Pearson.

O'Neill, M. (1961). *Hailstones and halibut bones.* New York: Doubleday.

Perry, B. D. (2000). How the brain learns best. *Instructor, 110*(4), 34–35.

Perry, T., Steele, C., & Hilliard, A.G. (2003). *Young, gifted, and black.* Boston: Beacon Press.

Poincaré, H. (1905). *Science and hypothesis.* London: Walter Scott Publishing.

Popham, J. W. (2006, October). Defining and enhancing formative assessment. Paper presented at the Annual Large-Scale Assessment Conference, Council of Chief State School Officers, San Francisco.

Prince, G. (1968). The operational mechanism of synectics. *Journal of Creative Behavior, 2,* 1–13.

Reis, S. M., Burns, D. E., & Renzulli, J. R. (1992). *Curriculum compacting: The complete guide to modifying the curriculum for high ability students.* Mansfield, CT: Creative Learning Press.

Ringgold, F. (1999). *If a bus could talk: The story of Rosa Parks.* New York: Simon & Schuster.

Rosenthal, R., & Jacobson, L. (1968). *Pygmalion in the classroom: Teacher expectation and pupils' intellectual development.* New York: Holt, Rinehart and Winston.

Santa, C. (1988). *Content reading including study systems.* Dubuque, IA: Kendall Hunt.

Schraw, G., Flowerday, T., & Lehman, S. (2001). Increasing situational interest in the classroom. *Educational Psychology Review, 13*(3), 211–224.

Silver, H. F., & Perini, M. J., with Morris, S. C., Klein, V., Jackson, J. W., & Moirao, D. R. (2010). *Classroom curriculum design: How strategic units improve instruction and engage students in meaningful learning.* Ho-Ho-Kus, NJ: Thoughtful Education Press.

Smith, L. (2006). *John, Paul, George, and Ben.* New York: Disney-Hyperion.

Sousa, D. A., & Tomlinson, C. A. (2011). *Differentiation and the brain: How neuroscience supports the learner-friendly classroom.* Bloomington, IN: Solution Tree.

Spandel, V. (2012). *Creating writers through 6-trait writing assessment and instruction* (6th ed.). Boston: Allyn & Bacon.

Starko, A. J. (2013). *Creativity in the classroom: Schools of curious delight* (5th ed.). New York: Routledge.

Steele, C. (2011). *Whistling Vivaldi: How stereotypes affect us and what we can do.* New York: W. W. Norton & Company.

Sternberg, R. J. (2006). Recognizing neglected strengths. *Educational Leadership, 64*(1), 30–35.

Sternberg, R. J., & Grigorenko, E. L. (2007). *Teaching for successful intelligence* (2nd ed.). Thousand Oaks, CA: Corwin.

Stiggins, R., & Chappuis, J. (2011). *Student-involved assessment FOR learning* (6th ed.). Upper Saddle River, NJ: Pearson/Prentice Hall.

Strickland, C. A. (2007). *Tools for high-quality differentiated instruction.* Alexandria, VA: ASCD.

Strickland, C. A. (2009). *Professional development for differentiating instruction: An ASCD Action Tool.* Alexandria, VA: ASCD.

Tomlinson, C. A. (2002). Invitations to learn. *Educational Leadership, 60*(1), 6–10.

Tomlinson, C. A. (2003). *Fulfilling the promise of the differentiated classroom: Strategies and tools for responsive teaching.* Alexandria, VA: ASCD.

Tomlinson, C. A. (2005, July). *Keynote presentation: Differentiating instruction to meet the needs of all learners.* Presented at the Institutes on Academic Diversity: Summer Institute on Academic Diversity, Charlottesville, VA.

Tomlinson, C. A. (2009, February). Learning profile and student achievement. *School Administrator,* 28–34.

Tomlinson, C. A. (2014a). *The differentiated classroom: Responding to the needs of all learners* (2nd ed.). Alexandria, VA: ASCD.

Tomlinson, C. A. (2014b). Differentiated instruction. In C. M. Callahan & J. Plucker (Eds.), *Critical issues and practices in gifted education: What the research says.* Waco, TX: Prufrock Press.

Tomlinson, C. A., Brimijoin, K., & Narvaez, L. (2008). *The differentiated school: Making revolutionary changes in teaching and learning.* Alexandria, VA: ASCD.

Tomlinson, C. A., & Doubet, K. J. (2005). Reach them to teach them. *Educational Leadership, 62*(7), 8–15.

Tomlinson, C. A., Hockett, J., & Kiernan, L. J. (2001). *The common sense of differentiation: Meeting specific learner needs in the regular classroom* (Facilitator's Guide). Alexandria, VA: ASCD.

Tomlinson, C. A., & Imbeau, M. B. (2010). *Leading and managing a differentiated classroom.* Alexandria, VA: ASCD.

Tomlinson, C. A., & McTighe, J. (2006). *Integrating differentiated instruction and Understanding by Design.* Alexandria, VA: ASCD.

Tomlinson, C. A., & Moon, T. R. (2013). *Assessment and student success in a differentiated classroom.* Alexandria, VA: ASCD.

Tomlinson, C. A., & Murphy, M. (2015). *Leading for differentiation: Growing teachers who grow kids.* Alexandria, VA: ASCD.

Tyack, D., & Cuban, L. (1995). *Tinkering toward Utopia: A century of public school reform.* Cambridge, MA: Harvard University Press.

Walkington, C. A. (2013). Using adaptive learning technologies to personalize instruction: The impact of relevant contexts on performance and learning outcomes. *Journal of Educational Psychology, 105*(4), 932–945.

Webb, N. L., Alt, M., Ely, R., & Vesperman, B. (2005, July 24). *Depth of knowledge web alignment tool.* Wisconsin Center for Educational Research. Madison, WI: University of Wisconsin. Retrieved from http://wat.wceruw.org/index.aspx

White, E. B. (1952). *Charlotte's web.* New York: Harper & Brothers.

Wiggins, G. (2014, November 14). 5th graders speak out—survey results [Blog post]. *Granted, and . . . Thoughts on Education by Grant Wiggins.* Retrieved from https://grantwiggins.wordpress.com/2014/11/14/5th-graders-speak-out-survey-results

Wiggins, G., & McTighe, J. (2005). *Understanding by Design* (Expanded 2nd ed.). Alexandria, VA: ASCD.

Wiggins, G., & McTighe, J. (2011). *The Understanding by Design guide to creating high-quality units.* Alexandria, VA: ASCD.

Wiggins, G., & McTighe, J. (2012). *The Understanding by Design guide to advanced concepts in creating and reviewing units.* Alexandria, VA: ASCD.

Wiliam, D. (2011). *Embedded formative assessment.* Bloomington, IN: Solution Tree.

Wiliam, D. (2012). Feedback: Part of a system. *Educational Leadership, 70*(1), 30–34.

Williams, B. (2006, May 25). Steve Jobs: Iconoclast and salesman. Apple founder's newest store wows fans in Manhattan. Interview transcript from *NBC Nightly News with Brian Williams.* Retrieved from http://www.nbcnews.com/id/12974884/#.V84inWWYwZ4

Willingham, D. T. (2009, Spring). Why don't students like school? Book excerpt in *American Educator,* 4–13.

Willis, J. (2006). *Research-based strategies to ignite student learning.* Alexandria, VA: ASCD.

Willis, J. (2007, Summer). The neuroscience of joyful education. *Educational Leadership, 64.* Retrieved from http://www.ascd.org/publications/educational-leadership/summer07/vol64/num09/The-Neuroscience-of-Joyful-Education.aspx

Wolfe, P. (2001). *Brain matters: Translating research into classroom practice.* Alexandria, VA: ASCD.

Wulffson, D. (2000). *Toys! Amazing stories behind some great inventions.* New York: Henry Holt and Company.

Index

Note: Page references followed by an italicized *f* indicate information contained in figures.

About the Authors

Dr. Kristina J. Doubet is a professor in the College of Education at James Madison University in Harrisonburg, Virginia, where she has received the Distinguished Teacher Award, the Madison Scholar Award, and the Sarah Miller Luck Endowed Professorship for Excellence in Education. As an independent consultant and ASCD Faculty member, Kristi has partnered with more than 100 schools, districts, and organizations around initiatives related to differentiated instruction, Understanding by Design, classroom assessment, digital learning, and classroom management and grouping. In addition to numerous journal articles, book chapters, and educational blogs, she is the coauthor (with Jessica Hockett) of *Differentiation in Middle and High School: Strategies to Engage All Learners*—the companion book to this volume—and of *The Differentiated Flipped Classroom: A Practical Guide to Digital Learning* (with Eric Carbaugh). She is also the coauthor (with Carol Ann Tomlinson) of *Smart in the Middle Grades: Classrooms That Work for Bright Middle Schoolers*. Kristi taught middle and high school language arts for 10 years and has also served as an instructional coach and a curriculum developer in elementary and middle school classrooms. You can connect with Kristi via her website (http://www.kristinadoubet.com), Twitter (@kjdoubet), or e-mail (kjdoubet@mac.com).

Dr. Jessica A. Hockett has been a full-time education consultant for 12 years, specializing in interactive and differentiated instruction, standards-aligned curriculum and performance task design, classroom grouping practices, and program evaluation. Her work with numerous schools, districts, departments, and organizations has supported a wide range of initiatives centered on improving teacher and student learning. She is the coauthor (with Kristina Doubet) of *Differentiation in Middle and High School: Strategies to Engage All Learners* and (with Chester E. Finn Jr.) of *Exam Schools: Inside America's Most Selective Public High Schools*, a big-picture look at a high-performing but understudied niche of U.S. education. Her other publications include academic articles and book chapters, journal articles, news editorials, and education blogs. Jessica lives Evanston, Illinois, with her husband and two children. You can connect with Jessica via her website (http://www .jessicahockett.com), Twitter (@jahockett), or email (jessicahockett@me.com).